The Basilica of
St. Mark in Venice

The Basilica of
St. Mark in Venice

edited by
ETTORE VIO

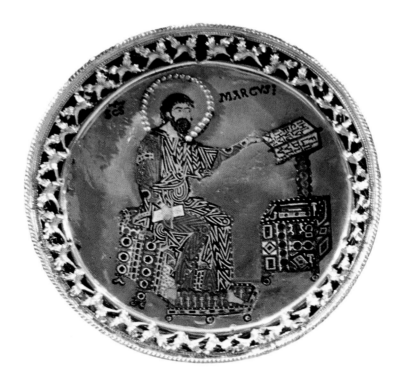

SCALA / RIVERSIDE

THE BASILICA OF ST. MARK IN VENICE
edited by *Ettore Vio*

Authors of the texts
Prof. Ennio Concina, *director of the department of art history at the*
  IUAV
Dr. Umberto Daniele, *art historian*
Dr. Maria da Villa Urbani, *chief librarian of the Basilica*
Mgr. Antonio Niero, *procurator of St. Mark and instructor in history at*
  Ca' Foscari University
Prof. Guido Tigler, *instructor in history of art at Florence University*
Arch. Ettore Vio, proto *of St. Mark and responsible for the conservation*
  of the Basilica
Prof. Licia Vlad Borrelli, *chief inspector of the Ministry of Cultural*
  Assets

Editorial coordination and graphic design
Andrea Grandese

Editing
Patrizia Bevilacqua

Video paging
Colophon srl, Venice

Translation
Huw Evans

Photographs
Archivio Fotografico SCALA (M. Falsini, M. Sarri, Cameraphoto)
except: pages 9, 34, 66, 69, 91, 143 (Cameraphoto) and pages 19,
56, 58, 62, 112, 135, 152, 153 (Procuratoria di San Marco).

The drawings on pages 29, 50, 54, 56, 59, 77, 78, 94-5, 97, 145
and 166 have been kindly provided by the Procuratoria di
San Marco and the architect Ettore Vio.

The axonometric projections on page 89, drawn by Ettore Vio,
are taken from the book *San Marco. I mosaici. La storia.*
L'illuminazione, Fabbri Editore, 1990.

© 1999 SCALA GROUP, Antella (Florence)
Printed in Italy

Published by Riverside Book Company, Inc.
250 West 57th Street
New York, N.Y. 10107
www.riversidebook.com

ISBN 1-878351-55-9

Contents

History and Art

9   St. Mark: a Biographical Profile

21   Liturgy in St. Mark's: the Mosaics and the Rites

35   The Art of St. Mark's

Tour of the Basilica

51   The Tour of the Basilica

53   The Exterior of the Basilica

66   The Gothic Decoration of the Copings

68   The Arches of the Central Portal

70   The Horses of St. Mark's

77   The Atrium

86   The Mosaics

90   The Porta da Mar

93   The Interior of the Basilica

108   The Iconostasis of the Dalle Masegne Brothers

110   The Baldachin

114   The Inscriptions of the Mosaics

134   The Tessellated Floor of St. Mark's

142   The Crypt

145   The Chapels

152   The Inlaid Cabinets in the Sacristy

154   The Angels in the Baptistery

158   The Mosaics of the Mascoli Chapel

163   The Pala d'Oro and the Treasury of St. Mark's

173   The Tapestries

174   Essential Bibliography

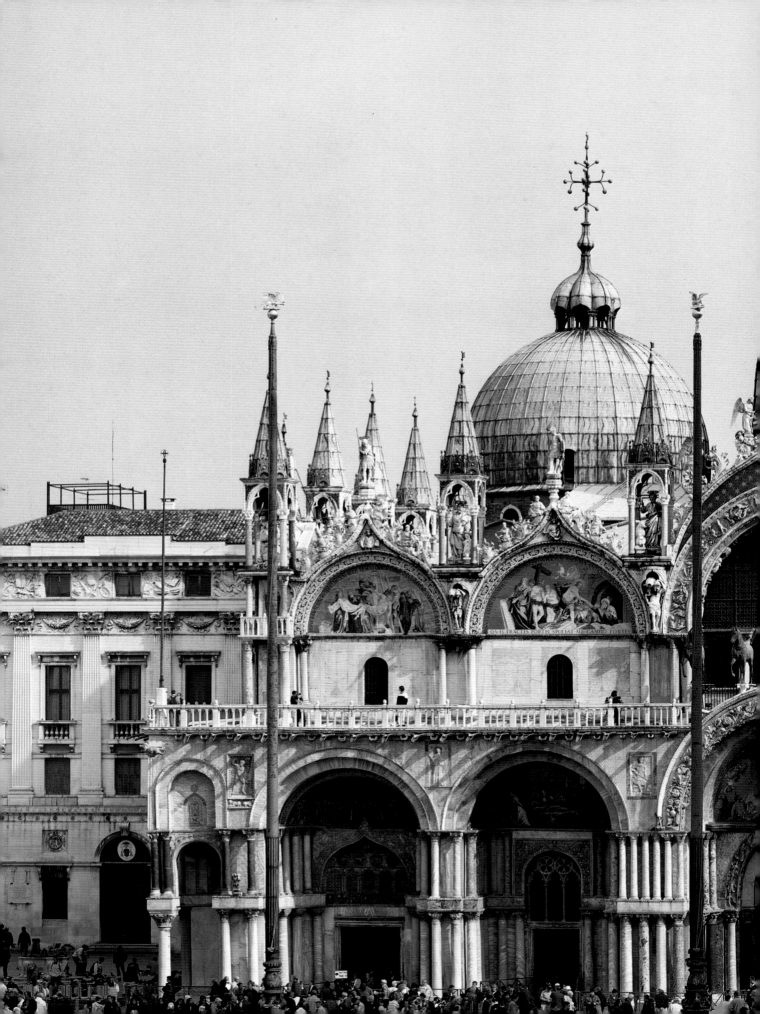

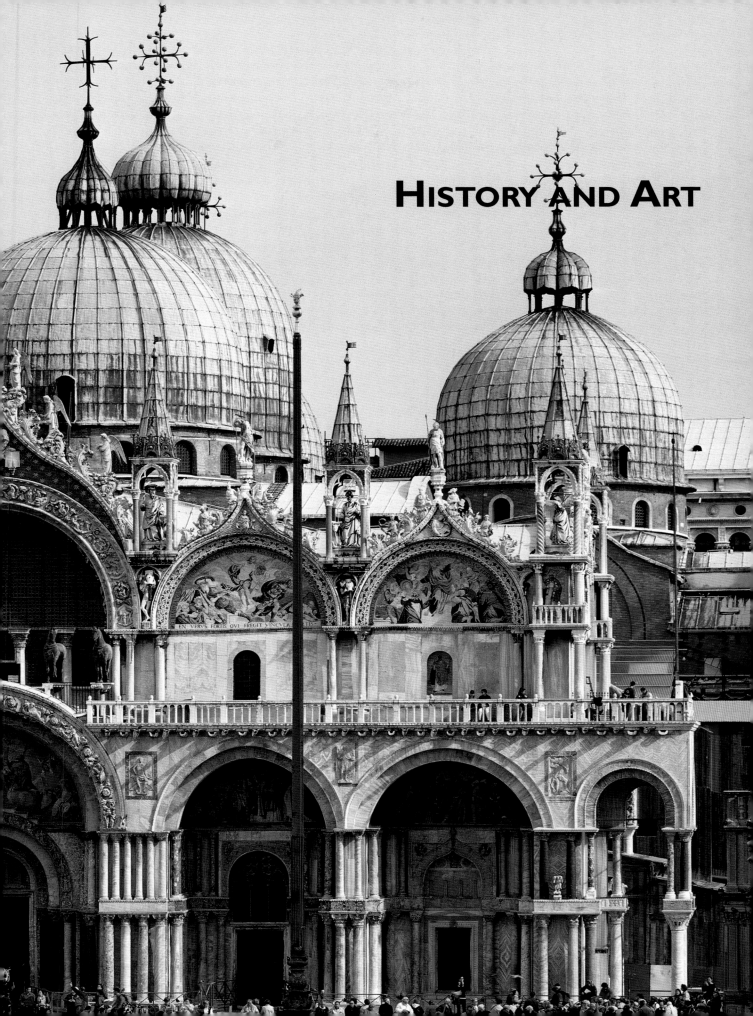

HISTORY AND ART

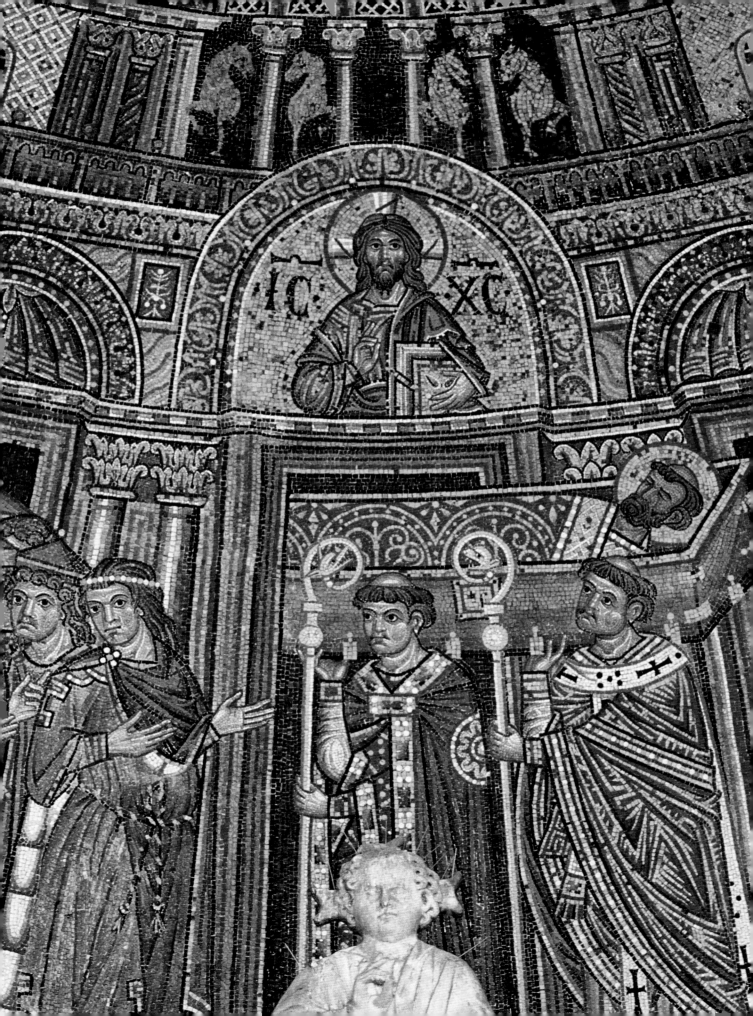

ST. MARK: A BIOGRAPHICAL PROFILE

Antonio Niero

The evangelist Mark first stepped on to the stage of history in the year AD 43 or 44, when the apostle Peter, after escaping from prison in miraculous fashion, took refuge in "the house of Mary, the mother of John, whose surname was Mark" (Acts of the Apostles, 12, 12). Double names like this were not uncommon in Jewish circles at the time. The first and strictly theophoric name (*Yohanan*) meant "God is gracious" in Hebrew, whereas the second (*Marcus*) was a Roman name derived from the god Mars and used by prosperous clans, although Tertullian (*c*. AD 200) used it almost like a common noun, corresponding roughly to our "fellow," or "person." It was to the house of Mary and John Mark that the apostle Saul, as he was then still known, and his friend Barnabas, born in Cyprus and a relative of Mark's (whether an uncle or a cousin, we don't know) went in the early months of 45. They took with them a substantial sum of money raised by the Christian community of Antioch to aid that of Jerusalem, which was struggling economically as a result of the food shortages from which the Roman Empire had been suffering for years.

The young and now fatherless Mark was probably born a few decades after Jesus. There is a lively passage in his Gospel (14, 51-52) which is thought to relate to his own life. In a few, brief lines, it describes a dramatic scene. While the soldiers arrested Jesus in the garden in the dead of night, a young man wrapped in a linen cloth suddenly appeared, following the Master. The soldiers, disturbed by the presence of an inconvenient witness, tried to seize him, perhaps to find out who he was. But the young man instinctively slipped off the linen cloth and fled from them, naked. A number of scholars have interpreted this passage as a reference to the evangelist himself, serving as a sort of signature to his Gospel. Analysis of some of the details suggests that he came from a middle-class family, for only the wealthy could afford linen. Such affluence agrees with the references in Acts to the house of Mark's mother Mary, where the early Christian community in Jerusalem used to gather after the Ascension of Christ.

Again according to Acts (12, 25), Saul and Barnabas took John Mark with them when they returned to Antioch from Jerusalem, a journey that may have been made at the beginning of 46. It is likely that Barnabas had chosen the young man as a companion because of their kinship. Given his plans to return to the island of his birth to preach the Gospel,

1

Placing of the Saint's Body in the Basilica, mosaic, west façade, Door of St. Alypius, detail, 13th century

2

Paolino da Venezia, plan of the city, copy by Tommaso Temanza from the parchment codex *Chronologia magna* of 1376

The boundaries of the ducal *castrum-castellum* in the area of St. Mark's are indicated by a battlemented enclosure. It was inside this that the first church of St. Mark, the Palatine chapel, was built between AD 829 and 832 to house the body of the saint.

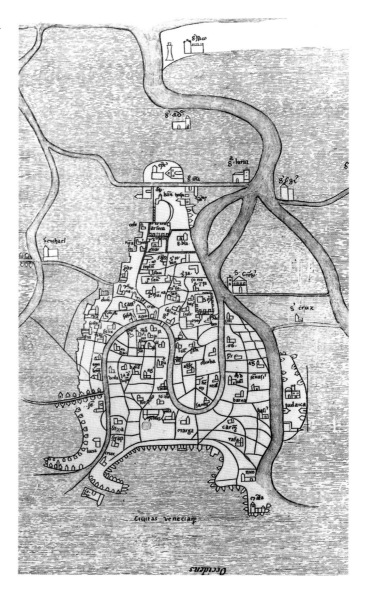

Barnabas probably thought that his quick and alert young relative would be useful to him as a secretary, diarist and general assistant. The other companion, though one of quite different stature, was Saul. The missionaries left the populous, wealthy and corrupt city of Antioch, through which the Orontes River flows, after a religious meeting briefly outlined in Acts (13, 2). The prophets and teachers of the local Christian community were told by the Holy Spirit: "Separate me Barnabas and Saul for the work whereunto I have called them." Acts continues (13, 4): "So they, being sent forth by the Holy Ghost, departed unto Seleucia; and from thence they sailed to Cyprus." Seleucia, Antioch's port, was some twenty-five kilometers from the city. The sea crossing was fairly quick, perhaps taking barely twenty-four hours. They landed at Salamis – the main port, largest city and former capital of

the island – where the Jewish colony, in existence for over two centuries, had many synagogues (Acts, 13, 5). At this point in the account John Mark is officially recognized as their assistant. The three missionaries set about preaching the Gospel in the local synagogues.

However, Salamis was just one leg of their journey, their final goal being the capital Paphos, on the other, western side of the island. Before reaching there, the three men had to cross the whole of Cyprus (Acts, 13, 6). We do not know what route they took: inland through the mountains or along the southern coast road that led to New Paphos. It was from here that the Roman proconsul Sergius Paulus governed the island. As he had the reputation of being a learned man and interested in spiritual matters, the missionaries felt that his conversion, or at least his support, would help Christianity

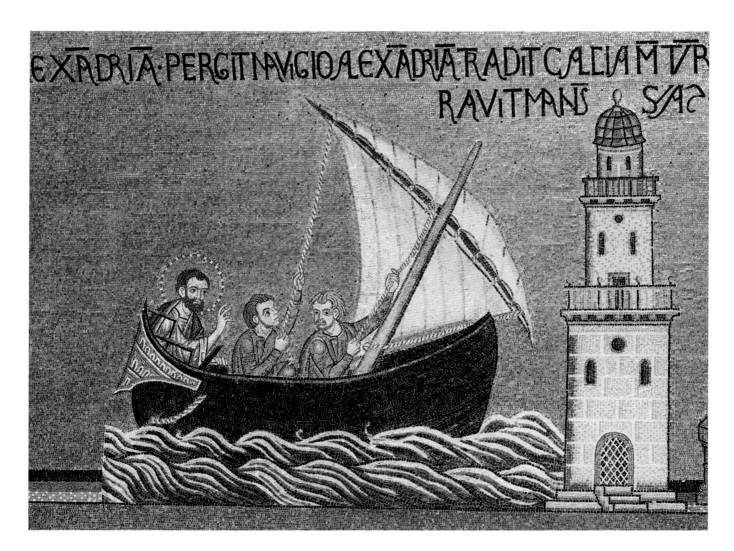

to gain a foothold in Cyprus. And in fact Sergius Paulus was an astonished witness to the dramatic events that took place between Saul and the sorcerer Bar-Jesus, also known as Elymas, who was half-scholar and half-soothsayer and claimed to be an intermediary between God and human beings. When Bar-Jesus tried to turn the proconsul away from Saul's preaching, he was temporarily blinded by the apostle. It is from this moment that Saul is always referred to as Paul (Acts, 13, 9–12). The episode made such an impression on the proconsul that he converted to Christianity. Indeed, it seems that he advised the preachers to leave Cyprus and head for the heart of Asia Minor (modern-day Turkey), to preach the Gospel at Antioch in Pisidia.

The missionaries set sail again, perhaps in the spring of 47, and after a brief crossing landed at the port of Attalia, in

Pamphylia on the coast of Asia Minor. From here they traveled inland, by river or along the road that ran alongside it, with the intention of crossing the forbidding Taurus Mountains. But at Perga, in the foothills, Mark suddenly decided to leave his two friends and return to Jerusalem (Acts, 13, 13). This was the famous crisis of Perga and, since the early days of Christianity, debate has raged over the reasons for Mark's decision. He may have been motivated by a desire to see his mother again, or perhaps he was not happy with the fact that Paul had become the leader of the mission instead of his relative Barnabas.

But Mark had not broken off all relations with the two missionaries. After the apostolic council held at Jerusalem in 49, he met his friends again at Antioch. On this occasion Barnabas proposed to Paul that Mark should accompany them on a second and longer apostolic journey. But Paul

3

St. Mark on His Way to Alexandria, mosaic, Zen Chapel, 13th century

The detail showing the saint traveling to Alexandria, where he would be made bishop and martyred in about AD 68, is part of the mosaics representing *Scenes from the Life of St. Mark.*

4

St. Mark Healing Anianus, mosaic, Zen Chapel, 13th century

The mosaic is one of the scenes from the life of the saint that adorn the ceiling of the chapel, formerly the Porta da Mar, through which Venetians landing at the wharf used to enter the church to pay their respects to St. Mark.

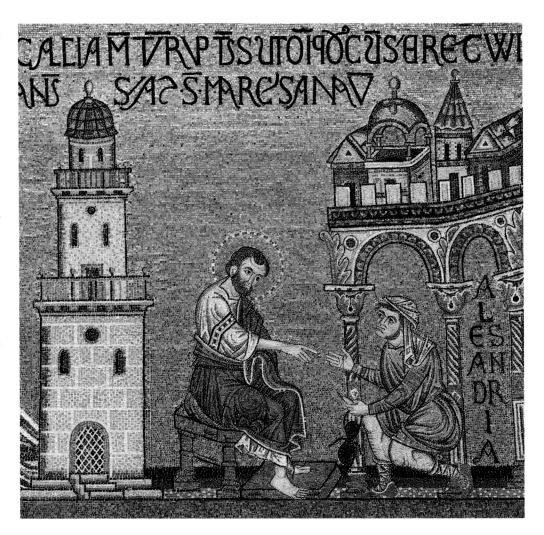

was unshakable in his refusal, leading to a fierce clash of words with Barnabas, for he regarded Mark as a weakling, not to say a traitor, for abandoning them at Perga. But this time Barnabas was adamant in his defense of his kinsman and broke off his long friendship and cooperation with Paul. The latter chose Silas as his new companion and left Asia Minor for the distant shores of Europe. Barnabas and Mark were left with no alternative but to retrace their previous journey and return to the island of Cyprus, which they were more than happy to do (Acts, 15, 37-41).

From here on, Acts has nothing further to say on the subject. There is an apocryphal text of little historical validity, the so-called *Acts of Barnabas* dating from the fourth century, whose account of the two missionaries' adventures in Cyprus is crammed with fantastical episodes, fabulous deeds, and tales bordering on the ridiculous. However, for reliable information about Mark we must return to the texts of the New Testament. By 54, Mark must have been back in Paul's

good graces, since the latter, writing to his friend Philemon of Colossae, did not omit to send his greetings to Mark. Paul was to have need of Mark in some of the most difficult moments of his life, such as the time of his second imprisonment in Rome, assuming that the references to Mark in Paul's Letter to the Colossians and in his Second Letter to Timothy are really his own work and not that of his school (and therefore written after his death). In the meantime Mark had become Peter's assistant in Rome, if we are to accept that Peter's mention of him at the end of his First Letter (5, 13) is genuine and should not instead be attributed to a late follower writing shortly before 100.

Mark's collaboration with Peter is further supported by non-Biblical evidence, such as that provided by the ecclesiastic writers active between the second and fourth centuries. If we accept the claims made by St. Irenaeus and St. Clement, both writing around 200, Mark transcribed Peter's sermons in Rome at the urging of members of the Roman social and

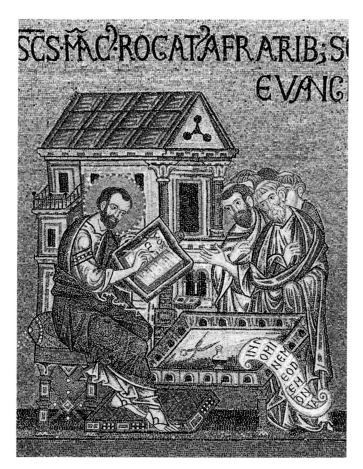

5 *left*
St. Mark Writing His Gospel, mosaic, Zen Chapel, 13th century
The mosaic is one of the scenes from the life of the saint that adorn the ceiling of the chapel, formerly the Porta da Mar.

6 *right*
The Saint Ordained as a Bishop, mosaic, left-hand choir of the presbytery, 12th century
The walls and ceilings of the two choirs, so-called because they are still used to house the organs and the choristers that accompany sacred services, are adorned with scenes from the life of the patron saint.

7 *following pages*
St. Mark Dragged through the City and Burial of the Saint, mosaic, Zen Chapel, 13th century
These mosaics are the last two scenes from the life of the saint that adorn the ceiling of the chapel, formerly the Porta da Mar. The images are accompanied by inscriptions: "Here he is dragged in chains toward the locality of Bucoli" and "St. Mark is buried by the followers of Christ."

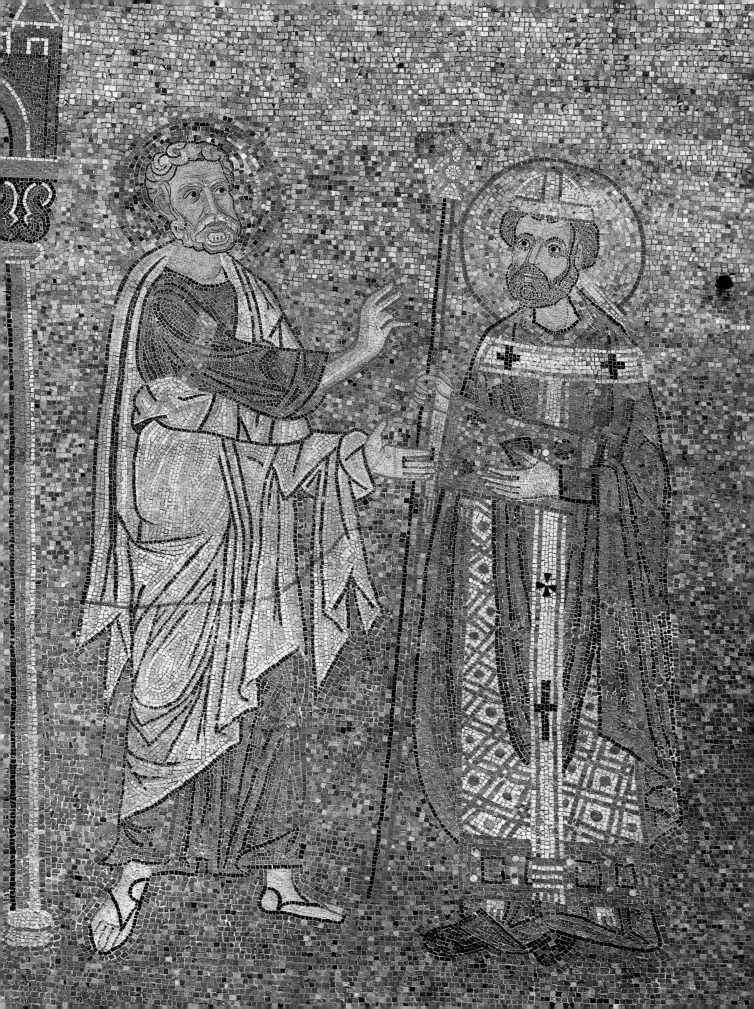

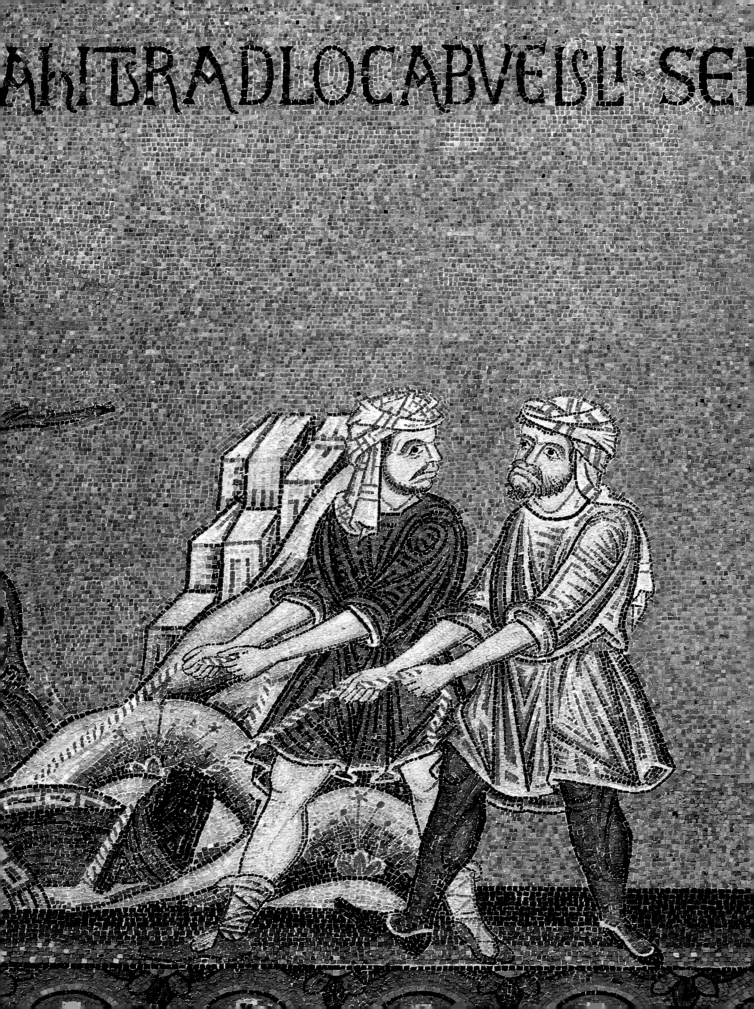

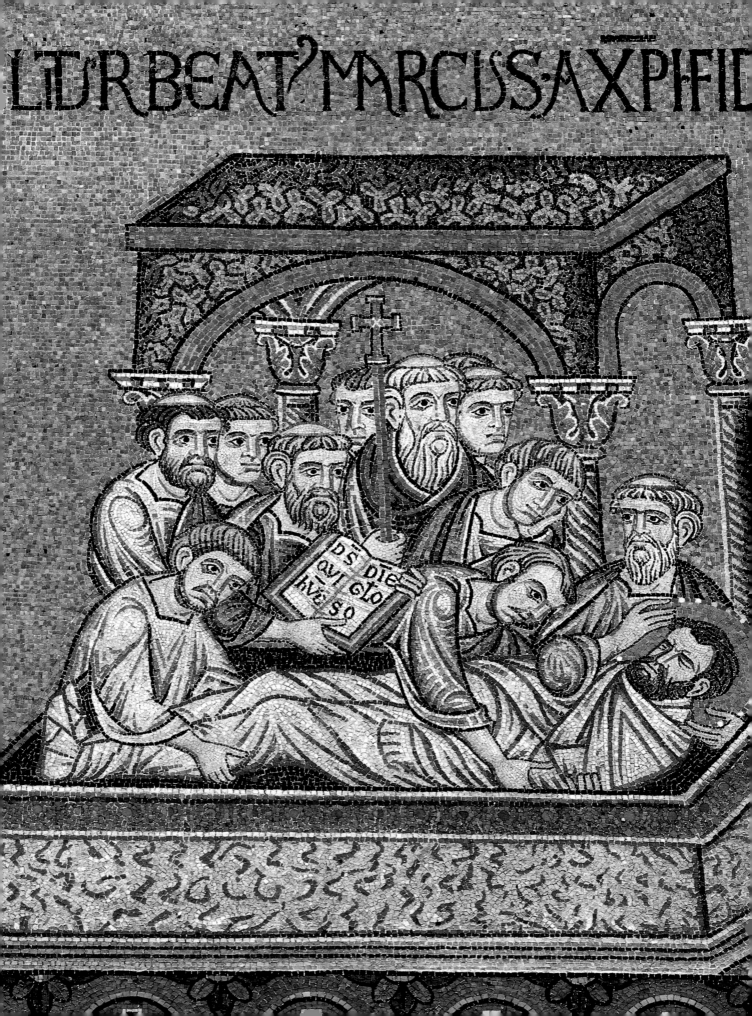

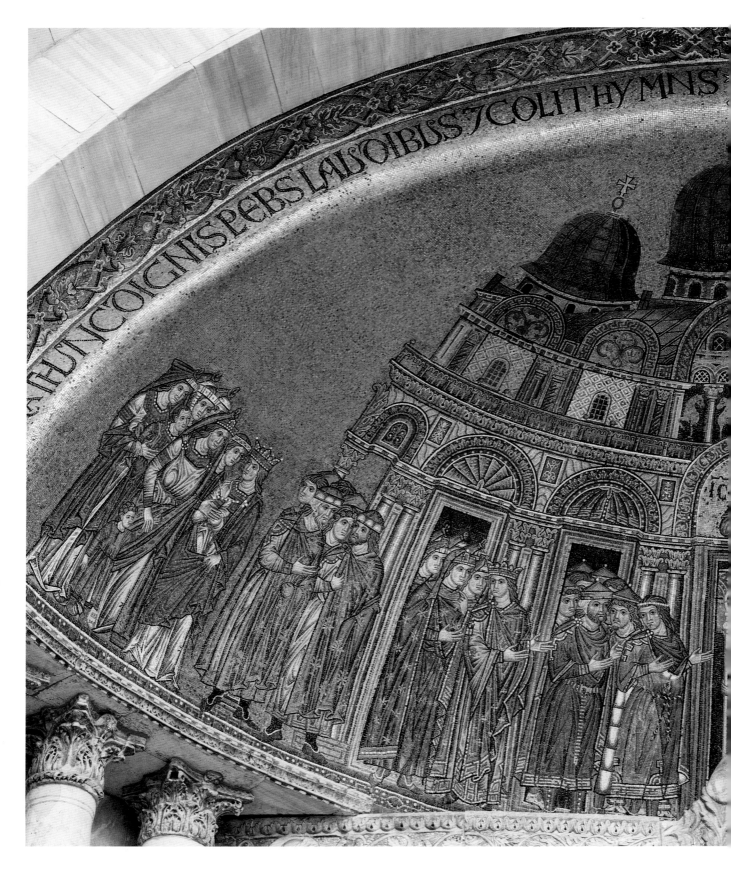

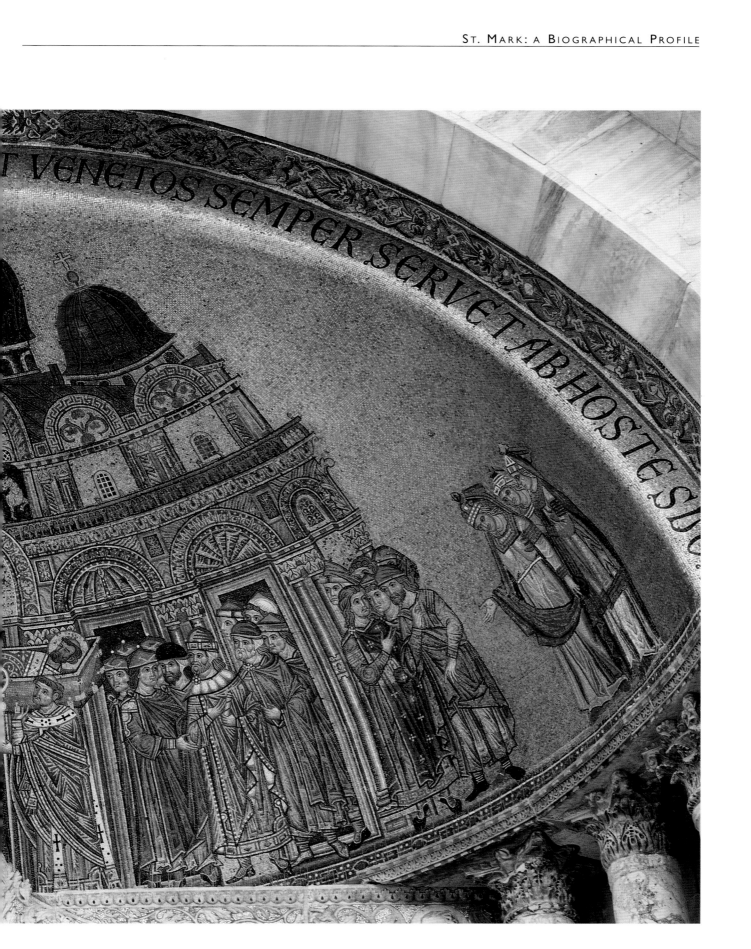

military classes and with the approval of the apostle himself. In practice, this must be a reference to Mark's Gospel (written prior to the year AD 70), the second of the four according to tradition from the time of St. Augustine onward.

This Gospel is a masterpiece in miniature, the shortest of the four, composed of just sixteen chapters in the Greek tongue. It shows a distinct preference for the story of Christ's life, insisting on the details and in particular the events that took place around the Sea of Galilee, which has led to St. Mark's Gospel being described as a "Gospel of the Sea." Mark also refers to the open countryside and scattered villages of the land around Galilee. Above all, however, he speaks of the crowds, at times vast, that invariably gathered around the Messiah in a desperate attempt to be cured of all sorts of ailments, to be freed of possession by devils, or simply to hear the good word. In essence Mark set out to demonstrate, through the recounting of numerous miracles, that Jesus was indeed the Son of God.

In his turn, Eusebius of Caesarea, the greatest historian of the ancient Church, wrote around 300 that Mark founded the Church of Alexandria, organizing it on a parochial basis, but he does not give more specific detail. Subsequently, local tradition built up a history of Mark's deeds in Africa, as an apostle first in Cyrenaica and then in Alexandria, up until his martyrdom on April 25 of what was probably the year 68. From an archeological viewpoint, we know that there was a tomb of St. Mark at Boucolis, an eastern suburb of Alexandria on the Mediterranean coast, in the fifth century. And we also know that the relics of the saint were moved from place to place in the Alexandrine region several times over the course of the centuries, before returning to Boucolis in the seventh century.

It was from here that, around 828, two traders from the Venetian lagoons, Buono da Malamocco and Rustico da Torcello, managed to carry off the body of the saint by means of a cunning stratagem. They had learned from the custodians of Mark's sanctuary in Boucolis that it was to be destroyed on the orders of the Arab governor of Alexandria and its marble used to build a palace at Al-Fustat, once called Babylon. To avert such desecration the two merchants offered to carry the remains of the evangelist to safety in Venice. Faced with reluctance on the part of the custodians, who raised a series of objections, not least the saint's patronage of the city, the merchants pointed out that St. Mark, before going to found the Church in Alexandria, had been sent by the apostle Paul to preach to the Veneti. Indeed they argued that Mark, on his way back to Rome with Hermagoras of Aquileia, whom he had chosen as his successor and bishop, had been caught in a storm in the marshes where Venice now stands and had received a heavenly vision: his body would not perish after death, but was destined instead for eternal repose and veneration in Venice. Though unwilling, the custodians agreed to the merchants' request, but not without first trying to substitute the remains of the martyred St. Claudia for those of Mark. Hiding the sacred relics between layers of pork, which the Muslim customs officers of Alexandria found repulsive, the traders were able to smuggle them out by declaring, when the time came for inspection, that what they were carrying was indeed *kanzir*, or pork. They were allowed to leave the port and, after an adventurous voyage across the Mediterranean and the Adriatic, stopping off at Cropani in Calabria, Zadar in Dalmatia and Umag in Istria, the navigators reached Venice, having warned Doge Giustiniano Particiaco of their precious cargo. When they arrived, the doge and his court, along with the local bishop and clergy, came to meet the bold adventurers. St. Mark's body, received with great pomp and ceremony, was placed in a corner of the Ducal Palace until such time as a suitable basilica could be built to house it. This took place on January 31, 829, according to later tradition.

Yet we have to ask how much truth there was in the claims about St. Mark's Venetian apostolate that the merchants used to persuade the custodians of Mark's tomb in Alexandria to hand over the sacred relics. Recent studies have shown that it was in fact a legend, which grew up over the course of the seventh century, and was gradually amplified until it took on the form in which it appears in Doge Andrea Dandolo's *Chronica*, written in the middle of the fourteenth century.

8 *preceding pages*

Placing of the Saint's Body in the Basilica, mosaic, west façade, Door of St. Alypius, 13th century

The doge, accompanied by the clergy and the people, brings the sarcophagus containing the saint's body into the church. This is the earliest picture of the basilica in its resplendent new guise, with marble and columns imported from the East, with the domes raised and covered in lead and the four horses already in place on the terrace. The date is between 1265 and 1270.

9

Antonio Visentini, *St. Mark's Basilica*, section through the Baptistery, engraving, 18th century

The print shows the wooden structures of the domes and the rooms above the atrium. Visentini made this engraving of the basilica in the 1720s. The artist took a scientific approach, investigating structures and parts of the basilica that were little known and rarely frequented.

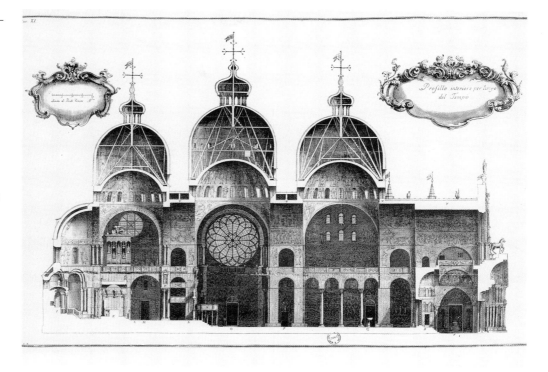

The small basilica that was erected as a martyrium in Venice to house the body of St. Mark became one of the most famous Christian sanctuaries of the early Middle Ages, drawing pilgrims from all over Europe. Damaged by a fire which broke out in August 976 and destroyed several areas of the city, it was quickly repaired by Doge Pietro Orseolo. Less than a century later, in 1063, Doge Domenico Contarini decided to demolish St. Mark's sanctuary and replace it with a larger and richer basilica, the present building with its five domes designed – it is supposed – by an anonymous Byzantine architect. The work did not proceed rapidly. It was not until 1094 that the building was finished, during the reign of Doge Vitale Falier. It was he who decided to have it consecrated, so that it could also serve as a palatine chapel or dogal church, annexed to the city's seat of government. The bishop of Venice, Enrico Contarini, was invited to conduct the ceremony. But when the time came to transfer St. Mark's body to the new building, it proved impossible to find. Many explanations were put forward, the most likely being that it had been consumed in the fire of 976, or that the location of its burial place had been forgotten. Prayers and days of fasting were proclaimed. In the end, on June 25, while the doge, bishop, nobility and populace were gathered in prayer and lamentation in the basilica, one of St. Mark's arms emerged from a pillar on the southern side of the church to indicate that his body rested there. It was true. The sacred relics were then moved to the center of the building, steeped in the sweet scent of roses. News of the discovery spread rapidly through the Veneto region and the rest of Europe. More and more pilgrims – inspired by the series of miracles that the saint had wrought, some of which had caused a great stir – came to visit the holy relics, among them nobles, common people and even the Holy Roman Emperor. On October 8, the body, housed in a precious sarcophagus, was placed inside the crypt that had been built by Doge Falier. There it remained until the first half of the nineteenth century when, to make it easier for the faithful to show their devotion, it was moved to a new location under the table of the high altar, where it still lies today. To such an extent did the saint's relics become the symbol of Venice and its government that the Florentine scholar Angelo Fiorenzuola (1493-1543) was moved to write, in his *Ragionamenti d'amore*, that in Venice the saint was honored more highly than God himself.

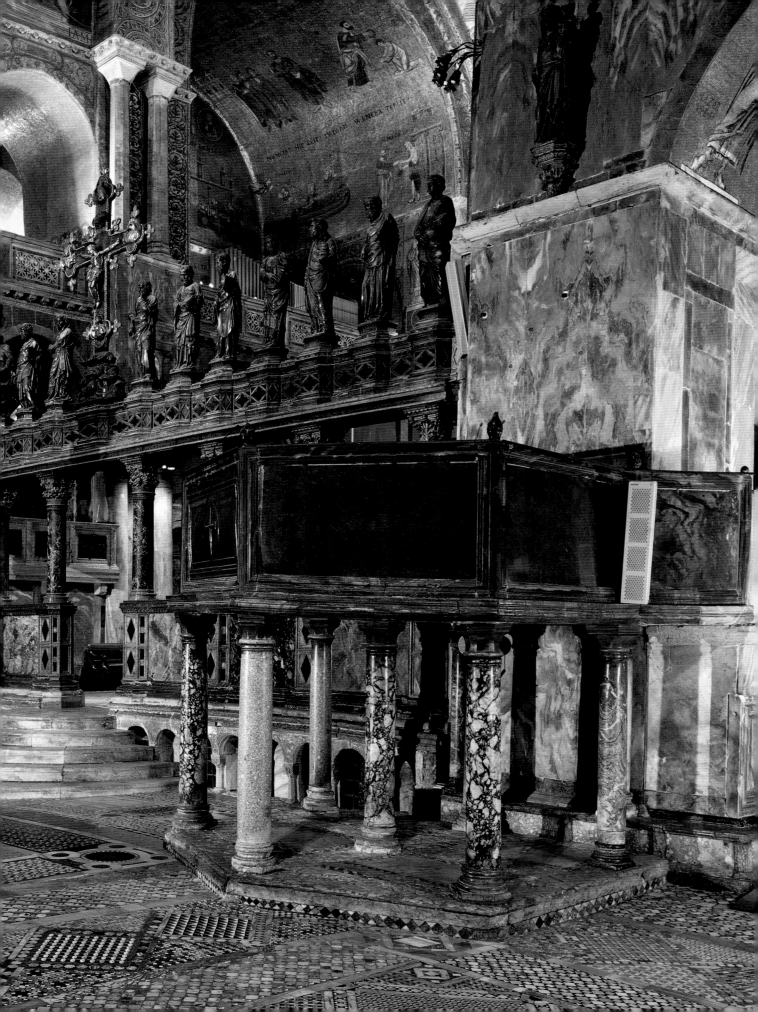

LITURGY IN ST. MARK'S: THE MOSAICS AND THE RITES

Antonio Niero

In the 8600 square meters of mosaics that cover the inside and outside of the basilica, it is possible to discern an underlying iconographic program drawn up by an anonymous Venetian scholar, perhaps the theologian Iacobo Venetico Greco, a canon of the basilica who was active around 1136.

Since the late fifteenth century and prior to the modern hypotheses on the subject, the program had been ascribed to Joachim of Floris (*c.* 1145-1202), the charismatic abbot of a Cistercian monastery in the Calabrian region of Aspromonte. It was said that he had come to St. Mark's and drawn up the entire scheme for the mosaics. Today it is difficult to find support for such a hypothesis, although some illustrious scholars, including most recently the Viennese Otto Demus, do

not exclude the possibility of Joachim's involvement at some stage. While it is possible to discern traces of Joachim's work (in the figures of the *Virtues* in the Dome of the Ascension, in the four Biblical rivers in its pendentives, in some details of the *Cycle of the Passion and Resurrection* and in the monks that appear in the aisles of the Dome of the Pentecost), the mosaics in St. Mark's can be divided entirely on the grounds of subject matter, into themes taken from the Bible and those drawn from the lives of the saints. The Biblical themes, in turn, are split between those from the Old Testament, arranged in strictly chronological order in the atrium, and those from the New Testament, which are located inside the church itself. There are just two exceptions: the *Scenes from the Story of*

10

Detail of the right-hand ambo known as the *pergolo grando*

The ambo, made from splendid plutei of imperial red granite supported by nine columns in antique breccia, is hexagonal and located in the doge's part of the church. It was used to present the doge to the people after he had been elected.

11

***Cain and Abel,* mosaic, Chapel of St. Clement, 12th century**

Set around the window from which the doge was able to attend Mass, the mosaic does not fit into any of the classical iconographies. The inscription,

"The Lord received Abel and his gift with favour; but Cain and his gift he did not receive" (Genesis, 4,4), serves as an admonition to the doge, warning him that he must always act in a disinterested and open way.

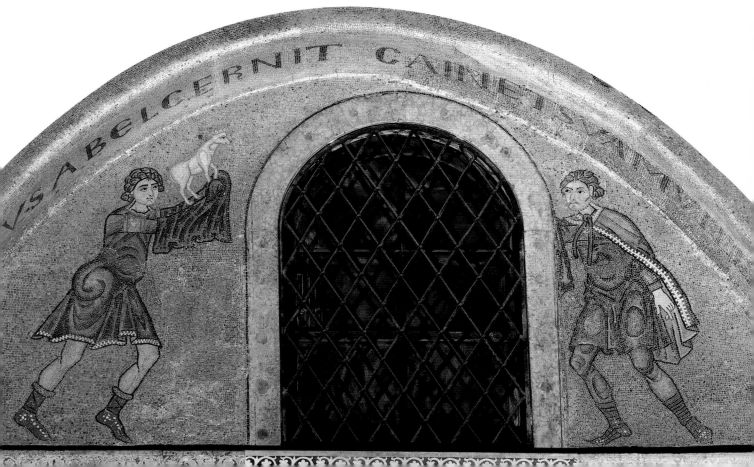

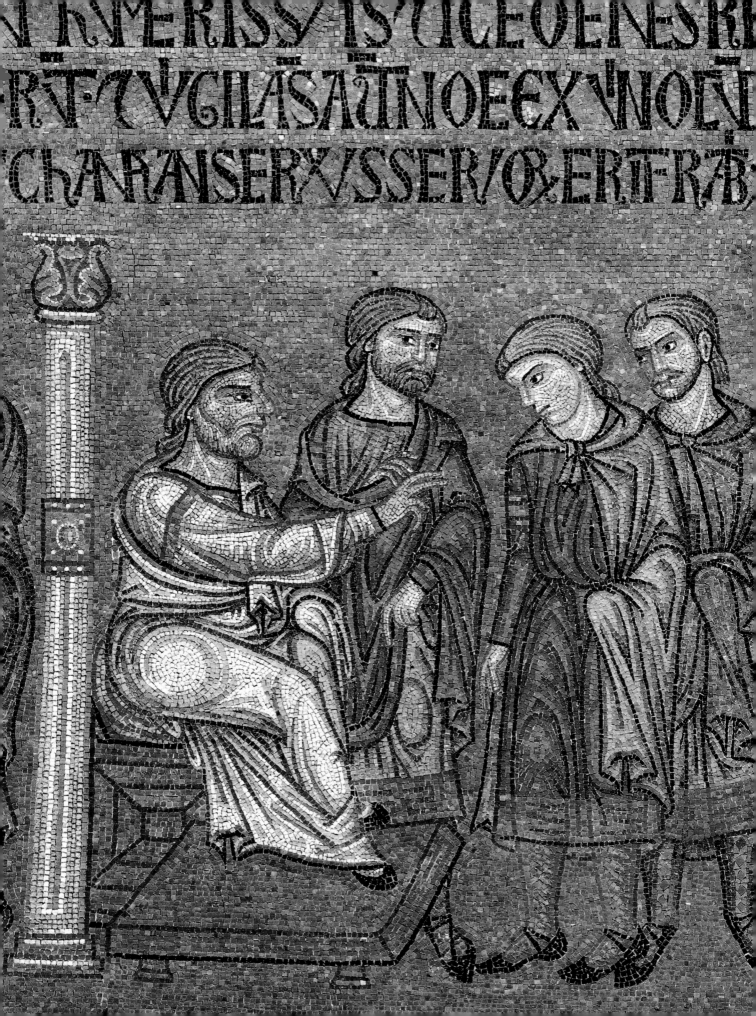

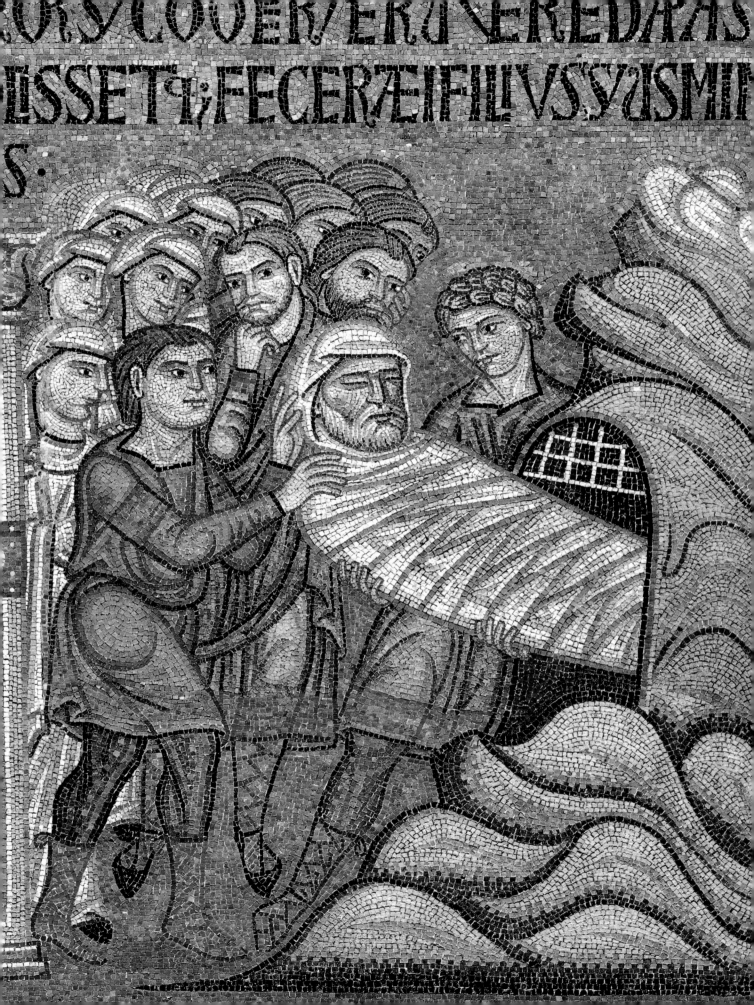

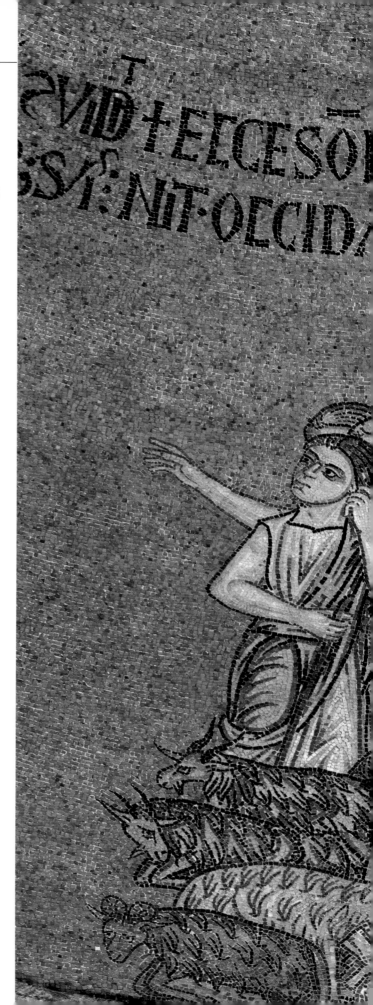

Susanna and Daniel, set on the west wall of the north transept facing the Altar of the Nicopeia, and a fragment of *Cain and Abel* (all that is left of a larger mosaic decorating the balcony from where the doge and his wife attended daily Mass up until at least the fourteenth century) on the right above the door in the Chapel of St. Clement leading to the Ducal Palace.

In all likelihood the mosaics in the atrium were begun in 1230, following the rebuilding of the structure after its destruction in an earthquake. They follow a scheme based on the choral liturgy, according to the rite of the Roman Curia that derived from the reform carried out by the Franciscan Aymon of Faversham between 1243 and 1244. The use of this liturgy at St. Mark's is documented in the contemporary *Antiphonal*, which has recently published by Cattin (*Musica e liturgia a San Marco*, II, Venice 1990). The liturgical sequence commenced with Septuagesima and then continued with Sexagesima, Quinquagesima and the Sundays of Lent. The reading of the *Creation of the World* commenced on Septuagesima, the third Sunday before Lent. This was followed by the *Story of Noah* at Sexagesima and that of Abraham at Quinquagesima. On the first Sunday in Lent, the reading of the Biblical text was omitted and replaced with a text from the writings of the Fathers of the Church. The Bible returned on the following Sundays with the *Story of Isaac and Jacob* (second Sunday in Lent); with the tale of how Joseph was sold by his brothers, became a high-ranking official of the Pharaoh and was later recognized by his brothers when they came to Egypt (third Sunday); and with the story of how Moses freed his

12 *preceding pages*

Judgment and Burial of Noah, Scenes from the Story of Noah, mosaic, west atrium, 13th century

Noah falls asleep naked after drinking wine made from the vine he planted after the Flood. His sons Shem and Japheth, watched by Ham, cover up their father's nakedness as they walk backward. Waking, Noah predicts that Ham will be his brothers' servant. He was buried at the age of 950.

13

Scenes from the Story of Joseph and His Brothers, mosaic, west atrium, First Dome of Joseph, 13th century

Joseph recounts a dream to his brothers, a premonition that one day he will be great. To rid themselves of him, his envious brothers first lower him into a well and then sell him as a slave to Midianite traders, who take him to Egypt.

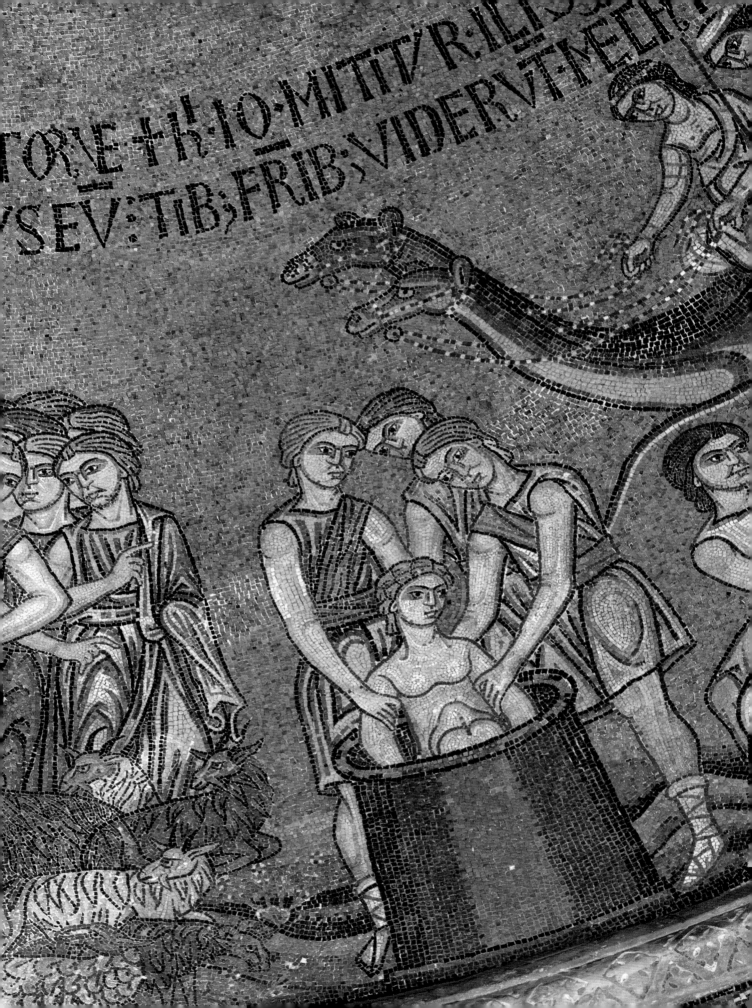

TORIE·TH·IO—MITTI/R·ILIS
/SEV:TIB;·FRIB;·VIDERVT·PELIC

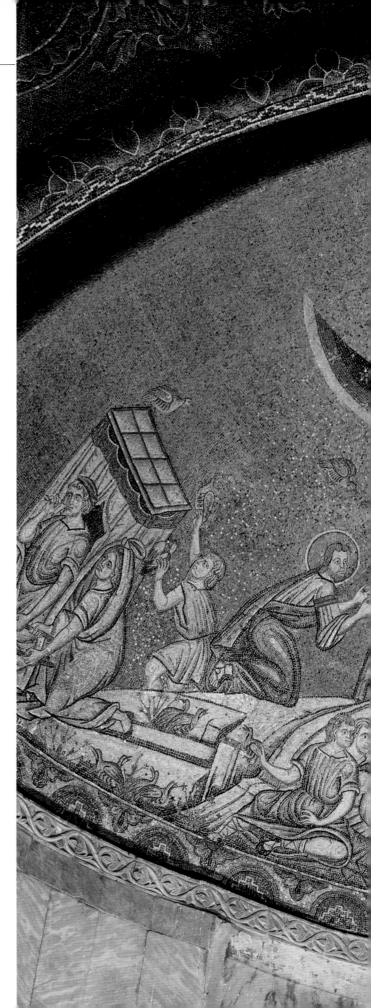

people from enslavement to the Pharaoh and led them across the Red Sea (fourth Sunday). These themes are all represented in mosaic, starting from the south end of the western arm of the atrium, on the inside of its domes and on the walls; they proceed along the northern arm with the *Scenes from the Lives of Joseph* and *Moses*. The mosaics are based on the Biblical texts. They have been continued, independently of the liturgical order, in an anthological manner in order to fill the spaces of the walls, which would otherwise have been left blank. Each story usually occupies a single dome. It is only that of Joseph which extends over three domes and a variety of interpretations have been given for this. One possibility is that greater space was given to the tale of Joseph, which is narrated moreover with superb artistic skill, as a mark of honor to the viceroy of Pharaonic Egypt, the land which St. Mark had converted to Christianity and from which his body was brought to Venice.

In some scenes it is possible to detect signs of Venetian nationalism. In the representation of the creation of the animals, for instance, in the second circle of the dome at the south end of the west atrium, the first creatures to prostrate themselves in worship before God are a pair of lions, symbol of the Venetian Republic, in an apparent sign of divine predestination. In the *Scenes from the Flood*, the ark contains not only peacocks, symbol of the Persian Empire, and eagles, alluding to the Byzantine Empire, but also lions, a reference both to the Kingdom of Judah and to the Republic of Venice, its ideal heir. On the subject of the iconographic sources, the arguments put forward by the Finnish scholar Tikkanen are now universally accepted. He maintains that the mosaicists in the atrium took their inspiration largely from the *Cotton Bible*, a biblical codex of Egyptian origin dating from the reign of Constantine and now in a British museum, while those who represented the *Scenes from the Life of Moses* were influenced by the so-called *Gerona Bible* from the time of the Paleologan renaissance that took place after 1261.

14

Scenes from the Story of Moses, mosaic, north atrium, lunette above the Porta dei Fiori, 13th century

The left-hand scene represents the miracle of the manna and on the right is that of the water flowing from the rock.

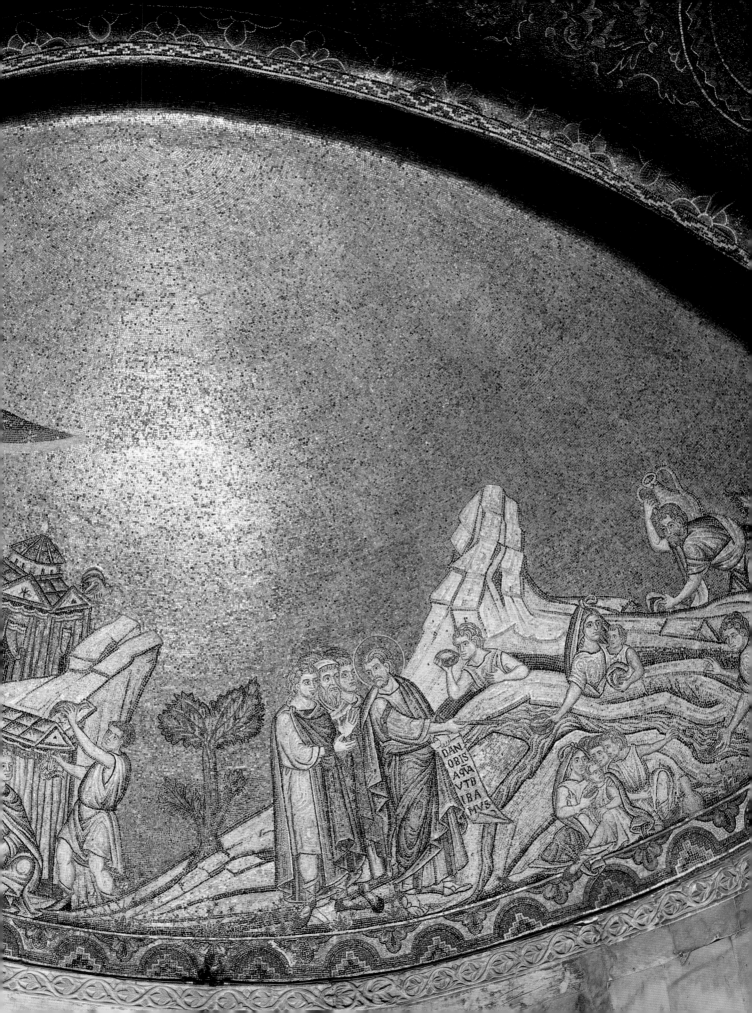

DAN
OBIS
AQA
VTB
IBA
MVS

The mosaic decoration of the atrium was completed around 1275. That of the interior commenced shortly after 1094, as soon as the basilica was finished. Work on it continued up until 1204, though it is now recognized that some of the mosaics were executed as late as the middle of the century.

Demus has put forward an interesting hypothesis, based on the actual topographical arrangement of the scenes, that the mosaics of the interior are a development of the so-called *historia salutis*, along the longitudinal axis starting from the Dome of the Presbytery, or Dome of the Emmanuel. The story begins here with the people eagerly awaiting the envoy of the Eternal Father (hence the name Dome of the Father) and continues more or less as far as Epiphany. The following mosaics, to the right and left, are loosely based on the passages from the Gospels used on the Sundays after Epiphany and on weekdays during Lent. Exemplary, in this respect, are the extremely elegant mosaics on the arch to the left of the Dome of the Ascension as we walk away from the altar, drawn from the Gospel text of the first Sunday of Lent and representing the *Temptations in the Wilderness*. These are followed by scenes from the *Passion, Crucifixion, Resurrection, Ascension* and *Christ in Glory*, in the mosaics on the walls and ceiling of the Dome of the Ascension. The period after Easter was dominated by readings from the Acts of the Apostles. These are represented in the vaults of the aisles to either side of the Dome of the Pentecost, where the stories of the twelve apostles are narrated, drawing on reliable historical sources as well as on apocryphal writings. The text of Revelation, the last book in the Bible and final chapter in the history of the human race, is depicted between the Dome of the Pentecost and the way out of the basilica.

On a smaller scale are the liturgical cycles of the Holy Communion and the Life of Mary. At least from the middle of the fourteenth century up until 1517, the tabernacle was placed on the wall to the left of the entrance to the presbytery, as was the custom at the time. As a consequence the surrounding mosaics focus on the mystery of Communion, in terms both of its prefiguration in the Old Testament and of its institution in the New Testament. Above the steps leading to the tabernacle rise the majestic figures of Moses and Elijah with eucharistic inscriptions. Nearby, on the east vault of the north transept, we find scenes from the Gospel story of the centurion praying for his ailing servant, *Domine non sum dignus...* – which is echoed in the liturgy of the Mass at the moment of Communion – and the *Last Supper*, with its evident eucharistic significance. The extensive treatment of the story of the supper at Emmaus in the Nicopeia Chapel continues the eucharistic theme.

The Marian cycle, on the other hand, is laid out fanwise on the western walls of the two transepts and ends in the entrance bay of the atrium. The *Scenes from the Birth of the Virgin*, based on apocryphal texts (the *Protevangelium of James*), are represented in the south transept, where the emphasis is placed on episodes involving the Virgin's parents, Joachim and Anna, while the scenes showing the *Childhood of the Virgin*, the *Marriage to Joseph* and the *Annunciation* appear on the corresponding western wall of the north transept. The Marian theme is taken up again in the *Death of the Virgin*, located in the so-called well in the entrance bay of the atrium, in a partially Byzantine scheme that juxtaposes the story of Mary with the Christological one of the *historia salutis*. The two sources of revelation – the Holy Scriptures and the

15

General plan of the basilica showing the location of the principal mosaics

1. west atrium	13. tribune of the Madonna of the Kiss	25. tribune of the procurators
2. north atrium	14. Mascoli Chapel	26. east vault of the Ascension and iconostasis
3. Baptistery	15. Chapel of St. Isidore	
4. Vault of the Apocalypse	16. Dome of St. John the Evangelist	27. tribune of the patriarch
5. tribune of St. Peter	17. north vault of the Ascension	28. Nicopeia Chapel
6. tribune of St. Clement	18. Dome of the Ascension	29. Chapel of St. Peter
7. Dome of the Pentecost (or of the Holy Spirit)	19. south vault of the Ascension	30. presbytery
8. north vault of the Pentecost	20. Dome of St. Leonard	31. Dome of the Presbytery (or the Prophets or the Emmanuel)
9. south vault of the Pentecost	21. Treasury	
10. west vault of the Ascension	22. Sanctuary	32. Chapel of St. Clement
11. capital of the Crucifix	23. Chapel of St. Leonard	33. apse with Christ the Pantocrator
12. Virgin of the Gun	24. pillar of the Finding of St. Mark	34. Sacristy

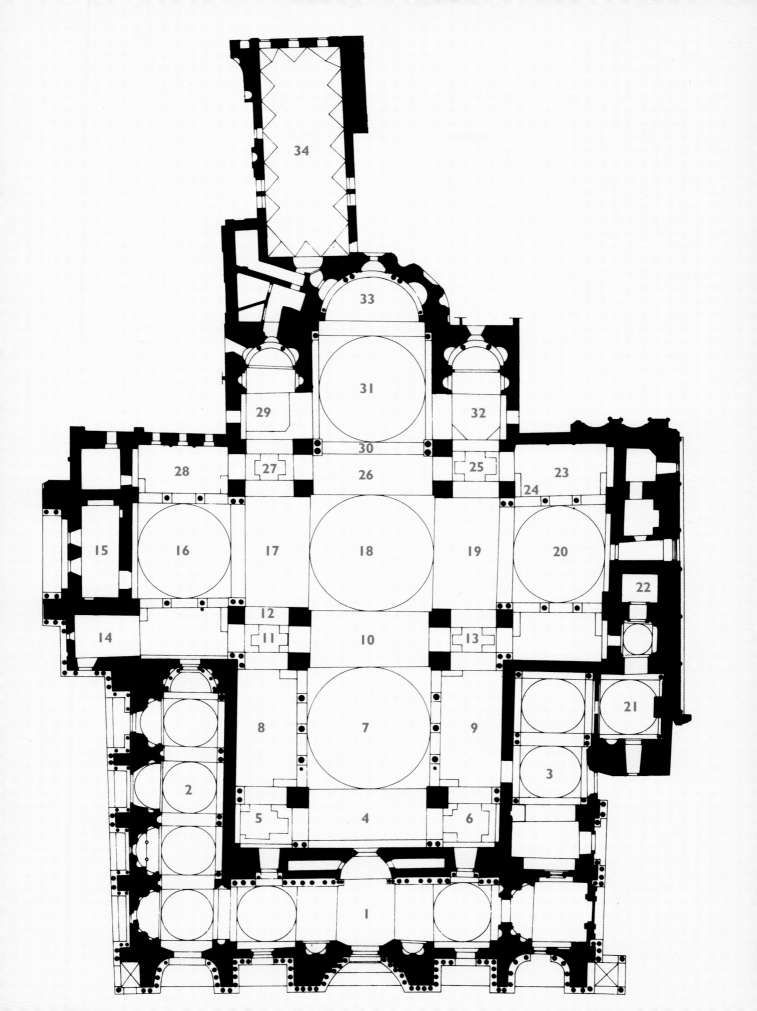

Tradition of the Doctors of the Church – represented respectively in the pendentives of the Dome of the Ascension and of the Dome of St. John the Evangelist should be seen in relation to these liturgical themes. Today theology, after the Second Vatican Council, accepts the union of the Holy Scriptures and Tradition as the sole source of divine revelation, whereas in classical doctrine, and in particular in that of the Middle Ages, the two sources were regarded as distinct. The presence of the four evangelists and the rivers of the Garden of Eden associated with them in the pendentives of the Dome of the Ascension is intended to show that divine revelation flows to the Church and to humanity through the written Word of God, or the Holy Scriptures. In the pendentives of the Dome of St. John the Evangelist, on the other hand, we find the four classical Doctors of the Western Church – Ambrose, Augustine, Gregory the Great and Jerome – alluding to Tradition. The interaction between Holy Scripture and Tradition is also reflected on the outside of the basilica, with the statues at the top of the north front representing the four Doctors of the Church and those on the west façade depicting the four evangelists.

We now come to the cycles of scenes from the lives of the saints. Whether arranged to form a *continuum historicum* – as in the case of St. Mark, St. Peter and the other apostles, St. John the Evangelist, Pope Clement I and St. Leonard of Limoges – or as isolated images, they total 181 figures. The presence of many of these saints can be connected with the political and trade links established by the Republic with markets in the East and West, such as St. Leonard (France) and St. Boniface (the German-speaking lands).

Numerous religious festivals were held in the basilica and are recorded in the *Ordo*, the specific liturgical calendar. Four feast days were devoted to the patron saint, Mark: January 31, commemorating the arrival of his body; April 25, the day of his martyrdom; June 25, the day on which his relics were found; and October 8, in memory of the dedication of the basilica. On January 31 the city's clergy walked in procession around the saint's altar, singing psalms. Since the early part of the nineteenth century and right up to the present day, the feast of April 25 has come to be known as *San Marco dei bocoli* (St. Mark of the Buds), after the custom of presenting a rosebud to your beloved or to women in general. On April 25, the faithful used to come and venerate the so-called marble

throne of St. Mark, now in the Treasury but previously kept in the basilica. The throne, on which the saint was believed to have once sat, was brought to Venice in 1451 from Grado, where it had been received as a gift – it is said – from the Byzantine emperor Heraclius around 630. In Venice it was regarded as a precious relic and was said to cure or relieve anyone who sat on it from the pains of rheumatoid arthritis.

The other festivals have also been given popular names that have been in use since at least the early seventeenth century. That of January 31 was known as *San Marco dei mezéni*, in memory of the fact that the saint's relics had been transported to Venice concealed in the middle (*in mezzo*) of layers of pork (or lard) and cabbage leaves. This was very similar to the old technique for preserving meat, widespread in the Venetian countryside up until the beginning of the twentieth century, which involved alternating meat with layers of lard and cabbage leaves. The feast of June 25 was called *San Marco dell'acqua rosata* (St. Mark of the Rosewater), as on this day a priest went round the basilica with an altar boy, sprinkling first the high altar, then the clergy in the chancel and finally the congregation with rosewater, to commemorate the strong scent of roses that was given off when the saint indicated where his remains were buried.

16

View of the interior of the basilica

The sequence of vaults and domes reflects an essentially Byzantine scheme of construction. It permitted the Greek architects, summoned to Venice by Doge Domenico Contarini in 1063, to adapt the requirements of the new building to the existing structures that the doge wished to preserve, such as the one that is now the crypt but was originally the place where the body of St. Mark was kept.

The domes of the transept and the ones in the church's longitudinal axis differ in size, as do the north and south

ones in the transept itself. This provides clear indication that changes were necessary to adapt the plan of the basilica to the existing structures to the north and south, as well as to incorporate the first church of St. Mark, which is now the crypt.

Finally, another significant factor in Venice was the need to distribute the weight of the church's walls, piers and domes over the largest area possible. The solution of repeating the same structural pattern many times achieves the effect of grandeur that the Venetians so admired in the basilica of Hagia Sophia in Constantinople.

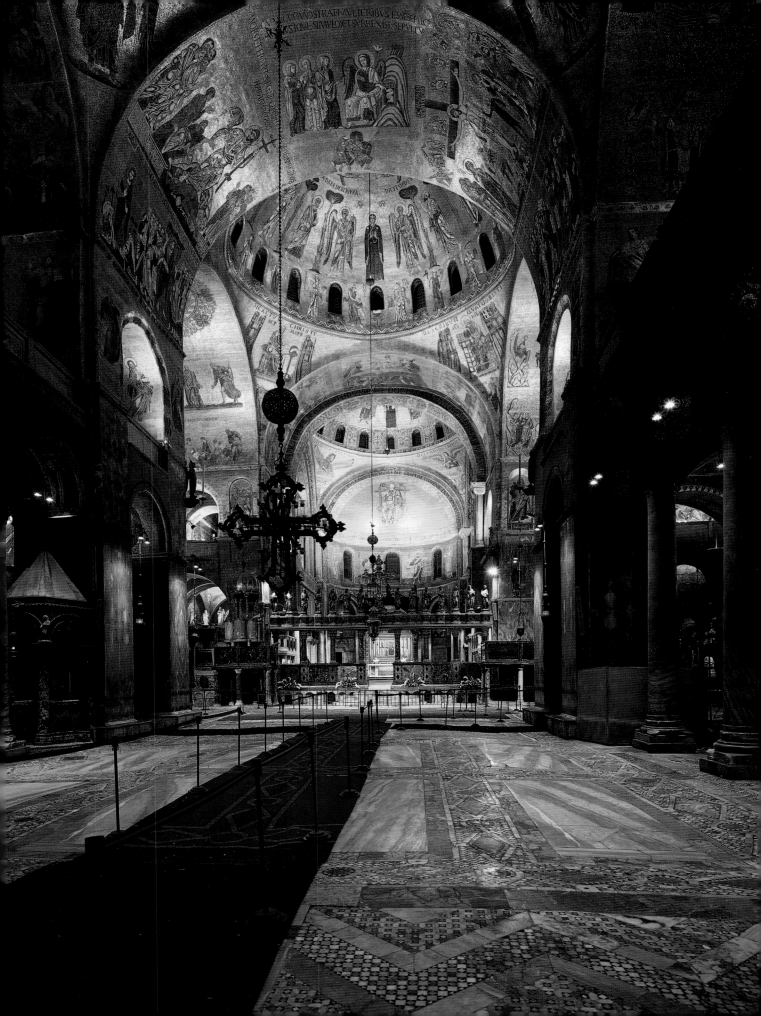

The custom, recorded up until the middle of the nineteenth century, slowly died out. On the same feast day, the clergy used to incense the pillar where the saint had appeared, the one on the right as you come out of the Chapel of St. Leonard next to the entrance to the crypt. The feast of October 8 was known as *San Marco delle zízole* (St. Mark of the Jujubes), as this was the time when the red berries were ripening in the hedges of Venetian gardens.

Some of the solemn rites celebrated in the basilica and recorded in the manuscript and printed ceremonials of St. Mark's were attended by the doge and his court. It should be remembered that the doge considered himself to be the vicar of Mark the Evangelist, with jurisdiction over the basilica and several other Venetian churches that was independent of the authority of the pope. He had almost the powers of a bishop, who was his representative in spiritual matters, and, where liturgical rights were concerned, authority was exercised through the *canonicus primicerius*. As well as attending Mass, the doge took part in various other phases of the celebrations, commencing with the procession in which he was accompanied from the Ducal Palace along the Scala d'Oro and the Scala dei Giganti by staggered groups of his twelve dogal canons dressed in copes of gold lamé, a parade of clerics and the dogal court. The procession left the palace through the door called the Porta della Carta and entered the basilica through the Door of St. Clement, continuing as far as the chapel of the same name. The doge then entered the presbytery, where he was awaited by the *primicerius* and the papal nuncio. The celebration of Mass would then begin at the foot of the altar, as depicted in the well-known eighteenth-century engraving by Antonio Visentini. The doge stood on the right, on the lectern side of the altar, in third place behind the *primicerius* and nuncio. While these two climbed the steps to the altar to recite the *Introit*, the doge ascended his throne, set in the middle of the entrance of the iconostasis.

In the more solemn rites of Holy Week, the doge would take part in the daily liturgical ceremonies, both in the morning and in the evening, as well as in the Procession of the Palms on Palm Sunday, in the services on Maundy Thursday and Good Friday and in the complicated ritual of the tomb on Easter Saturday. However, the doge was not present at the ceremony held on Maundy Thursday evening when the relics of Christ's Passion, conserved – as they still are – in the shrine next to the Treasury, were displayed in St. Mark's. This ended, as documented in a late eighteenth-century painting by Gabriele Bella, with a procession through the Piazzetta dei Leoni and St. Mark's Square itself, with the Scuole Grandi carrying their insignia. On Good Friday morning, the doge, dressed in mourning, attended the Mass of the Presanctified and the ritual of the Adoration of the Cross, accompanied by ambassadors, members of the signoria, magistrates and senators. And in the evening, after listening to the sermon on the Passion, he took part in the Procession of the Most Holy Sacrament through the basilica.

We find the most recent treatment of the so-called patriarchal rite, still the subject of much debate and practiced in the basilica up until 1807 when the Roman one was imposed, in the aforementioned work by Cattin (*Musica e liturgia a San Marco*, Venice 1990). The patriarchal rite was neither of Eastern origin, nor was it derived from the patriarchate of Aquileia, though this is where the name comes from. Instead, it was a Roman rite that was common in the Latin Church and had a number of unusual features. These included the use of the Roman Psalter, as in the Vatican basilica, while the rest of the Church followed the so-called Gallican Psalter, and liturgical colors that differed from those of the Roman rite. A few of the basilica's liturgical chants survived even after 1807 but were finally dropped when Latin was abolished in recent reforms. In essence they belonged to the current of Roman liturgy, embellished with virtuoso graces as in the chant of the *Epistle* and the *Gospel*, but producing a quite different effect in the chants of the *Lamentations* in Holy Week and in the readings at the first nocturn of the Christmas Matins. In these, the velvety softness of the voices and their melismas gave the impression, if not of remote origins in the Eastern Church or in the synagogue, at least of a respectful antiquity.

17

Christ the Pantocrator Giving His Blessing, mosaic, bowl-shaped vault of the central apse, replaced in 1506 by Maestro Pietro

Christ the Pantocrator, in accordance with the instructions of the *procuratori de supra*, is represented with the same figures and inscriptions as the original Byzantine mosaic. A later restoration was carried out by Leopoldo dal Pozzo, in 1716.

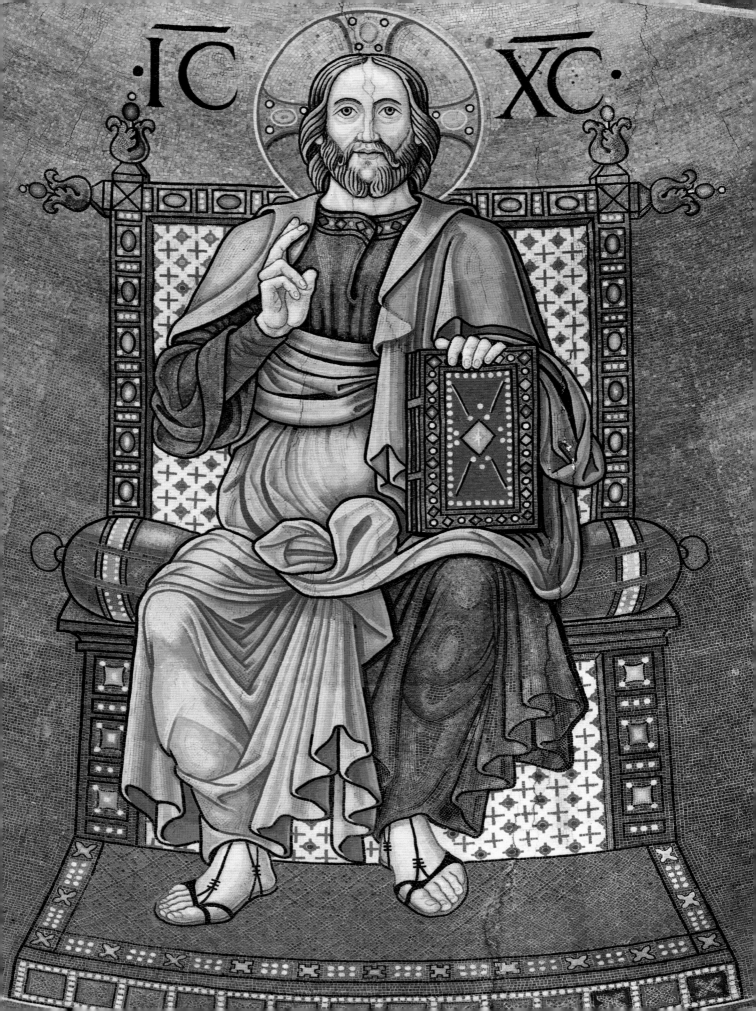

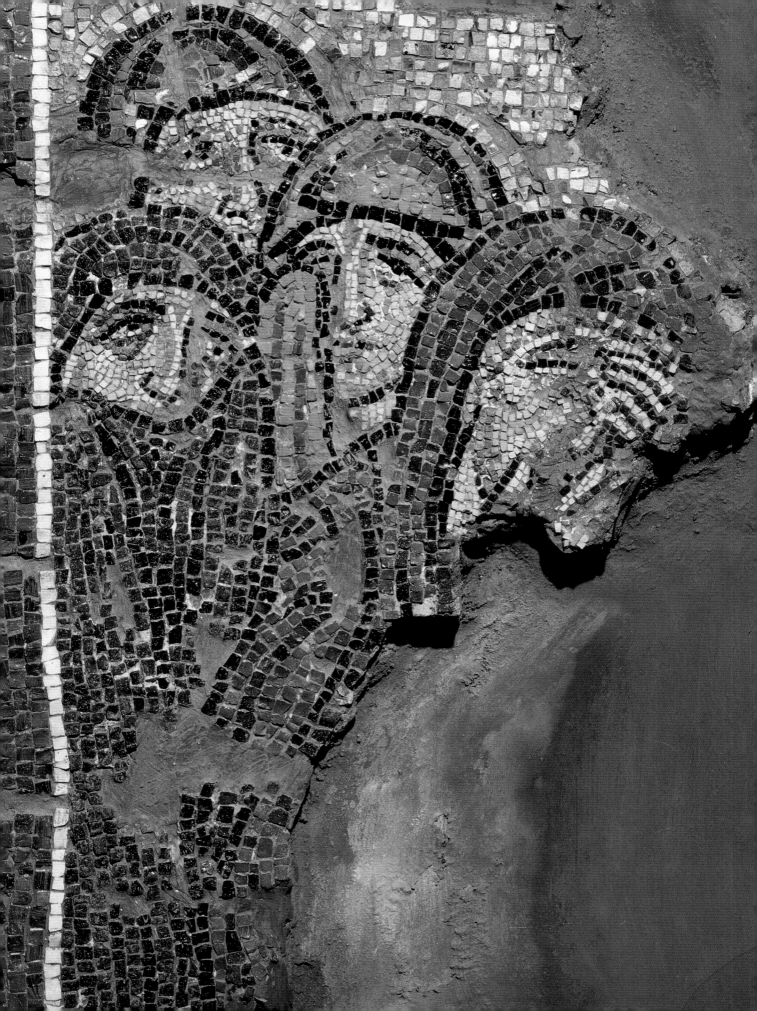

THE ART OF ST. MARK'S

Ennio Concina

St. Mark's does not stand at the geographic center of the city, which, for symbolic reasons, medieval and Renaissance accounts locate elsewhere. The site does not even coincide with the historical tradition of the *umbilicus urbis*, said to lie in the vicinity of San Luca or San Giacomo di Rialto. Nor is it a location dating from early times, since the church's foundation bears no connection to the miraculous appearances of Christ, the Virgin and the saints which induced St. Magnus, bishop of Venice, to choose the sites for the first churches to be erected in the city and around the lagoon. Up until the beginning of the nineteenth century, moreover, St. Mark's was not even the city's cathedral, a status that was assigned, throughout the Middle Ages and for most of the modern era, to the isolated church of San Pietro. And yet the basilica stands at the center of Venice's historical and cultural space.

The original St. Mark's was created as a place of worship closely connected with the authority of the doge, which was reinforced by his role as the custodian of the evangelist's body. This was done quite deliberately by an ancient dynasty of tribunes that, through a whole series of architectural commissions in addition to the basilica itself, set out to present itself as renewing the grandeur of the past. In doing so, it relegated the existing architecture in the area, the churches of San Teodoro and Santi Geminiano e Mena, into the background.

Medieval sources and accounts seem to underline both a sense of continuity and a break with the past. When Doge Giustiniano Particiaco laid down in his testament (829) that stones from Equilo and Torcello should be used for the new church, he was evidently not concerned solely with the salvage of materials, but wanted to incorporate important remains of the past into the building.

Though it was erected alongside the church of San Teodoro – domed, richly decorated and linked with he memory of the Eastern empire to which the Veneto province had been subject – the new basilica did not emulate the older building. As is specifically stated in the sources, it assumed a form of its own, an allusive one suited to the presence of the saint's mortal remains.

In fact, the first St. Mark's did not even copy the basilican structure of the principal episcopal churches in the Veneto, or even of the seat of the patriarch at Grado, the Nova Aquileia, depite the fact that this too was connected with the memory

18

The Holy Women, mosaic, Museum of St. Mark's, 10th-11th century

The mosaic used to be set on the southwest pier of the Dome of the Presbytery. Along with the weeping angel still visible on the pier, they formed part of the *Deposition from the Cross* which was destroyed and covered with marble at the time of the construction of the present and third St. Mark's.

The dimensions of the figures, their position on the pier and their height above the level of the crypt suggest that they were part of the mosaic decoration of the second church, the one rebuilt in the years 976-78.

19

Evangelists St. Matthew and St. Mark, mosaic, central portal of the west atrium, left-hand niches of the entrance, 11th-12th century

These are among the basilica's earliest mosaics and, owing to their position and the sturdiness of the walls to which they are attached, they were less affected by the series of fires and earthquakes that struck the church in the first half of the 12th century.

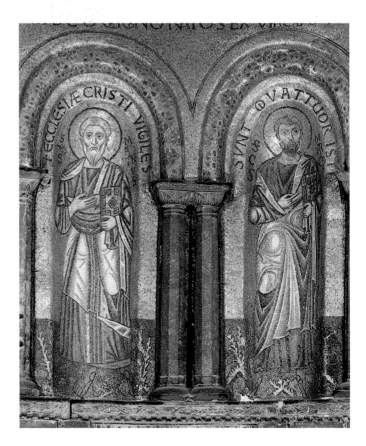

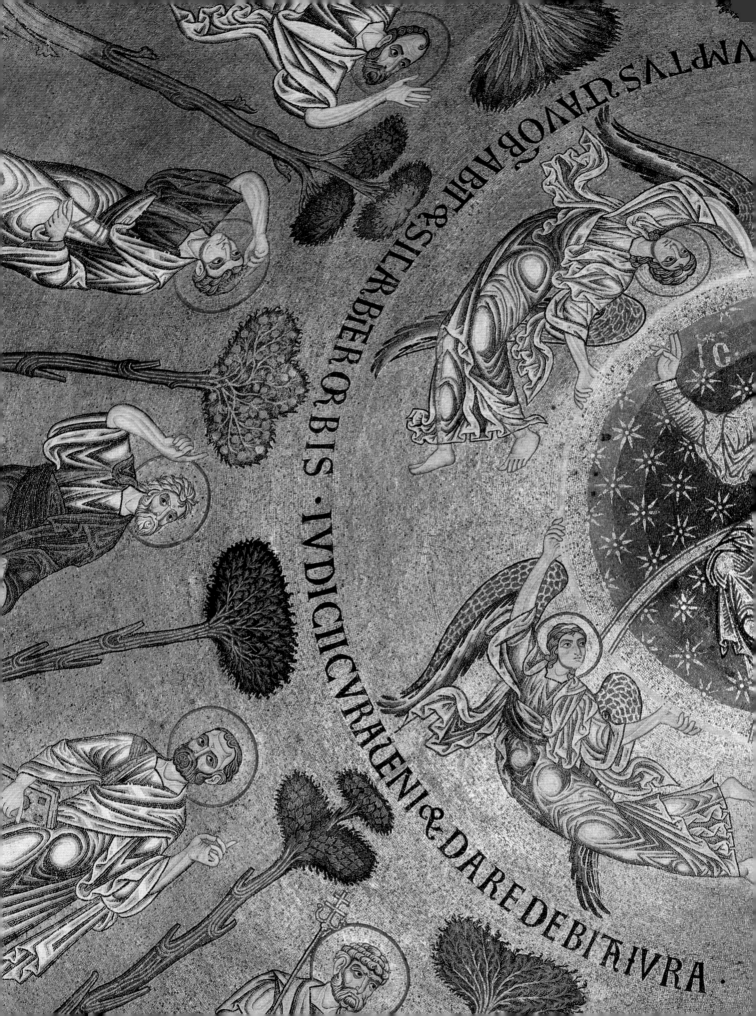

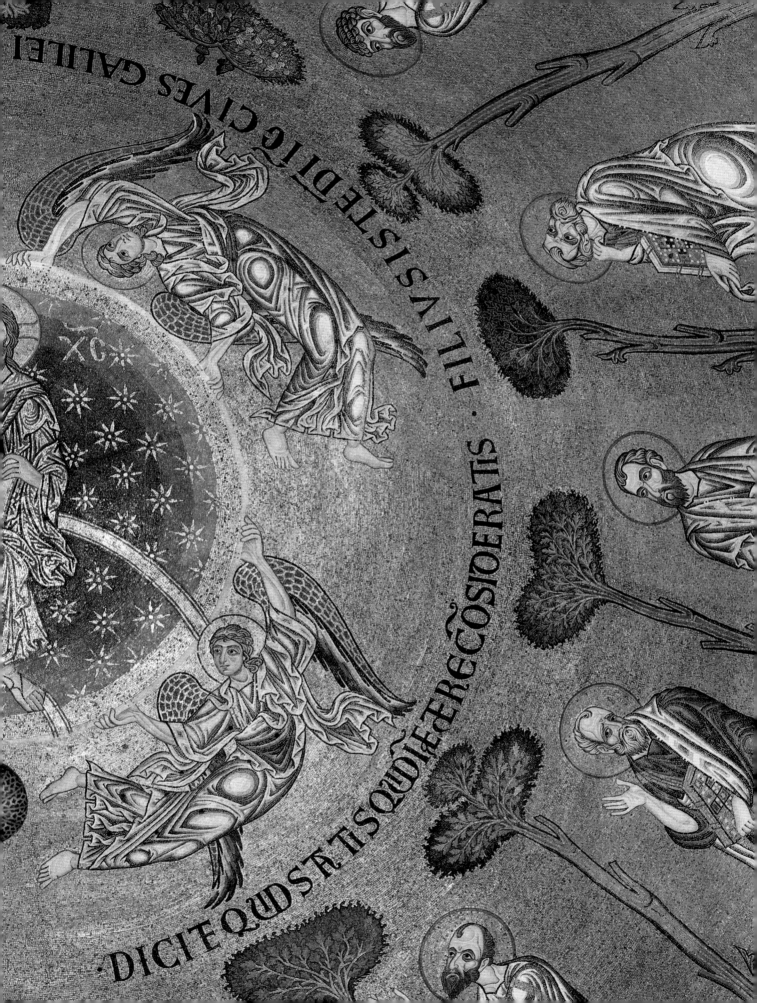

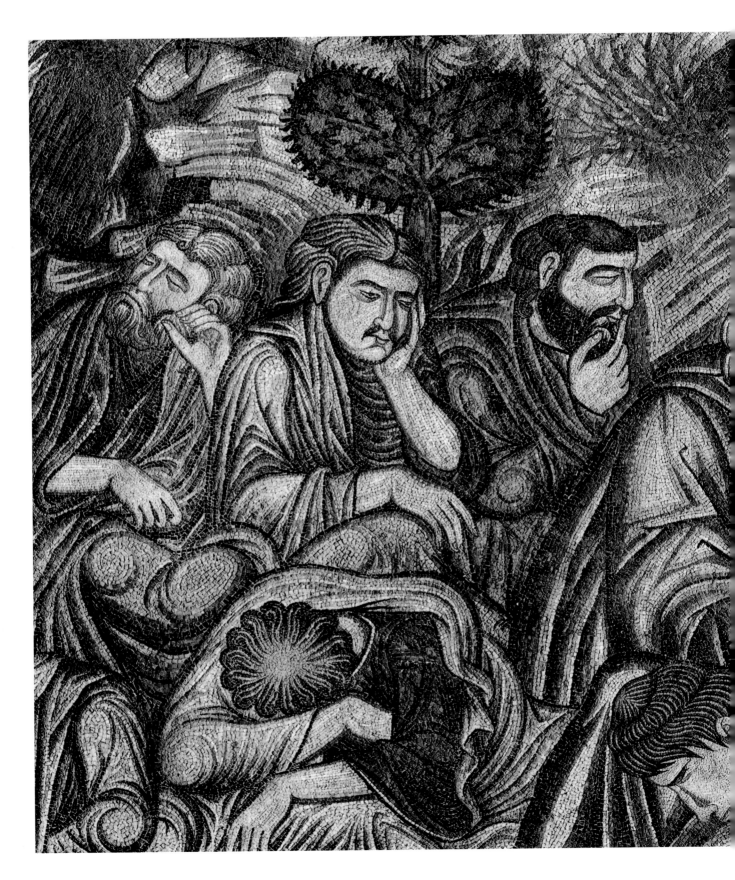

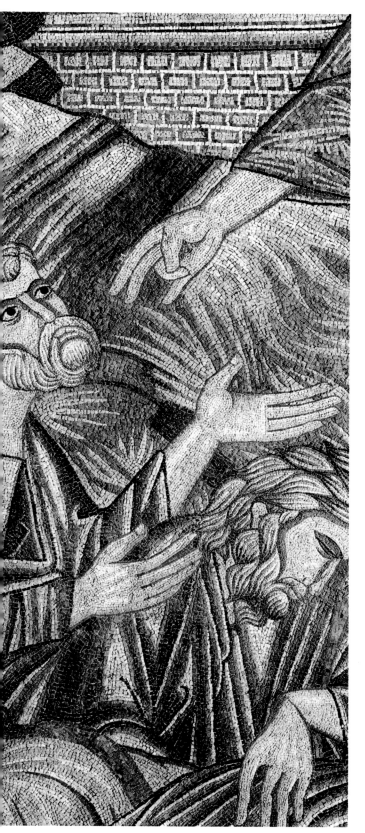

20 *preceding pages*

Dome of the Ascension, mosaic, detail, last quarter of 12th century

Four angels in flight support Christ in the celestial spheres.

21-22

Agony in the Garden, **mosaic, Dome of the Pentecost, south wall, 13th century**

The work of three different mosaicists and executed some time between 1214 and 1220, the image faithfully represents the story of Christ praying in the Garden of Gethsemane. Showing us the disciples' inability to stay awake and the intense suffering of Christ himself, it depicts the natural setting, and in particular the flowers, vibrating against the gold ground as the tension builds up to the momentous event. It is one of the most intense, dramatic and moving of all the mosaics in the basilica.

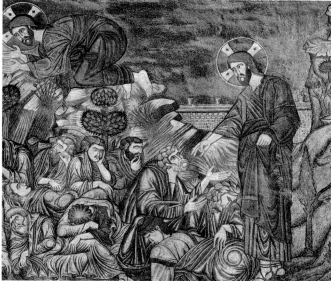

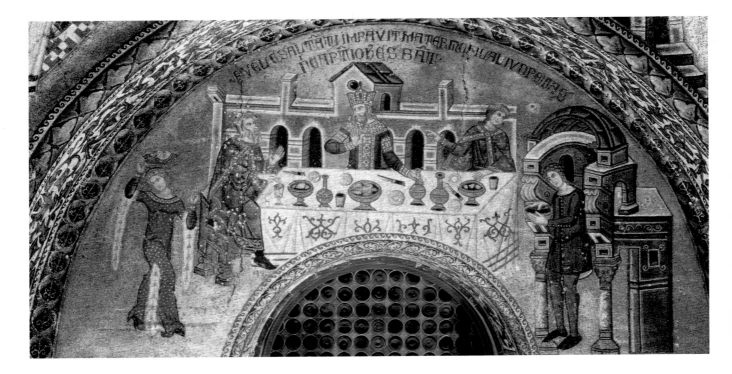

of St. Mark. Instead, the chronicles insist that St. Mark's was based on the Holy Sepulcher in Jerusalem. In other words, universal and sanctifying symbols were taken from the universal center of the world of devotion and transferred to the nascent power of Venice. These symbols served to create an artistic center that was to a certain extent autonomous, but was closely linked to the authority of the doge, whose *pietas* and *auctoritas* the building was also intended to represent. Later it was to become the decisive location for developing the image of the city-state, from the time of the medieval commune to that of the Renaissance Republic.

Following the renovations carried out by Pietro Orseolo, from 1063 onward, the dogal church was rebuilt and enlarged in a new architectural guise. The memory of the original *cappella ducis* was reinterpreted and redefined in undisguisedly courtly terms, taking as its prototype – or so it is claimed – Justinian's Church of the Holy Apostles in Constantinople. This church, a shrine for relics of the apostles and a site of imperial burials, was closely related to another church founded by Justinian, the Basilica of St. John at Ephesus. On the one hand, then, the building housing the remains of Mark the Evangelist was given the same architectural form as the ones with the remains of Luke the Evangelist – venerated in the Apostoleion, or Church of the Holy Apostles – and John the Evangelist,

buried at Ephesus. On the other, the new construction clearly symbolized Venice's imperial aspirations. From this time on, the great church in Venice was to breed, in a manner of speaking, a series of smaller-scale St. Mark's in the Venetian quarters of the Levant and even in Constantinople itself.

The chronicles' version of the reconstruction – probably of medieval origin and perhaps suggested by the bas-reliefs on the arch representing the crafts of the central portal – places great emphasis on the public participation that had been involved. The nobility contributed precious marble and money, while the commoners provided manual labor. St. Mark's was therefore seen as a collective effort on the part of both the *civitas* and commune, and not just as the chapel of the doge.

In the same way, the great cycles of mosaic, a Latin reinterpretation and translation of the decorations of Byzantium, and the complicated geometric patterns

23-24

Dance of Salome, mosaic, Baptistery, lunette above the north door, 14th century

Mosaic by the local workshop, dating from between 1343 and 1354. The mosaics in the Baptistery, the work of two different craftsmen, mark the transition between the Byzantine Romanesque and the fully Gothic period of Venetian culture. Elements of International Gothic can be discerned.

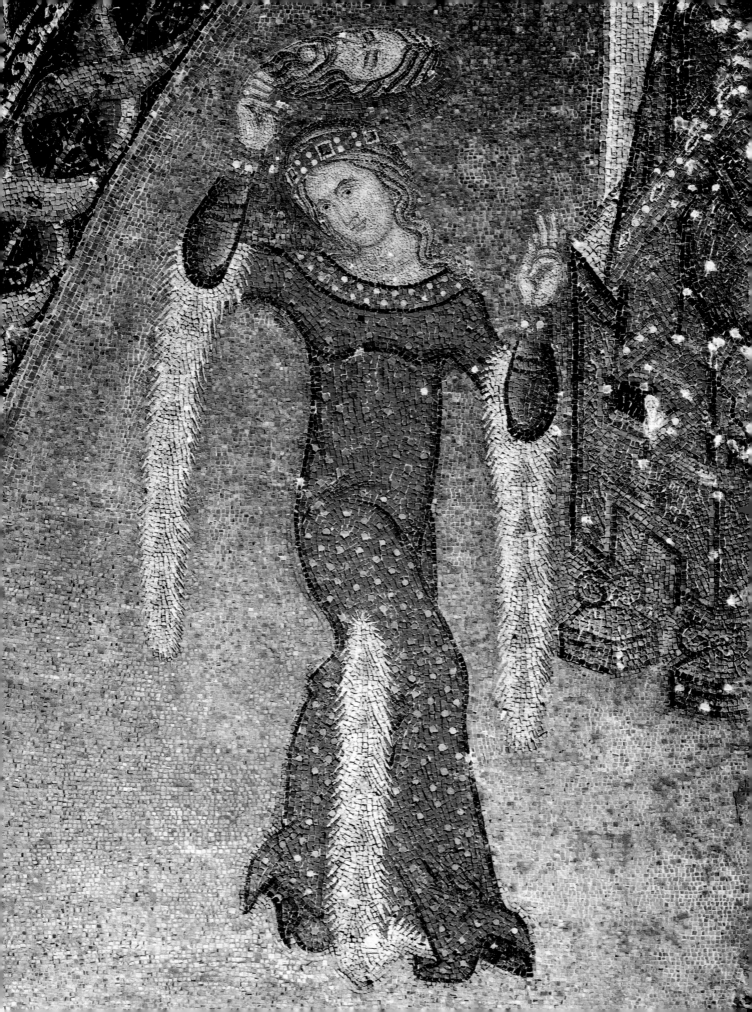

traced in *opus sectile* on the floor have led the collective imagination to attribute their design to Joachim of Floris and to see in them, inscribed for eternity, the mysteries of the destiny of humanity and the path toward its salvation.

From that time on, St. Mark's became the repository for the signs and symbols that reflected the rise of the *Comune Veneciarum* and its own sense of making history. The same feeling found expression in an extensive series of architectural projects, sculptures and stone and mosaic decorations that commenced in the early thirteenth century, during the time of the Eastern Latin Empire. The atrium was extended to both sides of the western arm of the church, and the external and internal walls were faced with precious marble, bas-reliefs and two orders of columns that framed the deep-set portals, concealing from view the surface of the twelfth-century walls with their niches and decorative motifs in brick. The central portal and the Porta da Mar were fitted with bronze doors made in Constantinople during the reign of Justinian and

25 *below*

Death of the Virgin, mosaic, Mascoli Chapel, east side of the vault, 15th century

Tuscan Renaissance in style, it should be compared with the *Birth of the Virgin* signed by Michele Giambono on the west wall, where the Venetian Gothic style is still evident in the architecture of the mosaic (see page 162). These are the earliest mosaics in the basilica for which a cartoon was used, a technique that seems to have been introduced by Paolo Uccello, the Tuscan artist sent from Florence to Venice (1425-33) to reestablish the school of mosaic, which had recently died out.

26 *right*

Tree of Jesse, mosaic, north transept, north wall, 16th century

The Virgin and Child appear at the top of the tree, also known as the Family Tree of the Virgin, that has Jesse at its root. The top is the place of Christ's union with humanity. The mosaic is the work of the mosaicist Vincenzo Bianchini to a design by Giuseppe Porta known as Salviati (1542-52).

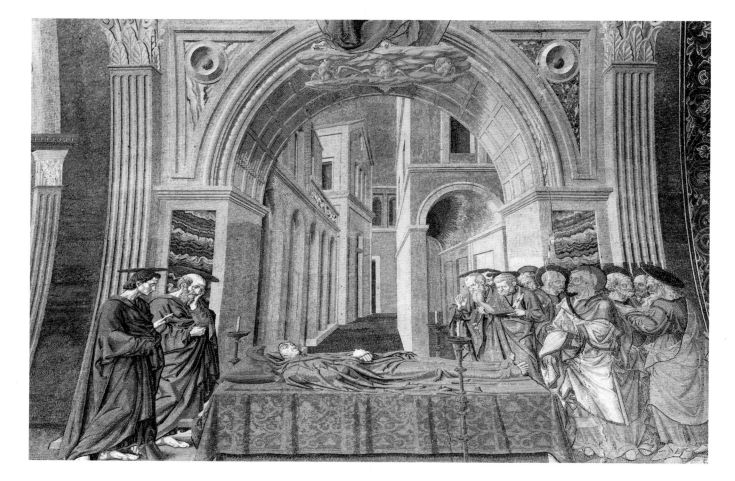

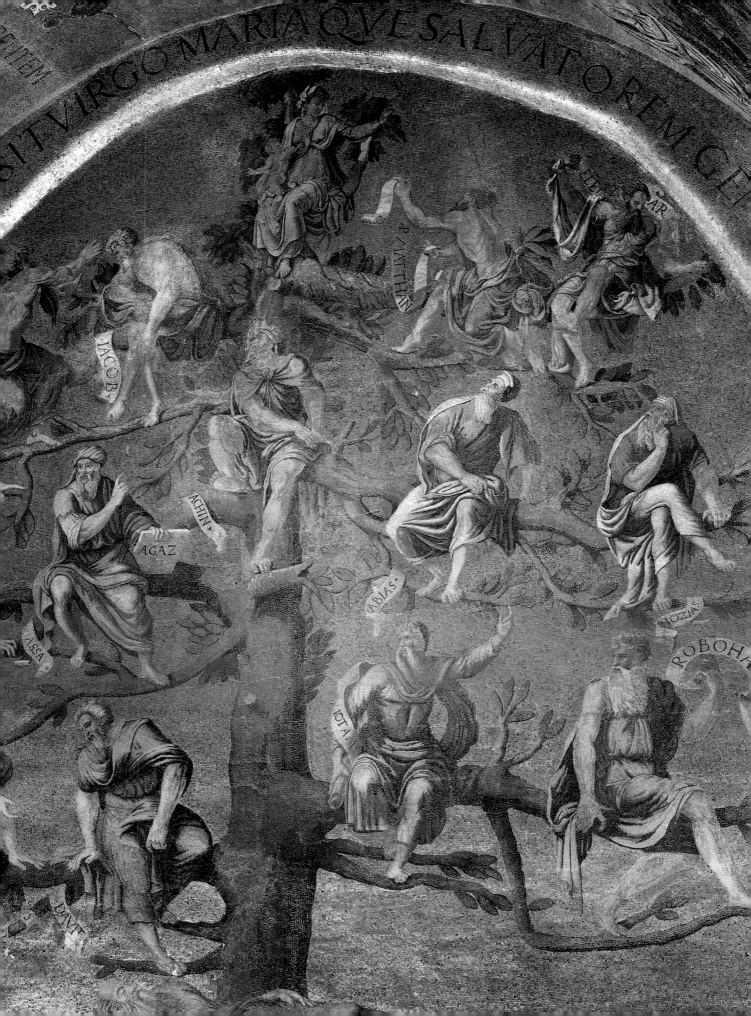

above them were placed the four horses of the quadriga looted from the hippodrome of the Eastern capital. The sculptural group of the *Tetrarchs*, carved out of porphyry and taken from the square of the Philadelphion, was placed at the corner, between the palace and the church. Two elegant pillars that may once have stood in the Church of St. Polyeuctus in Byzantium were erected just a few paces away, so as to lend even greater magnificence to the southern ceremonial entrance to the basilica. Another addition to St. Mark's was the icon of the Virgin known as the *Nicopeia*. Venerated as the sacred painting that had occupied a central place in the imperial liturgy as the protector of the Romans and "leader of the legions," it had once been housed in a chapel of the imperial palaces.

So the structural and decorative renovation of the basilica should be seen as appropriating the *regalia insignia* on the part of the city. It certainly has to be interpreted as an artistic affirmation of the *translatio imperii*, of the conquest and surpassing of Byzantium, whose memory, sovereign magnificence and splendid emblems Venice now flaunted in triumph. Actually the symbolism extended even further. The slabs of rare polychrome stone – it is claimed – came from Aquileia and Ravenna as well as from Byzantium, in other words, from the three cities that epitomized both the history and the grandeur of the imperial idea as well as the origins of Venice.

The symbolic role of the art stretched even further. A group of columns in the atrium were claimed to be genuine relics of Solomon's Temple, transferred from Jerusalem to Byzantium and then to Venice, an indication that the mantle of Nova Hierusalem had now passed to the city of the evangelist. Even the ritual of uncovering of the Pala d'Oro and displaying the church furnishings from the Treasury on the high altar under the honorific roof of the baldachin appears to imitate a similar ritual conducted in Jerusalem, when David offered the booty from his victories to the Temple of Solomon.

The relationship between the church, the urban landscape and the square was also changed. The profile of the domes was altered, emphasized by the high extrados so as to impart an even greater visual impact to the sacred site of the city-state. The marble decorations and cycles of mosaics, that herald the iconographic system of the interior from the outside, transform the opaque screen of the front of St. Mark's into a luminous surface, as a reflection of the relationship between the basilica's exterior and its sacred and liturgical recesses. With the *Scenes of the Retrieval of St. Mark's Body*, the façade becomes an unroofed ceremonial nave to the square, taking on the role of an immense and precious iconostasis.

From this moment on, throughout the Middle Ages and beyond, the art of St. Mark's would be seen as the heart of Venetian artistic culture. In the basilica "gleaming with Parian marble," Raffaello Zovenzoni would seek Antiquity, finding works equal to those of Scopas, Zeuxis and Polyclitus, which he knew from their literary descriptions. The art historians of the sixteenth century would see it as a yardstick and model of magnificence, whose influence had already spread (San Giovanni in Oleo had a "structure … modeled on the middle part of the golden temple of St. Mark" and Santa Maria Formosa was "brought to perfection … on the model of the middle section of the church of St. Mark," wrote Francesco Sansovino) and was to endure beyond the threshold of the Renaissance. According to Sansovino again, San Salvador, a renovation of great symbolic significance that began in 1506 was "rebuilt … to a model … copied from the middle part of the church of St. Mark's." And it was no coincidence that the church was built at the very center of the city which it served to reconsecrate.

27 *above*

Descent into Limbo, mosaic, west façade, second lunette from the left

The work of the mosaicist Luigi Gaetano, to a cartoon by Maffeo da Verona. In 1617-18 the artist completed the entire upper level of the main façade, with the four lunettes illustrating the *Deposition from the Cross*, the *Descent into Limbo*, the *Resurrection* and finally the *Ascension*.

28 *below*

Homage Paid by the Signoria and the Doge to the Body of the Saint, mosaic, west façade, lower level, second portal from the left, 18th century

This mosaic, which covers both the lunette and the vault of the arch, is the work of the mosaicist Leopoldo dal Pozzo, to a design by Sebastiano Ricci (*c.* 1730).

29 *following pages*

Last Judgment, mosaic, bowl-shaped vault of the central portal, lower level

The mosaic is the work of the mosaicist Liborio Salandri, to cartoons by Lattanzio Querena (1836-38).

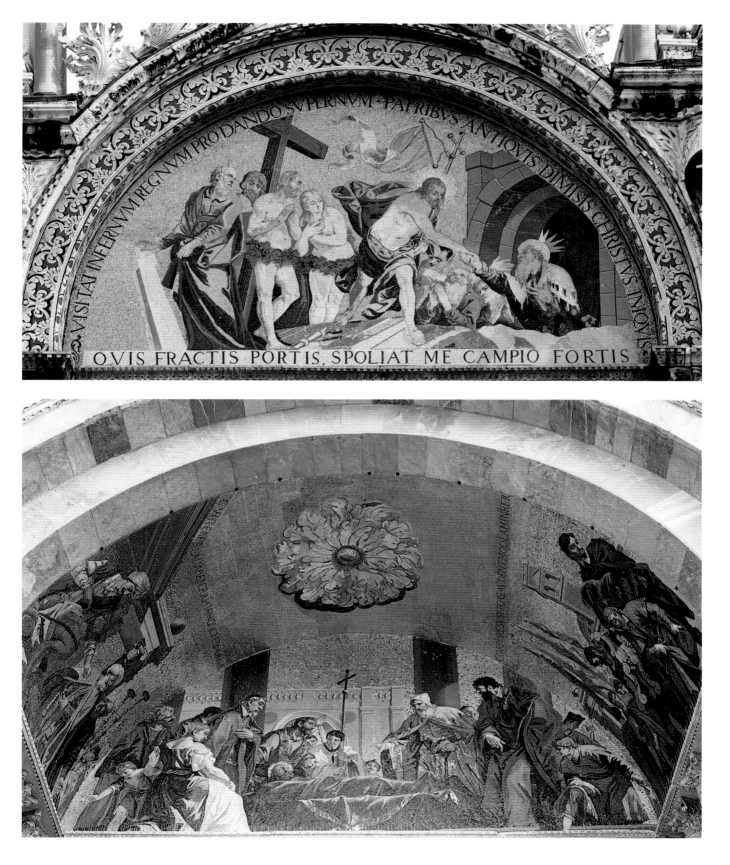

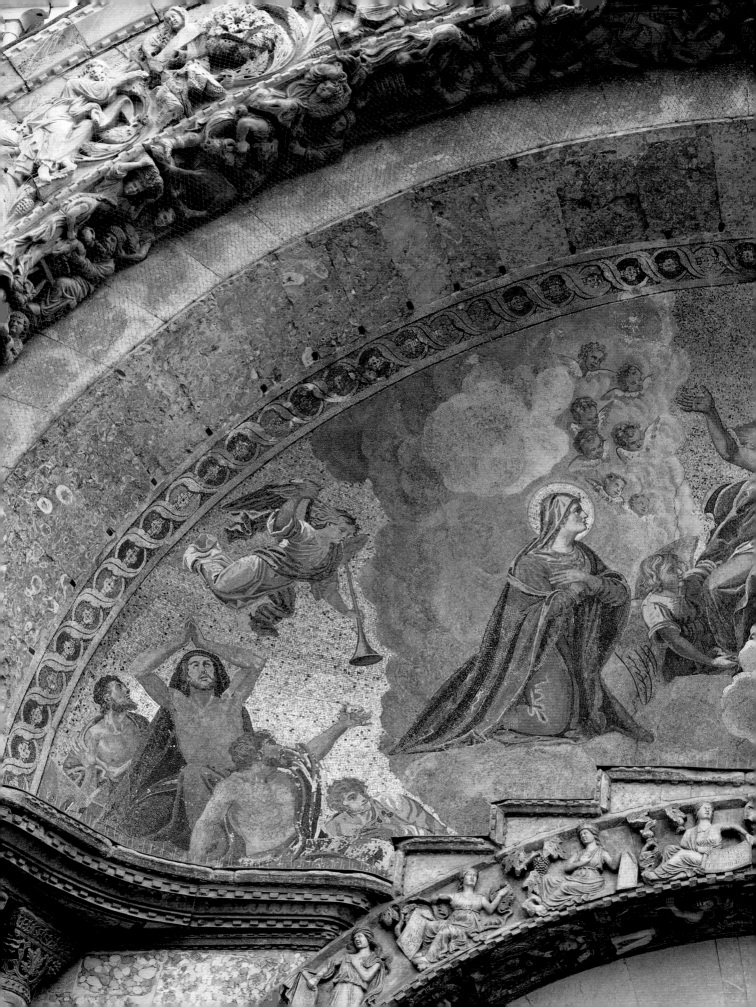

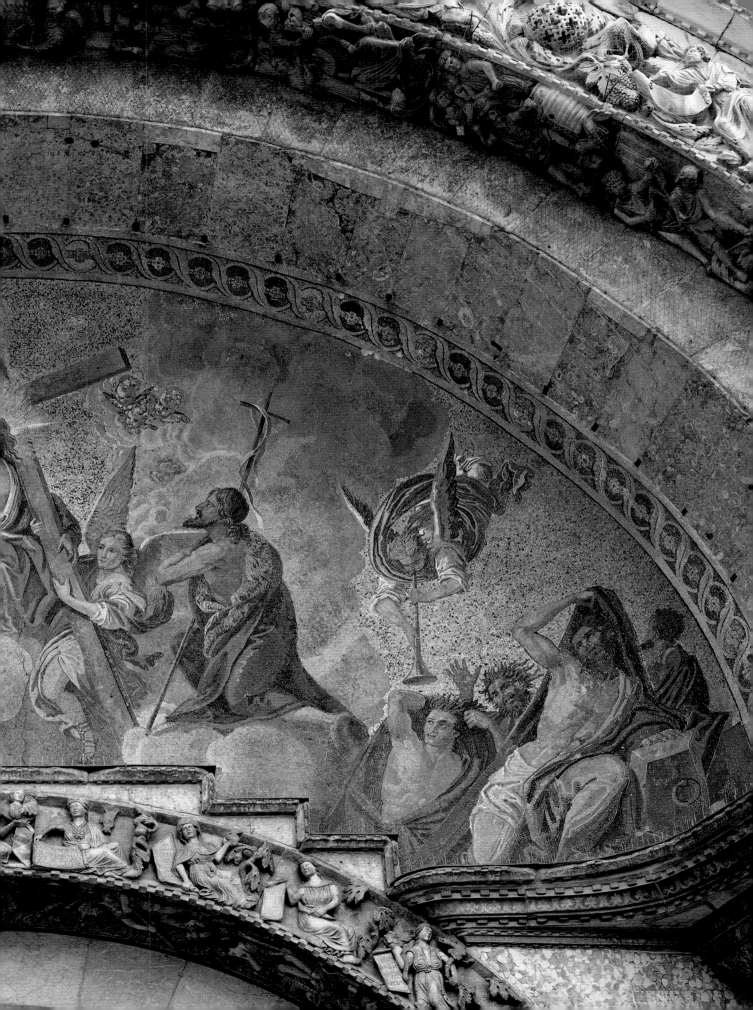

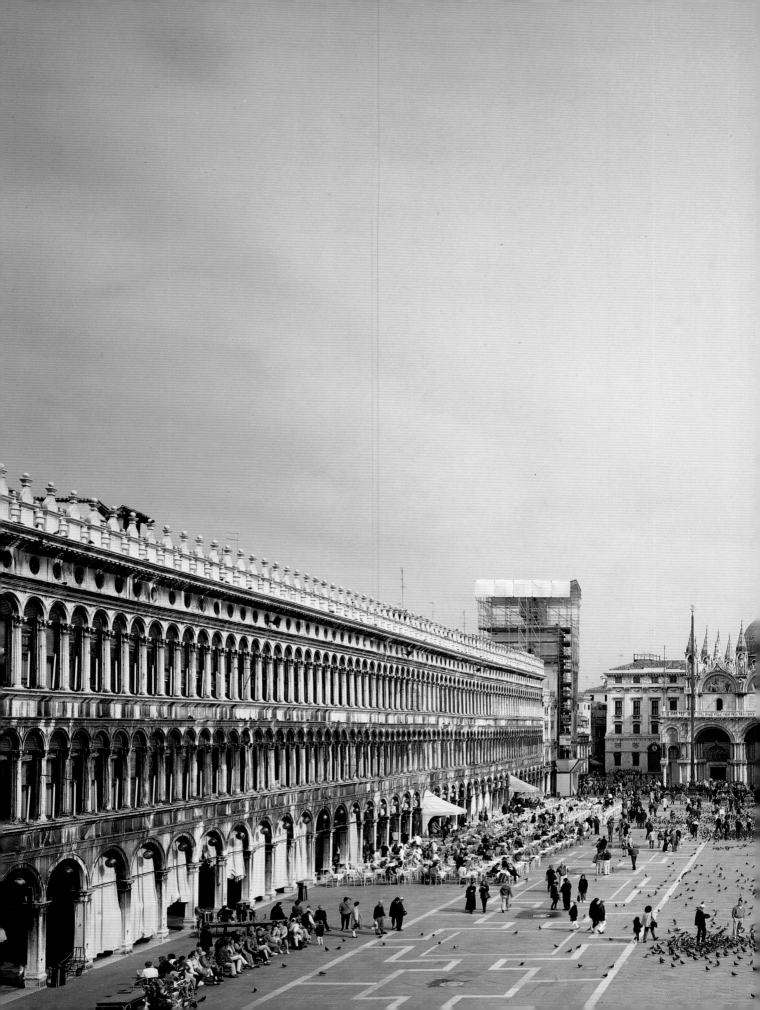

TOUR OF THE BASILICA

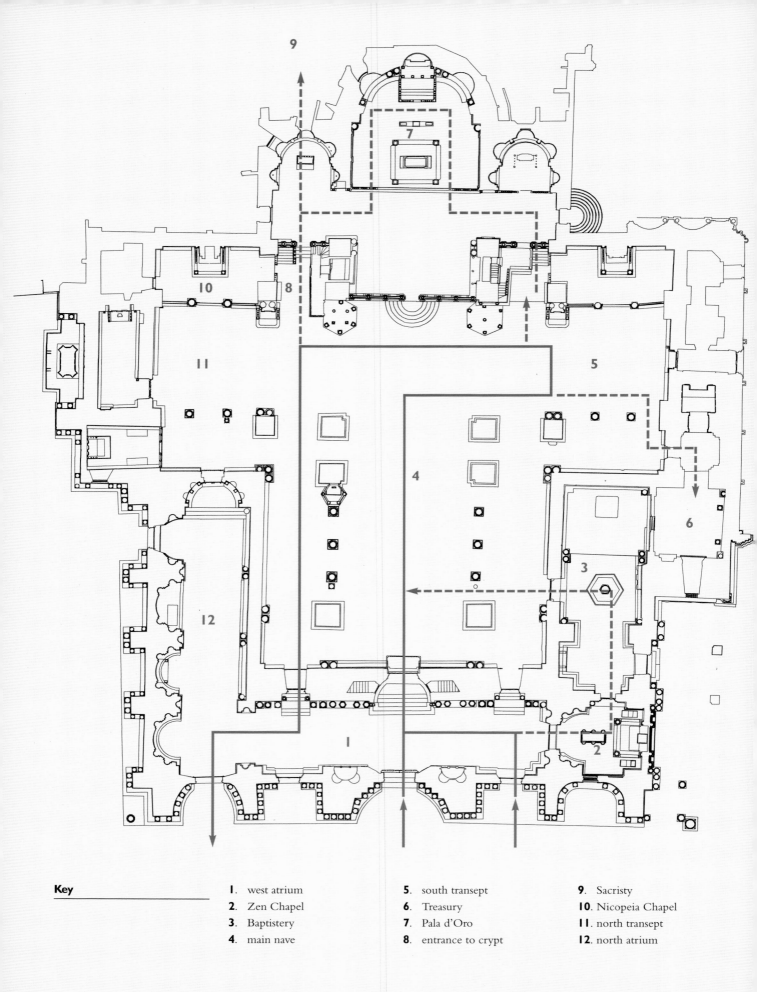

Key

1. west atrium
2. Zen Chapel
3. Baptistery
4. main nave
5. south transept
6. Treasury
7. Pala d'Oro
8. entrance to crypt
9. Sacristy
10. Nicopeia Chapel
11. north transept
12. north atrium

THE TOUR OF THE BASILICA

Ettore Vio

We shall start our tour from the south front, the most enigmatic and extensively modified of the basilica's façades, and the one that appears in all views of the city. From there, we shall move to the west front, opening on to St. Mark's Square, to view the key elements of the building's architecture: the great arches that support the terrace, the lunettes of the structures above the basilica's atrium, the four bronze horses and the Gothic friezes with statues of saints, with that of St. Mark in the middle. The façade is crowned by large domes faced with lead, in an unparalleled Western interpretation of a Byzantine model.

The Porta dei Fiori (Door of the Flowers) is set in the north front, facing on to the Piazzetta dei Leoni. It leads into the atrium at the entrance to the north transept (used only by people going to pray). We shall enter the basilica from the main façade.

The atrium or narthex, which was once entered from the south through the Porta da Mar (Sea Door), now turned into the Zen Chapel, is decorated with mosaics representing scenes from the Old Testament. Passing through the Porta della Madonna after the *Crossing of the Red Sea* at the far end of the northern arm of the atrium, we enter the northern transept facing the Altar of the Nicopeia, an ancient icon brought to Venice as part of the booty from the Fourth Crusade.

The main entrance is through the portal with doors of damascened bronze, which house the oldest mosaics in the basilica. As you enter, you are immediately struck by the preciosity of the marble and mosaic facings and the proportions of an unrivalled architecture.

What you see is a succession of arches, vaults and domes, whose facing of golden mosaics catches the light entering through the windows in the dome, the large openings of the rose windows and the stained-glass Window of the Horses on the west façade, scattering reflections endlessly.

From the inside it is possible to appreciate the underlying structural system of the Greek-cross layout of the basilica's architecture. It consists of four piers united by four vaults with a dome on top, a pattern that is repeated five times.

The mosaics in the domes that line the longitudinal axis tell the *Story of Salvation* and indicate, in the Dome of the Presbytery above the altar, the promise of a Savior. At the center of the crossing, the Dome of the Ascension shows us the historical Christ and his witnesses, the four evangelists,

in the pendentives that support it. The Dome of the Pentecost, with the throne for Christ who will come at the end of time (*Hetoimasia*), presents the apostles assembled and filled with the Holy Spirit.

The south transept, a part of the basilica used particularly by the doge, is surmounted by the Dome of St. Leonard, with Saints Nicholas, Blaise, Clement and Leonard. Up until 1981, the altar dedicated to Leonard to the east of the dome housed the Holy Sacrament. In the north transept – an area used by the church's priests, headed by the *primicerius* who lived in what is now the patriarchal palace – we find the Dome of St. John the Evangelist. Epitome of priesthood, the latter strengthened the faith, overthrew idols and brought aid and succor to believers. In the area to the east of the north transept, we find the Altar of the Nicopeia, with the ancient icon of the Blessed Virgin.

Our tour now takes us toward the crossing, allowing us to appreciate the scale of the transept and to admire the iconostasis and the altar that houses the mortal remains of St. Mark, underneath a baldachin.

The entrance to the Treasury is located in the southwest corner of the church. It is housed in a tower that used to be part of the Ducal Palace, but was later annexed to the basilica.

From here it is possible to visit the golden altar screen known as the Pala d'Oro (for which a fee is charged), located behind the altar. A prior appointment is needed to see the Sacristy, with its mosaics dating from the early sixteenth century and inlaid work by the brothers Paolo and Antonio Mola, and the crypt, recently restored and reopened in 1993. From the western atrium you can enter the Museum of St. Mark. Going out into the Corte Canonica, a staircase leads up to the museum, housed in the former banquet hall.

30

General plan of the basilica showing the internal and external routes
The text follows the route, where the interior is concerned, from the right-hand (south) side of the nave to the south transept, the presbytery and the two side chapels, the north transept and the north wall of the nave on the way out. The exterior and the atrium or narthex are described separately.

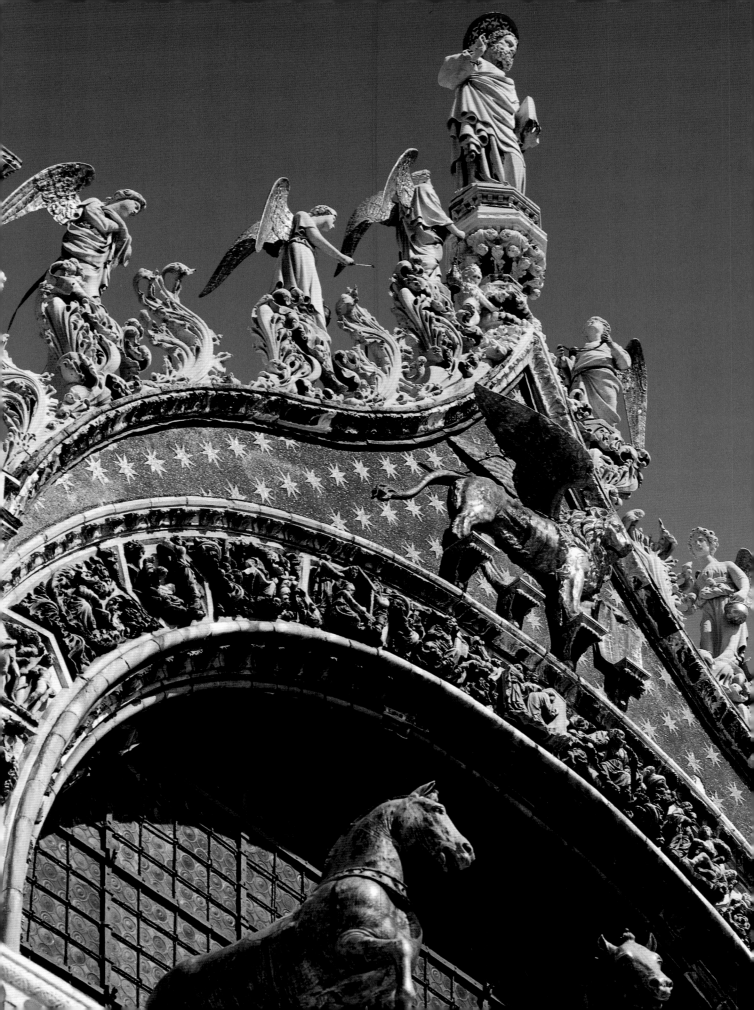

THE EXTERIOR OF THE BASILICA
Ettore Vio

The basilica is not an easy building to grasp, owing to the substantial modifications and renovations of the magnificent structure that were carried out over the first five centuries of its existence. This tour underlines the key points of the basilica's architecture and decoration.

We approach the building from the south, where it faces on to the original square of St. Mark, the Piazzetta – as opposed to Piazza – San Marco. For seven hundred years, this square provided a scenic backdrop for when the doge and the Signoria Serenissima made their grand exits in the direction of the wharf, the square or the basilica itself through the adjoining Porta della Carta of the Ducal Palace.

The southern front is characterized by key elements of the basilica's architecture: the tower set at the corner between the Ducal Palace and the church that used to stand on the site before the construction of the first St. Mark's (829-32); the Porta da Mar, the entrance used by all kinds of navigators from

31
St. Mark with his Gospel, west façade, top of the central pediment
Set above the large stained-glass Window of the Horses, the statue represents the political authority expressed in the quadriga of St. Mark's and the religious faith that in Venice gave special emphasis to the veneration of the city's patron saint.

32
Exterior of the basilica, west façade
Here we see the basilica and all the harmony of its composition, in which every element tends to draw the observer's attention toward the central doorway. Above, the three domes of the nave emphasize the importance of the façade's median axis. Between the central portal and these domes, the large window and the four horses increase the significance of the main entrance. At the sides, the portals create a visual link between the façade and the sequence of arches in the Procuratie Vecchie and Nuove.

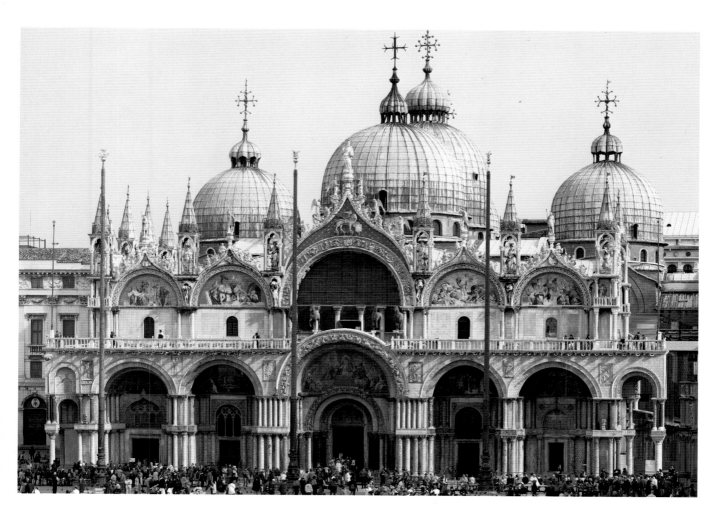

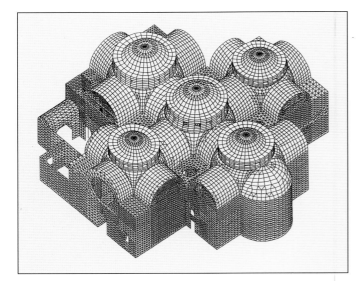

33

Structural model of St. Mark's, made by the Institute of Structural Studies and Research of Bergamo, 1992-93

This model, showing all the basilica's elements, is used to assess the level of stress on the wall structures.

34

View of the domes

The domes were built out of wood and covered with lead – just as we see them today – on top of the Byzantine ones in brick. Their inner surfaces are decorated with the basilica's famous mosaics.

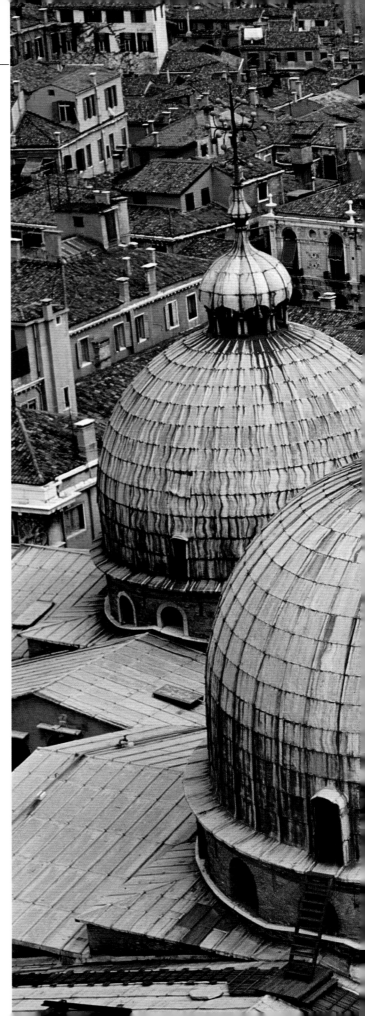

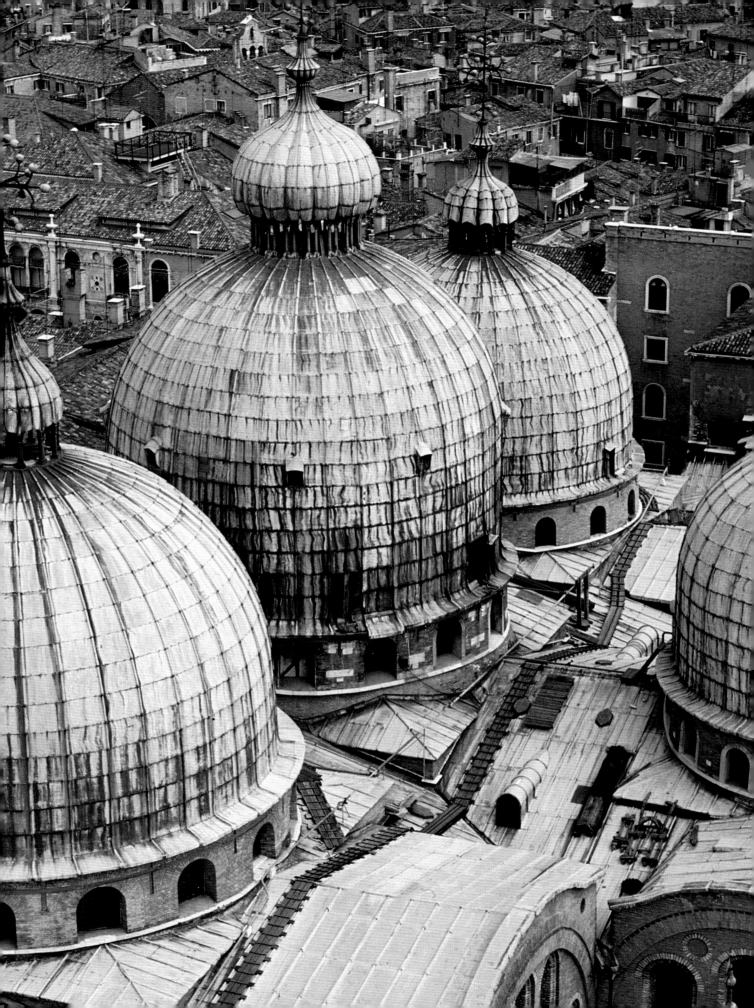

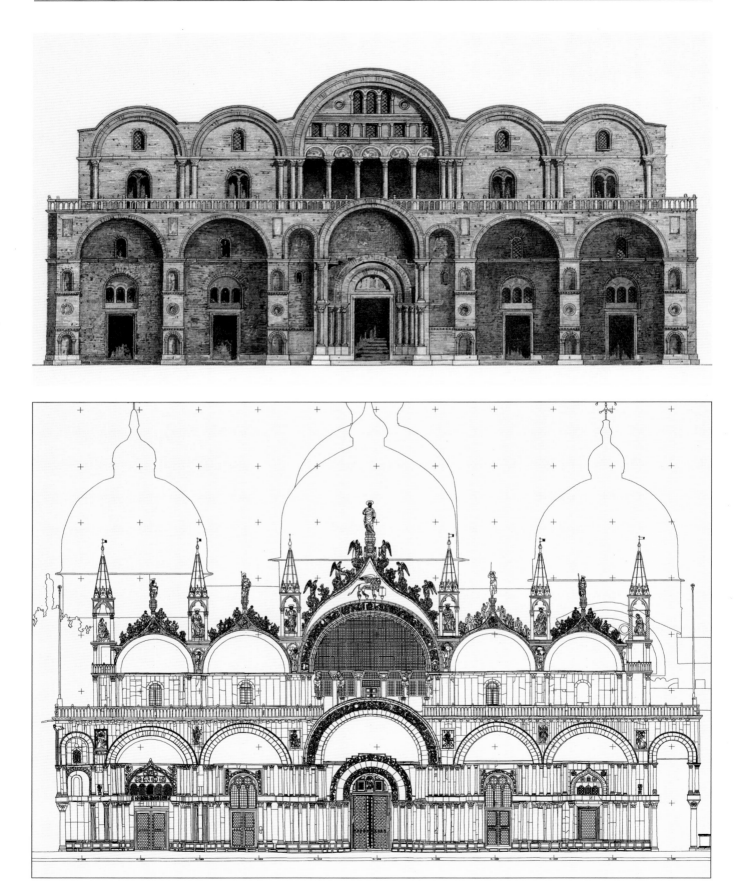

the twelfth century up until the beginning of the sixteenth, when it was walled up to house the tomb of Cardinal Zen; and between the two lies the Baptistery, formerly the *giesia dei putti* (Church of the Putti). Initially it had a portico, which at the beginning of the eleventh century was frescoed with an *Ascension*, whose remains were uncovered during the restoration carried out in the 1960s. The present structure dates to the restoration of 1865–75 and to further repairs executed in the years between 1890 and 1895.

The terrace is supported by a double order of three columns and at the corner, at the feet of the columns, stands a block of red granite called the *pietra del bando*, or proclamation stone. This leads us to the main west façade, which has five large portals dating from the twelfth century, each surmounted by a lunette. The central portal, adorned with three large arches carved in the lower level, is topped, above the terrace,

35 *above left*
W. Scott, after a drawing by A. Pellanda, *Conjectural Original Design of St. Mark's Basilica*, watercolor
The work shows the west façade before the restoration work carried out in the second half of the 19th century. It presents a hypothetical reconstruction of the appearance of the present basilica in the time of Doge Vitale Falier (1094), before the brick walls were clad with marble.

36 *below left*
Photogrammetric survey of the façade as we see it today, 1985-94

37
***Arrival in Venice, Scenes of the Retrieval of St. Mark's Body*, mosaic, west façade, lower level, second lunette and vault from the right, 17th century**
The mosaic was executed to a design by Pietro Vecchia (*c.* 1660).

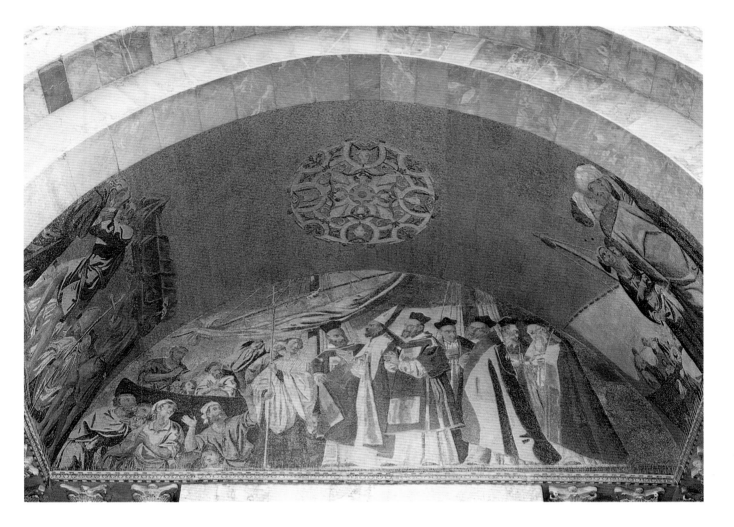

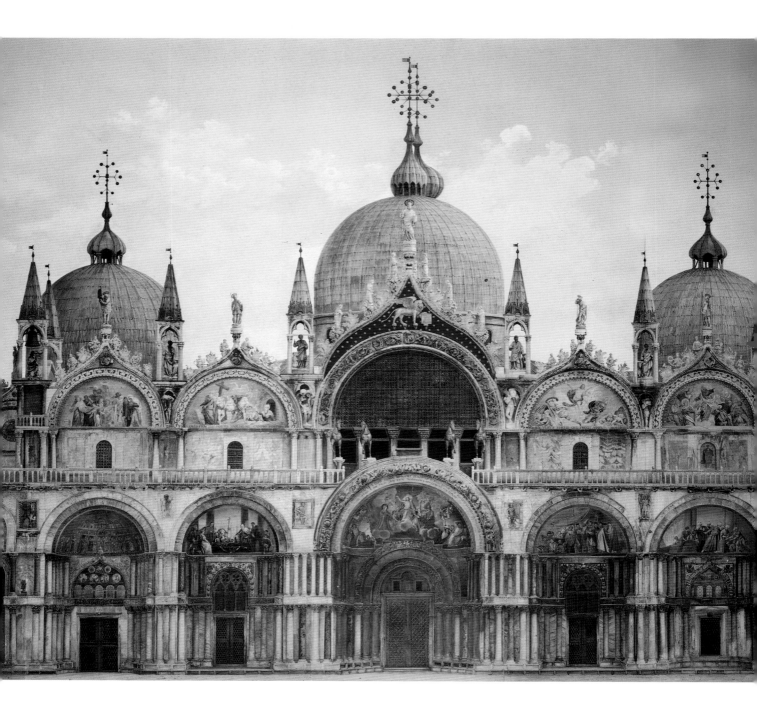

by the large Window of the Horses. This in turn is surmounted by an arch, molded on both the front and inner surfaces. The statue of St. Mark stands at its apex.

The present structure is laid over the original masonry of the eleventh century; it was clad with marble and adorned with columns in the thirteenth century. Gothic pediments were added by Tuscan stonecutters, active in the basilica in the early fifteenth century. They also created the Window

38

Alberto Prosdocimi,
West Façade of the Basilica,
watercolor, 1885-87

The artist painted this view of the façade and one of the interior of the church in preparation for the chromolithographs illustrating the great work on St. Mark's,

published by Ferdinando Ongania: *La basilica di San Marco in Venezia, illustrata nella storia e nell'arte da scrittori veneziani,* edited by Camillo Boito, 1888-92.

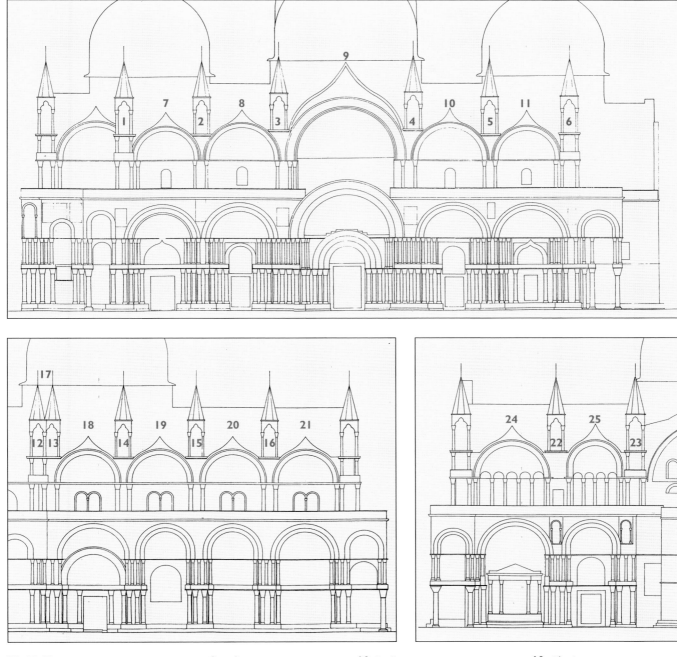

39-40-41

**Schematic drawings showing
the location of the sculptures**

west façade

1. archangel Gabriel
2. St. Matthew
3. St. Mark
4. St. John
5. St. Luke
6. Virgin Mary
7. St. Constantine
8. St. Demetrius
9. St. Mark

10. St. George
11. St. Theodore

north façade

12. archangel Michael
13. St. Gregory
14. St. Ambrose
15. St. Augustine
16. St. Jerome
17. Hope

18. Charity
19. Faith
20. Temperance
21. Prudence

south façade

22. St. Anthony Abbot
23. St. Paul the Hermit
24. Justice
25. Courage

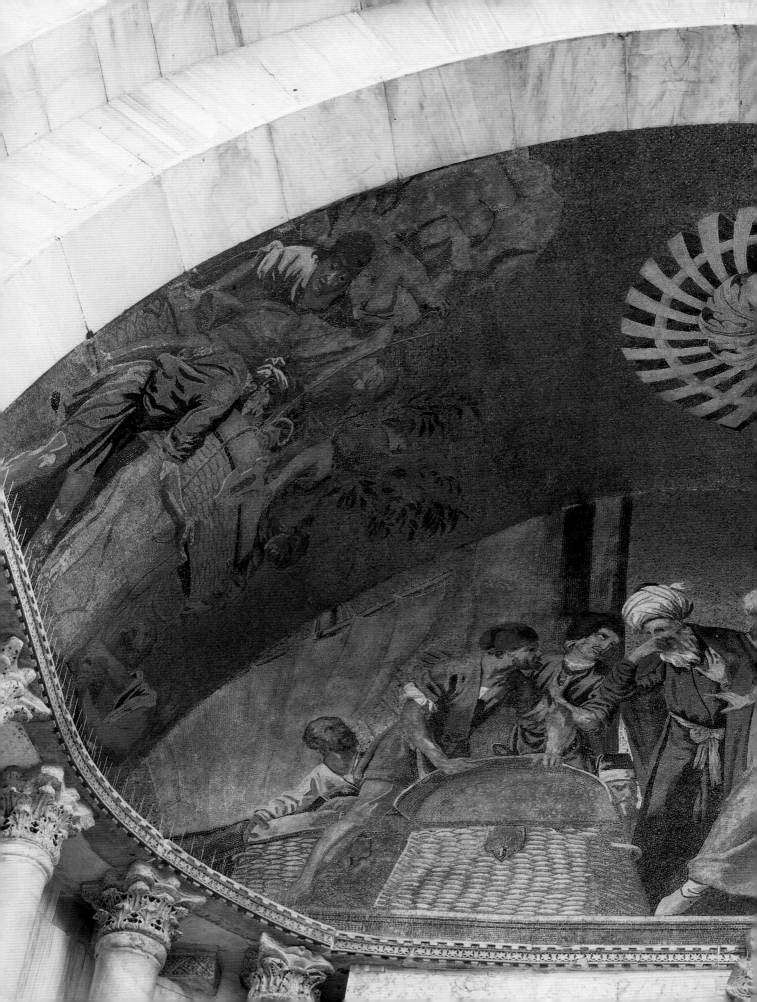

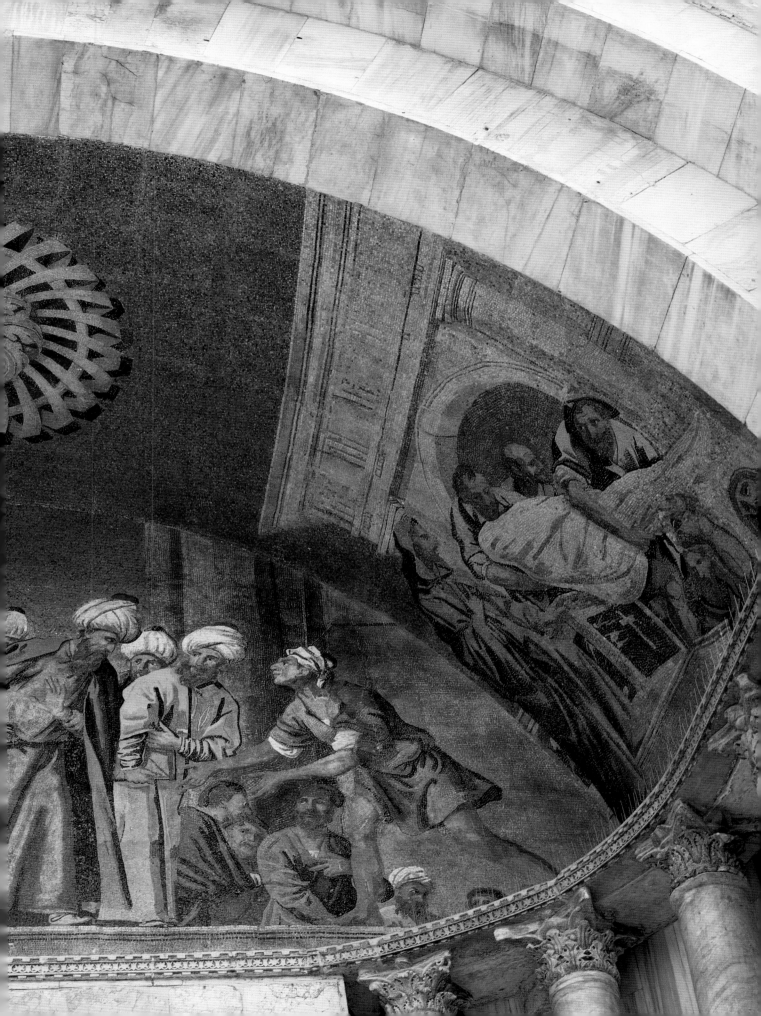

of the Horses (1420-22) and the Gothic rose window in the south transept facing on to the courtyard of the Ducal Palace.

The image of the west façade is completed by the lead-covered domes that were erected in the thirteenth century above the Byzantine hemispherical vaults. The effects of the restoration carried out in 1855-65 can be seen on the north façade. Its layout echoes the scheme of the western façade, but large expanses of the original marble have been replaced. The Porta dei Fiori is located at the east end of the north atrium.

The mosaics in the vaults and lunettes of the portals on the main façade depict *Scenes of the Retrieval of St. Mark's Body*. In fact the first scene on the far right is the *Retrieval of St. Mark's Body from Alexandria*, while the lunette of the second door represents the *Arrival in Venice*. Both mosaics date from the seventeenth century. The fourth portal shows the *Homage Paid by the Signoria and the Doge to the Body of the Saint*, an eighteenth-century work by Sebastiano Ricci and the mosaicist Leopoldo dal Pozzo. The fifth door, on the far left, houses the only surviving mosaic from the original thirteenth-century series, depicting the *Placing of the Saint's Body in the Basilica*. This constitutes the earliest view of the basilica, showing its marble facings and columns and the horses on the terrace. The sole record we have of the rest of the original mosaics is the large canvas by Gentile Bellini, the *Procession in St. Mark's Square* (1496), now in the Gallerie dell'Accademia. Bellini presents the basilica gleaming with gold and laden with sculptures, after the Tuscan additions and the repairs following the devastating fires of 1419 and 1489 had been made.

On the upper level, the four lunettes, all the work of Maffeo da Verona in the seventeenth century, illustrate, from left to right, the *Deposition from the Cross, Descent into Limbo, Resurrection* and *Ascension*. The bowl-shaped vault over the central portal represents the *Last Judgment* with Christ and the Virgin.

42 *preceding pages*

Retrieval of St. Mark's Body from Alexandria, mosaic, west façade, lower level, first lunette and vault on the right, 17th century

The saint's body is placed in a basket with pork meat. The mosaic was executed to a cartoon by Pietro Vecchia (c. 1660).

43 *below*

Red porphyry head called the Carmagnola Head

In the light of recent comparative studies of images of Justinian, the head is now considered to be that of the Byzantine emperor. The cut-off nose, which has also given the head its name of *rinotmetos*, may simply be the result of damage to the sculpture. The head is located in the southwest corner of the balustrade of the loggia above the atrium.

44 *right*

The Tetrarchs, sculpture in imperial red granite, 4th century

Set at the base of the corner tower of the Ducal Palace, the sculptural relief representing four tetrarchs, a product of Egyptian art, is placed, as if it were the cornerstone of the palace, to defend its chapel, the church of St. Mark, to which the tower was eventually annexed. It was also a symbol of the duchy's loyalty to the Byzantine Empire and subsequently of the inheritance of its mantle and the continuation of its history. In popular tradition, they are identified as four Moors, or Saracens, who attempted to rob the Treasury of St. Mark's.

45 *following pages above*

Deposition from the Cross and Descent into Limbo, mosaics, west façade, upper level, first and second lunettes to the left of the central arches

Both are the work of the mosaicist Luigi Gaetano (1617-18), to cartoons by Maffeo da Verona.

46 *following pages below*

Resurrection and Ascension, mosaics, west façade, upper level, first and second lunettes to the right of the central arches

Both are the work of the mosaicist Luigi Gaetano (1617-18), to cartoons by Maffeo da Verona. A remarkable feature is the presence of the lion of St. Mark on the flag held by the risen Christ, instead of the traditional red cross on a white field.

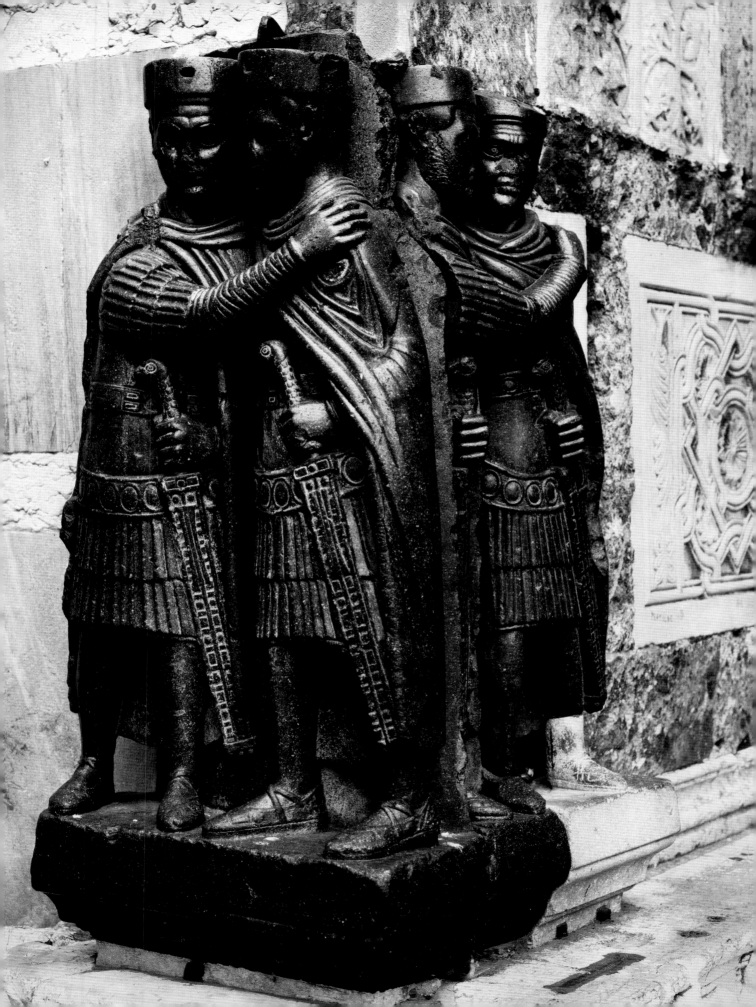

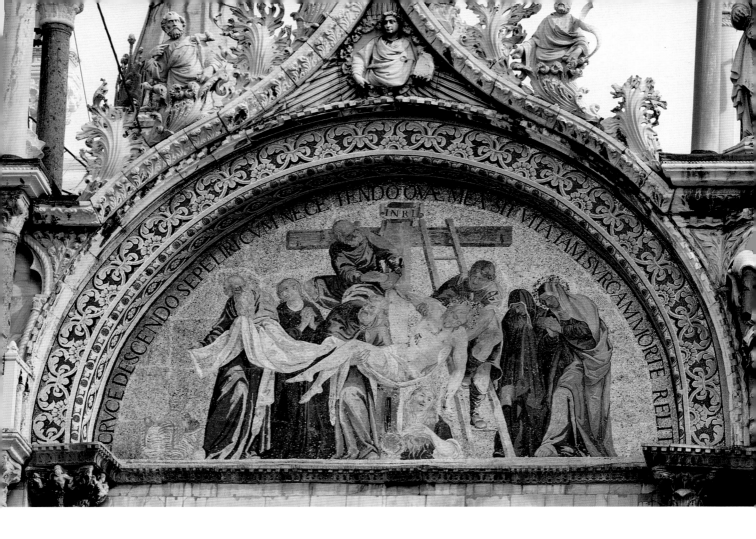

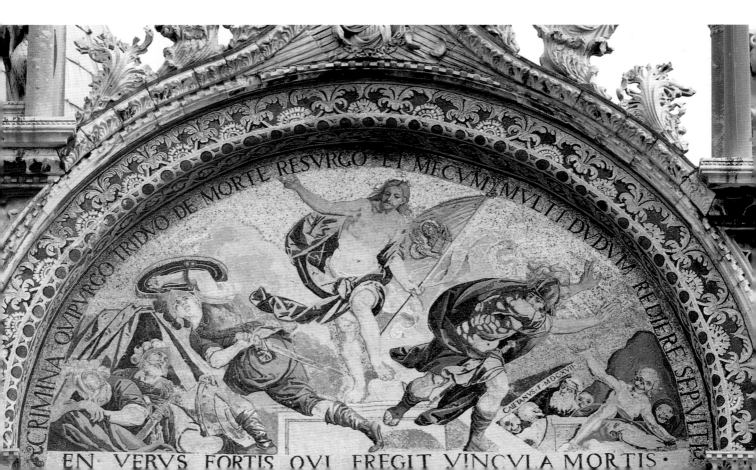

EN VERVS FORTIS QVI FREGIT VINCVLA MORTIS·

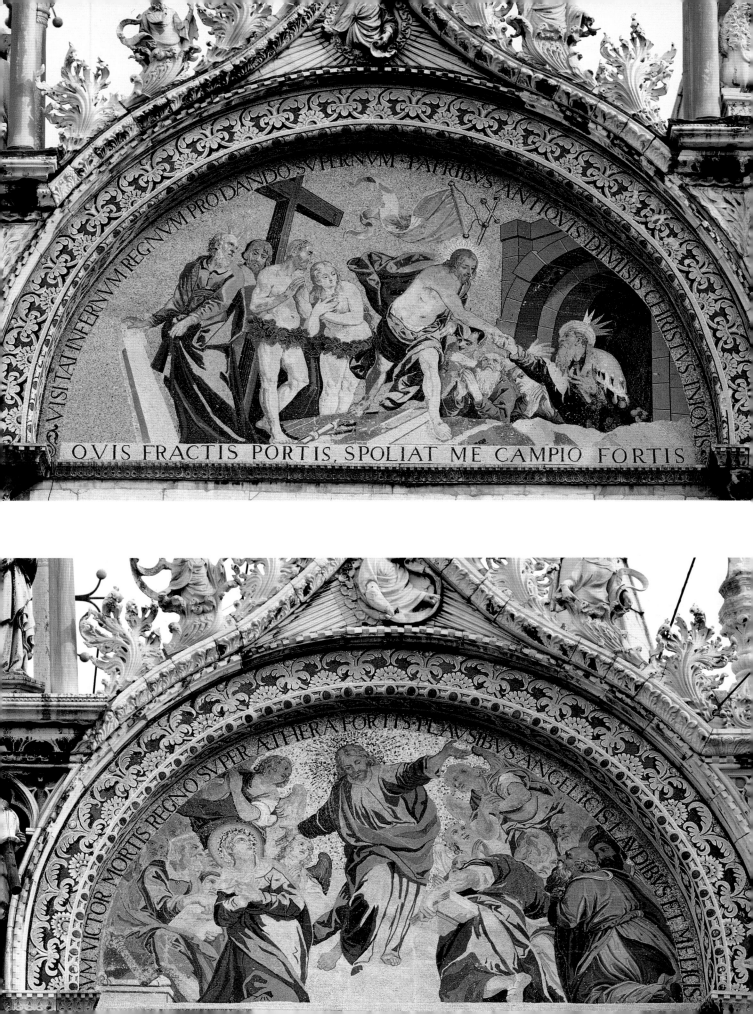

VISITAT INFERNVM REGNVM PRODANDO SVPERNVM PATRIBVS ANTIQVIS DIMISIS CHRISTVS INIQVS

OVIS FRACTIS PORTIS, SPOLIAT ME CAMPIO FORTIS

IM VICTOR MORTIS REGNO SVPER ÆTHERA FORTIS PLAVSIBVS ANGELICIS LAVDIBVS ET MELICIS

THE GOTHIC DECORATION OF THE COPINGS

Guido Tigler

The complex profile of the basilica's façades is ringed at the top by what is effectively a crown of white marble, giving the solid block of the building an ethereal and fragile late Gothic finish. Semicircular arches are set within ogee arches (busts of saints are placed in the resulting spaces), decorated on the outside with carvings of large serrated cabbage leaves stirred by the wind, alternating with busts of prophets. On top of each ogee arch stands a statue of a saint venerated in Venice or the personification of a Virtue. Four of these figures (Constantine, Demetrius, George and Theodore) were brought down by an earthquake in 1511 and replaced in 1618 with statues by Giorgio Albanese. The arch in the middle of the main façade is larger and has a taller external profile. In the space between the ogee and semicircular arches is set a lion of St. Mark against the background of a starry sky, a nineteenth-century cast-iron reproduction of the original one, destroyed in 1797. This higher arch is surmounted by a statue of the evangelist to whom the church is dedicated, while six adoring angels with gilded wings are ranged along the sides.

Between the arches are tall Gothic aedicules (the one at the northwest corner, which also houses a bell, is dated 1384 and marks the beginning of work on this part of the basilica). Each of the aedicules (known as *capitelli* in the Venetian dialect) contains a statue. The aedicules at each end of the west façade house the Annunciant Angel and the Virgin, repeating the arrangement of the slabs carved in relief on the lower part of the façade and alluding to the Venetian New Year and the mythical origin of the city on March 25, 421. The other four central aedicules on the west façade contain the four evangelists, while those on the northern side house the Fathers of the

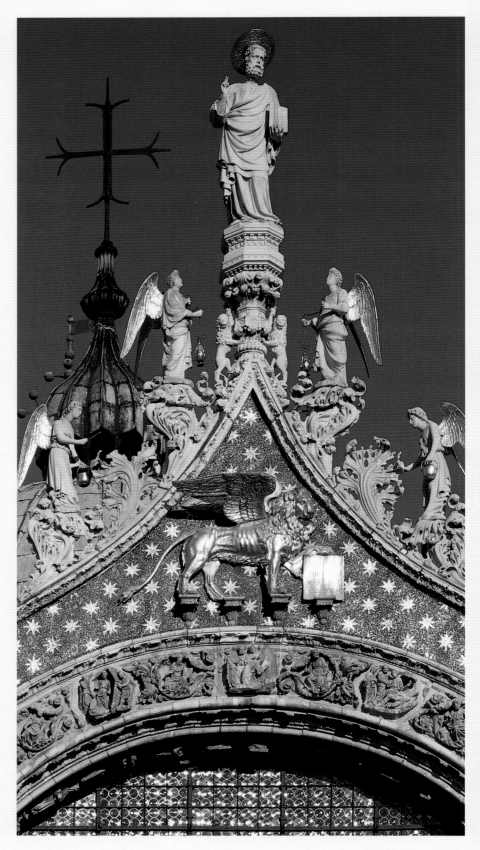

Church and on the southern façade, two saints (Anthony Abbot and Paul the Hermit). Under the four central aedicules of the western side stand sturdy human figures holding amphorae, squeezed into the restricted space of the niches set in the spandrels. These are the spouts or gargoyles that must have once served to collect the rainwater from the roofs behind, while evoking the concept of the Rivers of Paradise (four more Rivers, though only two of them now survive, were located on the lower, thirteenth-century part of the west façade). The high reliefs of the arch around the central window, behind the horses, date from the same period. Those in the soffit of the arch represent the four Patriarchs of the Old Testament and the evangelists beneath canopies, while the ones on the front depict episodes from the Old Testament inside hexagonal panels alternating with foliage.

The greater part of the sculptural decoration – some of it carved from Carrara marble – must have been executed after the two recorded deliveries of marble from Lucca in 1414 and 1419. The documents also tell us the names of the artists who were probably in charge of the undertaking, Paolo di Jacobello dalle Masegne in 1414 and Niccolò di Pietro Lamberti from Florence in 1419. We do not know whether the work was affected by the fire that broke out on the roof in 1419. The statues in the aedicules were carved in the first, Venetian phase of the work. However, the figure of St. Mark in the middle of the west façade and the reliefs of the central arch – which are full of references to Ghiberti and call to mind the tomb of Doge Tommaso Mocenigo at San Zanipolo (San Giovanni e Paolo), executed by Niccolò di Pietro Lamberti and Giovanni di Martino from Fiesole in 1423 – date from the second, Tuscan phase. One of the Tuscan sculptors who worked on these figures was Nanni di Bartolo, called Il Rosso, to whom three of the spouts on the north façade have been attributed. The gargoyles on the western side closely resemble those on Milan Cathedral, but their attribution to the Milanese sculptor Matteo Raverti is not certain. Nor can the hypothesis put forward by some, that Jacopo della Quercia may have worked here, be confirmed.

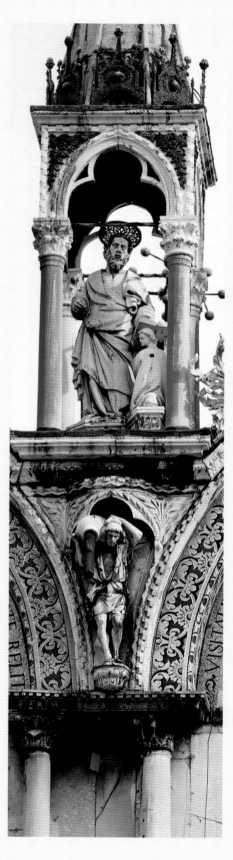

47

Detail showing the statue of St. Mark on top of the central pediment, west façade
The work of Niccolò di Pietro Lamberti (c. 1420), it includes a gilded stone lion, set at the saint's feet, against a blue mosaic background with gold stars.

48

Detail showing St. Mark the Evangelist inside a Gothic aedicule, west façade
At his feet is set a gargoyle, the figure of a man pouring water from an amphora on his shoulder. The statue was carved by Tuscan stonecutters in the first half of the 15th century.

THE ARCHES OF THE CENTRAL PORTAL

Guido Tigler

The main entrance of the basilica is ennobled by a solemn and complex structure of precious columns recessed into the wall. Its extrados rises above the level of the terrace, providing a visual base for the bronze horses. In all likelihood, therefore, it would seem that this unusual triumphal arch was designed for that very purpose, to be crowned by the statues from Constantinople, just as it is evident that the mosaic on the vault has always been intended to serve as the iconographic fulcrum of the decoration. The present mosaic, dating from the nineteenth century, is but a pale shadow of the previous, seventeenth-century one, which in turn was a replacement for the original thirteenth-century mosaic. We have some idea of the appearance of the latter, which represented the *Glorious Second Coming of Christ before the Last Judgment* and the *Raising of the Dead*, thanks to an accurate view of St. Mark's in a 1496 painting by Gentile Bellini, now in the Accademia.

The subjects represented in the crowded reliefs of the three arches, two of which directly encircle the sixteenth-century tympanum of the actual door while the third frames the upper vault, should be interpreted from an eschatological perspective. With this rich cycle of sculptures, embellished with gilding and polychromy of which extensive traces have recently been rediscovered (1982-87), thirteenth-century Venice – in the age of Scholasticism – set out to provide itself with an element that is typical of the great Gothic cathedrals of Northern Europe: a portal whose iconographic program is at once didactic and, in places at least, agreeably worldly.

On the underside of the innermost arch, the Devil and Lust, accompanied by Brutes, allude to the prevalence of evil in

the world. Set in that metaphorical dark forest which represented life for the people of the Middle Ages, the archivolt expands the theme of the vices, both through the allegory of hunting (on the left) and through the direct representation of ignoble acts (on the right). The intrados of the middle arch depicts the twelve months of the year, represented as was customary in medieval art by their personifications, most of them engaged in agricultural activities. They are accompanied by explanatory scrolls and the appropriate signs of the zodiac. The front, on the other hand, is decorated with female personifications of the Theological and Cardinal Virtues, the Beatitudes and Truth, some of them accompanied by attributes and scrolls with verses from the Bible. On the underside of the outermost arch, where higher relief has been used to compensate for the greater distance from the observer, we see the handicrafts of Venice (it is possible, though not supported by documentary evidence, that the various crafts correspond to the guilds who funded the work). Finally, the prophets and a sibyl are represented on the front of this arch. The concept that binds all these together is clear: while awaiting the return of Christ, humanity is offered a chance of spiritual progress by following a path that leads from sin to redemption through work and morality.

In their choice of compositional and iconographic models, the arch of the Brutes – which is based on a type of archivolt common in thirteenth-century Venetian palaces – and that of the Virtues, whose prototypes are to be found in the late twelfth-century mosaics of the central dome of St. Mark's, derive from local traditions. Even some of the crafts are based on mosaics in the basilica, this time the ones in the atrium dating from the

1220s. The lively little figures entwined by plant shoots on the front of the inner arch, the months and also the crafts plainly derive from the Emilian models of Benedetto Antelami and his followers. From a strictly stylistic point of view, however, all the sculptures on the portal, though varied, show signs of a Western influence that is associated with a sculptor known as the Master of the Months of Ferrara, who was active – in Venice as well – in the 1220s. The two inner arches were carved in 1240 by Master Radovan of Trogir in Dalmatia and the outermost – in view of subsequent developments in the sculptural decoration of St. Mark's – has to be placed no later than 1250.

49
Central portal

The center of the basilica is marked by four large, sculpted arches.

On the lower level, the first innermost arch surrounds the entrance and is decorated with scenes representing the struggle between humanity and nature. The underside of the second (early 13th century) depicts the months of the year and the signs of the zodiac, with an orderly sequence of activities connected with the seasons, while the front is adorned with the Virtues and Beatitudes. The outermost arch (mid-13th century), which concludes the lower level, illustrates the crafts on which the civil liberty of the people of Venice was founded, shown here supporting the Venetian community.

These three arches were restored between 1981 and 1987.

On the upper level, the fourth arch (first quarter of the 15th century) encloses the Window of the Horses. On its underside we see the evangelists and prophets, while the front is decorated with scenes from the Old Testament.

The fourth arch was restored between 1987 and 1994.

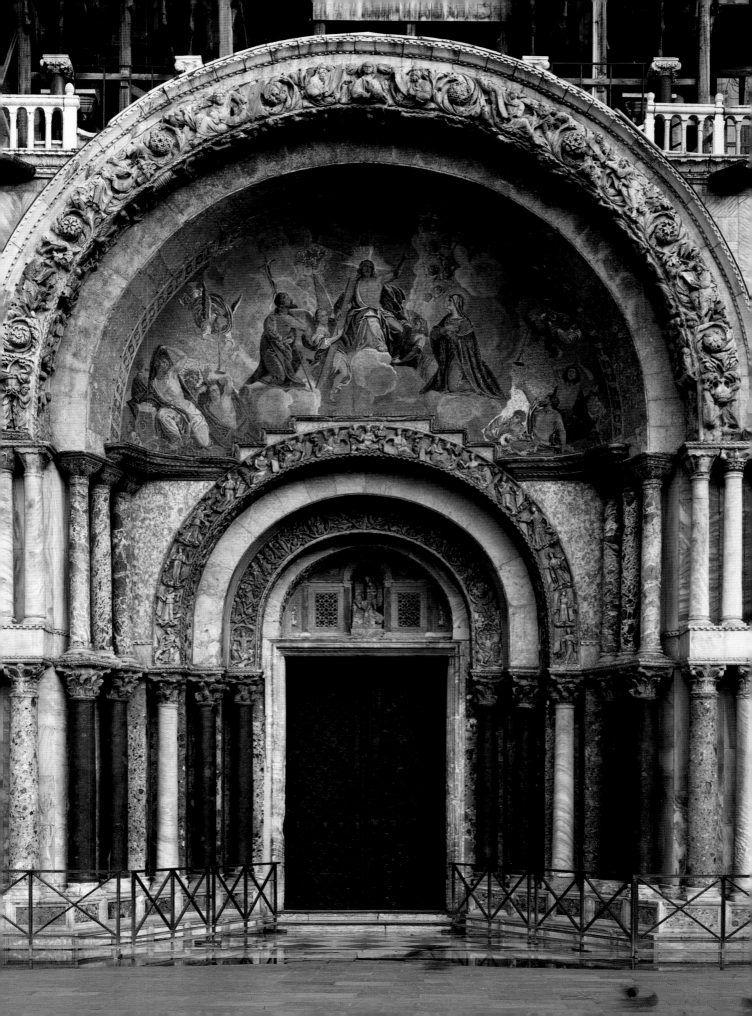

THE HORSES OF ST. MARK'S

Licia Vlad Borrelli

For seven centuries, the resplendent four bronze horses marked time on the façade of St. Mark's, overseeing so much of the history of the Repubblica Serenissima that they have become its proudest emblem. Yet their origins are far more remote. They came to the city among the rich spoils of war carried off by the Venetians, led by Doge Enrico Dandolo, after the conquest of Constantinople at the end of the Fourth Crusade (1204), along with other priceless works, many of them still conserved in the Treasury of the basilica. The sack of the ancient capital of the empire is described in dramatic tones by the historians of the time. Written both from the viewpoint of the Crusaders and from that of the Greeks, these texts bear witness to the massacres and other outrages that took place in the course of the amassing and sharing out of the precious booty, yet none makes explicit mention of the horses. According to a disputed claim made by writers in the Renaissance, they were dumped in the Arsenal for around fifty years, where they ran the risk of being melted down, until some Florentine ambassadors recognized their extraordinary quality. They were then placed on the façade of the basilica, probably during the office of Doge Ranieri Zeno (1253-68), as part of the long and complex process of transformation and embellishment of St. Mark's that was linked to the growing wealth and power of the Republic.

The mosaic that decorates the lunette over the Door of St. Alypius, dating from around 1265, shows the horses already installed on the façade in the position they were to retain for centuries. They have been celebrated by many Venetian artists, including Gentile Bellini in his huge canvas of the solemn *Procession in St. Mark's Square* (1496), in which the four steeds appear in all their glory on the basilica's central loggia as if standing on a great triumphal arch. An earlier, more oblique reference to the horses of St. Mark's can perhaps be found in the scene of the *Expulsion of the Merchants from the Temple* in the Scrovegni Chapel in Padua, where Giotto sets two lions and two horses on the four pillars of the temple. Petrarch was the first to wonder about their origins. In a letter written in 1364 he extols their beauty and recognizes that they are ancient works, "whoever may have made them." However, it was only with the resurgence of interest in antiquity during the Renaissance that attempts were made to assign the horses a paternity, by attributing them to one of the great Greek sculptors: Ciriaco d'Ancona suggested Phidias, while others put forward the names of Praxiteles and Lysippus. This last attribution was to prove the most enduring, for a series of historical and archeological reasons. Lysippus was known, in fact, to have created a bronze four-horse chariot for the people of Rhodes and many scholars have attempted to identify this with the horses of St. Mark's.

50

The four horses of St. Mark's before restoration, in a photograph taken on the terrace

There is a remarkable difference in the surface of the horses before and after restoration. The originals have now been replaced by bronze copies, whose surfaces are covered with an extremely thin layer of gold, applied with a wad, as they are considered an essential element of the façade's architecture and coloring.

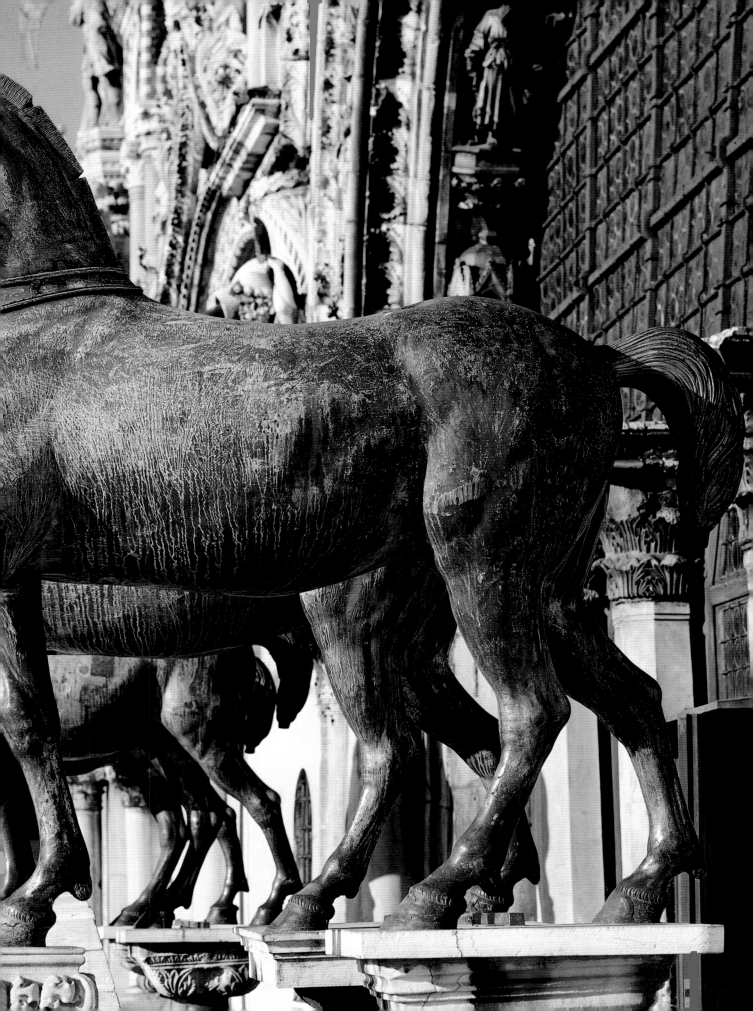

The various theories claim that they were first taken to Rome, or Persia, by one or another Roman emperor, and then transferred to Constantinople. The study of antiquity that developed in the late sixteenth and the seventeenth century unearthed new references to the presence of quadrigae, or four-horse chariots, made of gilded bronze in Byzantine sources. There were confusing mentions of four horses "covered with gold" set above the starting positions in the hippodrome in Constantinople, brought there from Chios during the reign of Theodosius II; of a four-horse chariot with the sun god Helios that the Emperor Constantine had erected in the square known as the Milion and then transferred to the hippodrome; and of yet another team of four horses, also gilded and accompanied by a chariot and driver, to which Constantine had added a statuette of Fortuna to commemorate the foundation of the city in an annual ceremony. Which of these sculptures is to be identified with the horses on the façade of St. Mark's is still a moot point. However, it is likely that the St. Mark's horses were located in the hippodrome, standing on four columns of porphyry, as described

51

The horses of St. Mark's, restored and placed in the Museum of St. Mark above the atrium in 1982

The quadriga has been recomposed in the same order as the horses were arranged on the loggia, in two pairs with their heads turned toward each other. Their height above the floor corresponds to a viewing distance of eight to ten meters.

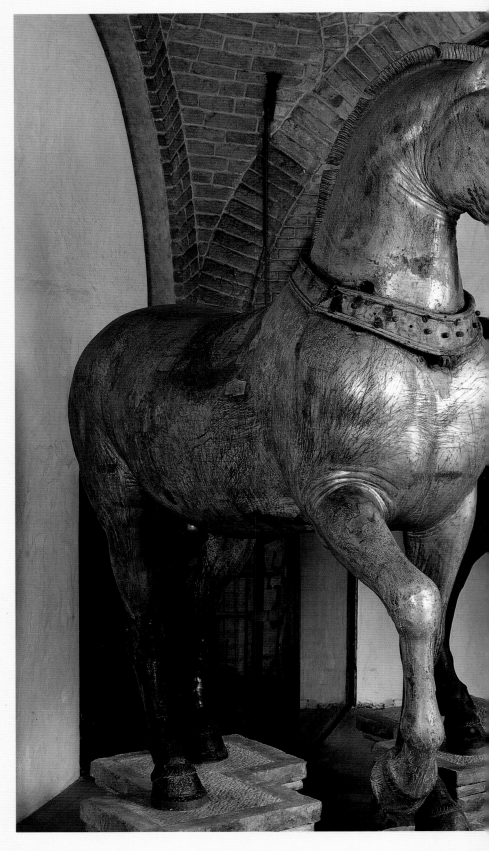

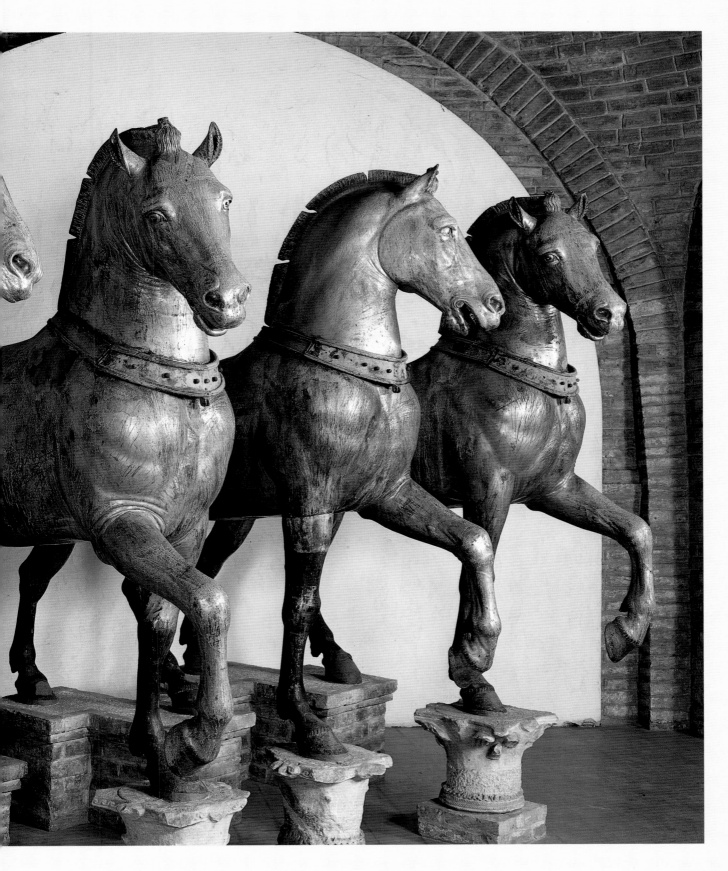

by two European travelers in the first half of the fifteenth century, in their account of the monuments of Constantinople. A more detailed interpretation of the sources and various aspects of the group would have to wait, however, for the erudite climate of the eighteenth century, largely shaped by the founder of modern archeology, J. J. Winckelmann. It has also been suggested that they were not a Greek work at all, but date from the Roman era, a theory that was debated throughout the nineteenth century and continues to be discussed today.

One sad December in 1797, the four steeds were brought down from the façade of St. Mark's for the first time in over five centuries and, along with many other masterpieces, carried off to Paris by Napoleon. We know from contemporary prints and descriptions that the magnificent trophy of war was paraded through the streets of Paris in a long procession, together with other booty brought back from Napoleon's successful campaigns. Given the role of decorating the Arc de Triomphe du Carrousel, they were harnessed to a chariot with two Victories and perhaps a statue of the Emperor. When the Parisian exile came to an end with the fall of Napoleon, Antonio Canova was given the job of recovering the looted works and bringing them back to Italy. In a magnificent ceremony attended by Francis I of Austria, the new ruler of Venice, that took place on December 13, 1815, "after eighteen years, and on the very same day that they had been removed," the horses were put back in place on the façade of St. Mark's.

Unfortunately, the precious team of gilded bronze horses, the only example to have survived from antiquity, did not come through these adventures unscathed. The horses had lost part of their collars, one head had been detached and they had

suffered other damage. The horses then had to spend a period in the Arsenal being restored before they could be put back in their rightful place. Further repairs proved necessary over the following years and the horses were again removed from their position above the main arch of St. Mark's during the two world wars, so that they could be stored in a safe place. As a consequence of these traumatic events, of the natural deterioration of the material over the course of the centuries and of the increase in air pollution – and above all of a more thorough understanding of problems linked with conservation – the Istituto Centrale del Restauro carried out a series of technical examinations on the horses in the 1960s. These revealed that the horses were in a precarious condition, but also provided a great deal of valuable data on the history and morphology of the sculptures. The subsequent restoration was the first to employ the latest technology, that science has now placed at the disposal of the arts, on large-scale bronzes. At the end of this long undertaking, it became apparent that in order to preserve the horses for the future it would be necessary to keep them inside the Museum of St. Mark and erect copies in their place above the arch, where for centuries they had stood as the proud emblem of Venice's power. As such, they had led the Genoese conqueror of Chioggia, Pietro Doria, to exclaim to the three Venetian ambassadors who came to sue for peace in 1379: "Venetians, we shall never make peace with you until we have placed halters on those unbridled horses set on top of the temple of the divine Mark." Removing the horses was a difficult and controversial decision, but the thin layer of gold that covered the bronze was wearing off in a number of places and pocked with tiny craters, cracks and scratches, harboring the products of

a long and irreversible process of corrosion, driven by the salts and acids present in the Venetian atmosphere.

The scientific analyses permitted a thorough examination of the sculptures. They had been cast in several pieces (head, trunk, legs and tail) by the so-called indirect method, using concave blocks carved out of a mould. These were then covered with a layer of wax that was melted and replaced by molten metal: the hundreds of different-shaped plugs used to fill the casting defects prove that this was a particularly difficult operation. In fact the alloy used in this case was made up almost exclusively of copper and had a much higher melting point than the usual form of bronze. It provides a very rare, if not unique, example of such a material being used for a statue of these dimensions, with the application of a layer of gold in mind. This proves that the gilding was intended right from the start, and was not applied subsequently, during the Roman era, as some had supposed. The gilding was probably carried out by two processes, using both gold leaf and gold powder mixed with mercury. The latter technique was in particularly wide use in the middle of the imperial Roman era. The artist toned down the gleam of the gold by engraving the areas most exposed to light with dense hatching, which explains the series of scratches. These had aroused a great deal of curiosity in the past, but electronic analysis now shows unequivocally that they were deliberate. Roman numerals, carved on the hooves and halters, have been attributed to measurements of weight, but their real function has never been clarified.

The recent detailed analysis of the horses has not brought any objective facts to light that would permit us to date them definitively, something which is made particularly difficult by the unique

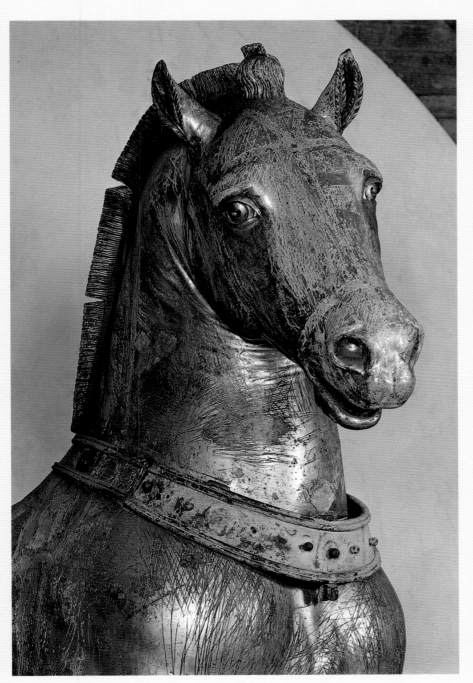

52

Restored head of a horse

The large expanse of gilded surface brought to light by the restoration is clearly visible. The artist who originally carried out the gilding used scratching to prevent reflections from the surface obscuring the modeling of the sculpture. The scratches were only applied to the parts exposed to sunlight.

character of these sculptures. Doubts remain and the date assigned to them by scholars – and there is no parallel to this in the history of ancient art – ranges from the fourth century BC to the fourth century AD. Yet there are a few clues – such as the use of mercury in the fusion, the form of the eyes, mane and ears and the complicated shape of the plugs used to repair casting defects prior to gilding, and therefore at the time of their execution – which suggest that the statues date from the Roman era, around the time of Septimius Severus, and were produced by a school of Greek-Oriental artists who had kept alive the great Hellenistic tradition. It is to be hoped that advances in the science of conservation will one day allow them to be put back on the front of the basilica, where Goethe saw them and was entranced by their powerful grace: "From close-up they look heavy, but viewed from below, from the square, they seem as slender and lithe as deer."

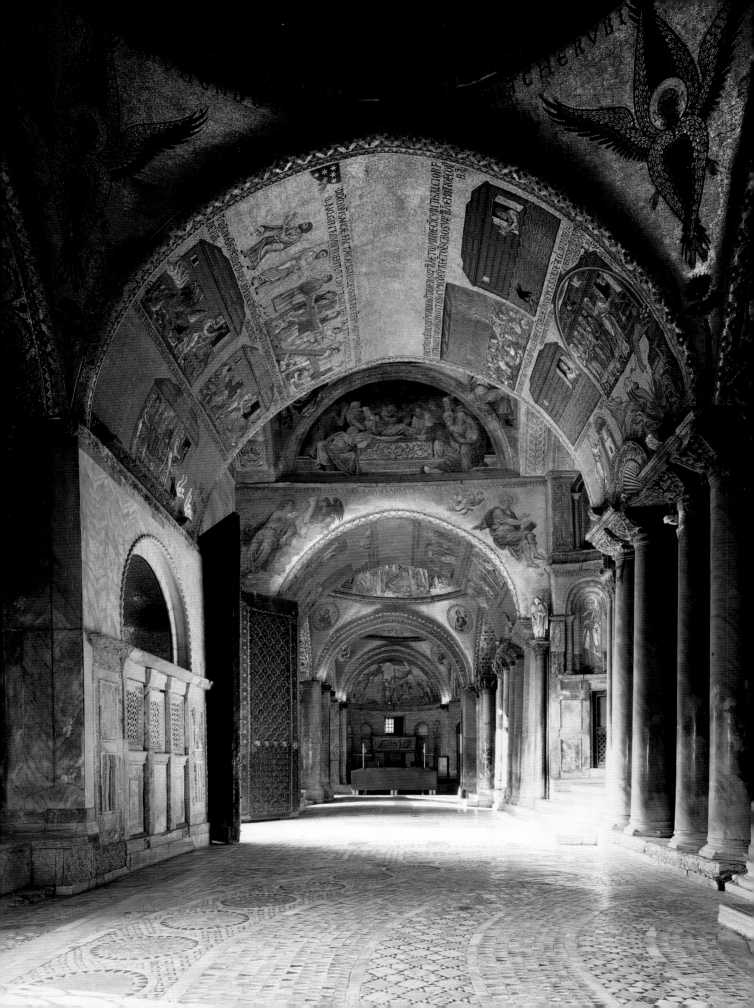

THE ATRIUM

Ettore Vio

The atrium or narthex plays a decisive role in the architecture of the north and west façades. The outer wall of the atrium is set against the large arches that support the terrace of the horses, from where one has a wonderful view of St. Mark's Square, the Piazzetta, the wharf and the lagoon with its islands. The structures that house the Museum of St. Mark rest on these arches.

The atrium contains the graves of a number of illustrious doges who contributed to the basilica. On the right as you enter is that of Vitale Falier (1086-96), who consecrated the church in 1094, while on the left is Felicita Michiel († 1101), the wife of Doge Vitale Michiel I (1096-1104) who, though engaged in continuous battles far away from Venice, dedicated much energy and effort to the completion of the basilica through his wife. Other doges present are Marino Morosini († 1253) and Bartolomeo Gradenigo († 1342) in the north atrium; opposite the Porta dei Fiori stands the tomb of the *primicerius* Bartolomeo Recovrati († 1420), who was involved with the great undertaking of modifying the outer parts of the façade in the Gothic style.

There are two more significant elements of the atrium: the Porta da Mar, walled up in 1501-15 to house the tomb of Cardinal Zen, and the great bronze doors of the outer portal, which have recently been dated to the end of the tenth century. Starting at the Porta da Mar, the domes, vaults and arches of the atrium depict scenes from the Old Testament.

In the bowl-shaped vault of the central portal, we find *St. Mark in Ecstasy.* Executed by the Zuccato brothers to a cartoon attributed to Titian or Lorenzo Lotto (1545), the mosaic shows him dressed in bishop's robes. Also in the entrance bay, the episodes of the *Crucifixion* and *Deposition from the Cross,* on the wall of the *pozzo* or well, are considered to be some of the finest mosaics of the sixteenth century. A substantial part of the magnificent Vault of the Apocalypse can be viewed through this opening. The nineteenth-century bronze doors on either side of the curve of the apse leading into the church take you to the museum above and to the terrace.

All the external gates have two leaves, each cast in a single piece with panels and arches, following the model of the first portal (that of St. Peter). Second from the left, this is dated and signed "MCCC - Magister Bertucius Aurifex Venetus me fecit." Only the central portal is closed by wooden doors faced

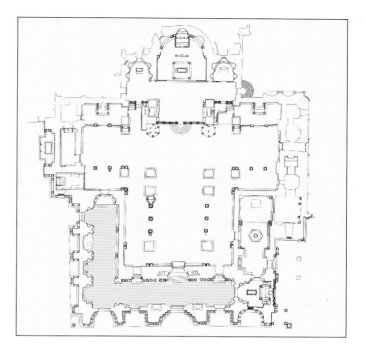

53 *left*
View of the west atrium
The sequence of mosaics with scenes from the Old Testament, based on the iconography of the *Cotton Bible,* decorates this space. As we see from the numerous columns supporting vaults and domes that are not part of the church's structure, the atrium is separate from the basilica.

54 *above*
Plan of the basilica showing the area of the atrium
The origins of the atrium have been the subject of inconclusive studies and hypotheses. It is certain that its structure is separate from that of the basilica, as we see from the columns set against the walls of the church, as both decoration and supports for its arches, vaults and domes. The slightly pointed shape of the arches in the north arm is reminiscent of the Byzantine architecture of the 7th-10th centuries, which has led some scholars to postulate that the first church was preceded by a cloister. It is not impossible that the present structure of the atrium derives from the transformation of an ancient portico, set against the boundary wall of the ducal *castrum-castellum.*

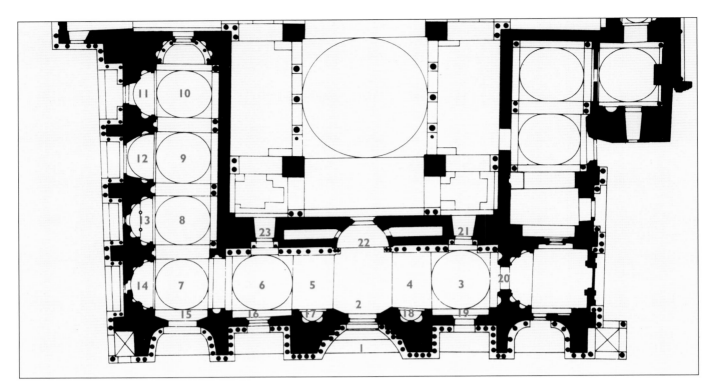

55

Plan of the atrium showing the location of the parts and the principal decorations

The mosaics represent in sequence: *The Creation* (1st dome), *The Flood* (1st vault), *Scenes from the Story of Noah* and the *Tower of Babel* (2nd vault), *Scenes from the Story of Abraham* (2nd dome), *Scenes from the Story of Joseph* (3rd, 4th and 5th domes), *Scenes from the Story of Moses* and the *Crossing of the Red Sea*, after which we enter the north transept through the Porta della Madonna surmounted by the *Virgin Enthroned with the Christ Child*. The mosaics were produced by a local workshop, active between 1220 and 1285 according to the scholar Otto Demus. By the main entrance, the architecture of the atrium is interrupted by an opening in the roof, known as the *pozzo* or well. This may have been created to preserve the integrity of the

apsidal vault of the central portal, whose doors of damascened bronze decorated with figures of saints are inlaid with silver foil. A Byzantine work from the first half of the 12th century, they are flanked by some of the oldest mosaics in the basilica (11th and 12th century) representing the *Four Evangelists*, with the *Virgin between the Apostles* above.

It is also worth drawing attention to the Renaissance design of the floor, by Paolo Uccello, in front of the Door of St. Peter, and to the large slab of red Verona marble that commemorates, at the entrance, the meeting between Pope Alexander III and Frederick Barbarossa to sign a peace treaty on July 23, 1177.

1. central portal
2. wooden door faced with bronze
3. Dome of the Creation
4. The *Ark* and the *Flood*
5. *Burial of Noah* and *Tower of Babel*
6. Dome of Abraham
7. First Dome of Joseph
8. Second Dome of Joseph
9. Third Dome of Joseph
10. Dome of Moses
11. Porta dei Fiori
12. tomb of *primicerius* Bartolomeo Recovrati
13. tomb of Doge Marino Morosini
14. tomb of Doge Bartolomeo Gradenigo
15. Door of St. Alypius
16. gate of St. Peter
17. tomb of Felicita Michiel
18. tomb of Doge Vitale Falier
19. gate of St. Clement
20. gate of the Zen Chapel
21. Door of St. Clement
22. central door
23. Door of St. Peter

56

Dome of the Creation, first on the right in the west atrium

The *Story of the Creation* is narrated in twenty-five scenes, all with inscriptions, and the sequence of days is identified by the number of angels present, from one on the first day to seven on the last. The mosaics were executed by the early local workshop in the first half of 13th century.

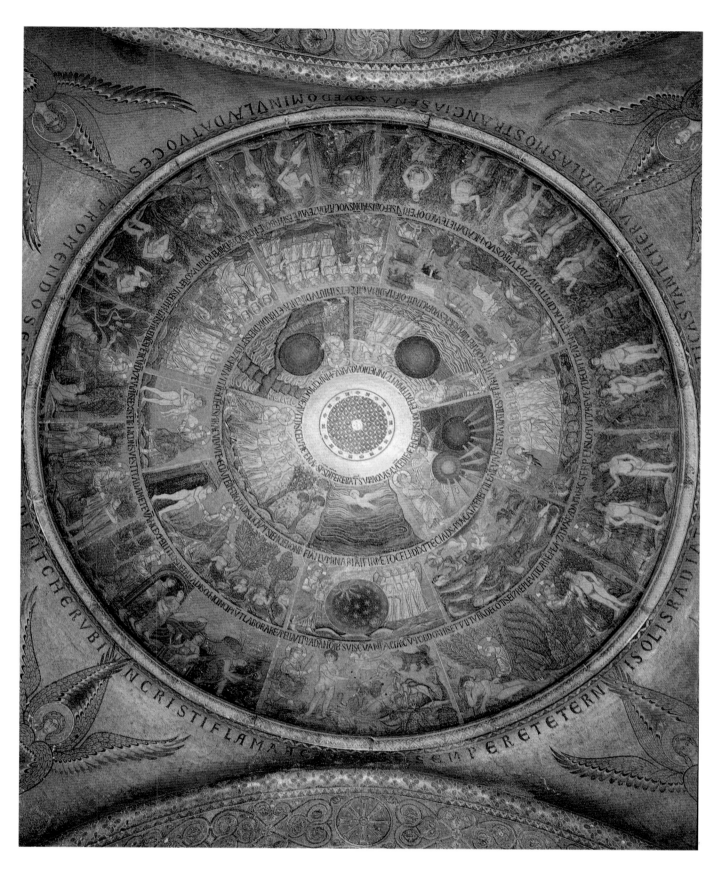

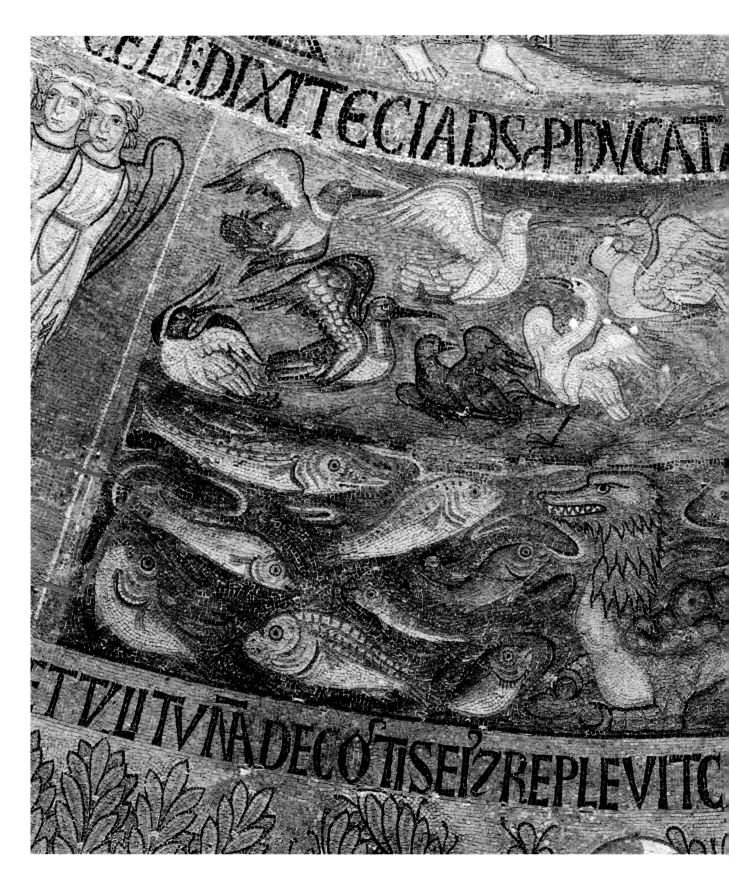

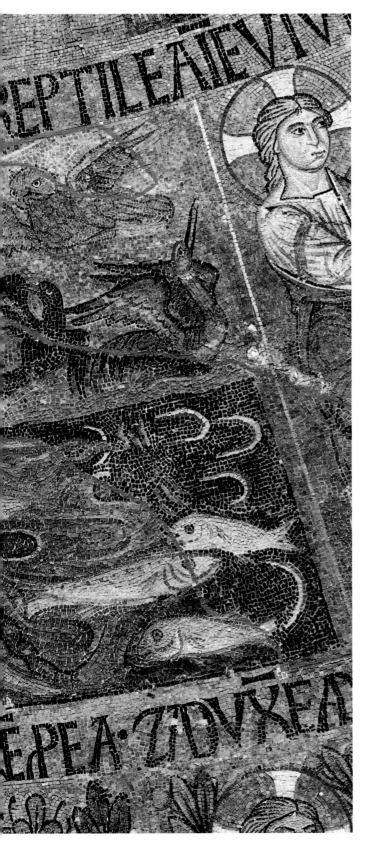

with bronze, to which two large seventh-century gratings are attached, along with ten stylized lions, nine of them of Persian origin (tenth-eleventh century) and one Venetian (twelfth-thirteenth century). The doors between the atrium and church are faced with sheets of bronze. In the north arm we find the nineteenth-century Porta della Madonna leading to the Dome of St. John. In the west arm, on the other hand, there is the Door of St. Peter on the left – with its twelfth-century Byzantine panels set in a sturdy frame – and the Door of St. Clement on the right. Probably the middle door of the earlier church (976-78), this is made of damascened bronze like the late eleventh-century central one. Finally, there is the large entrance gate to the Zen Chapel with small arches, made out of seventh-century gratings identical to those fixed on the outside of the main central portal.

The floor of the atrium presents a great variety of designs, as does that of the interior.

57

Creation of the Fish and the Birds, mosaic, west atrium, Dome of the Creation, 13th century

58

Creation of Eve, mosaic, west atrium, Dome of the Creation, 13th century

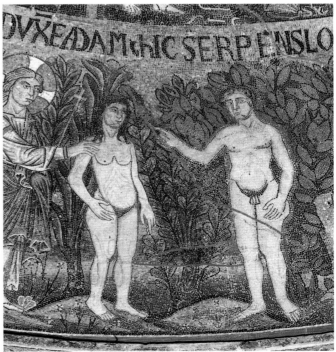

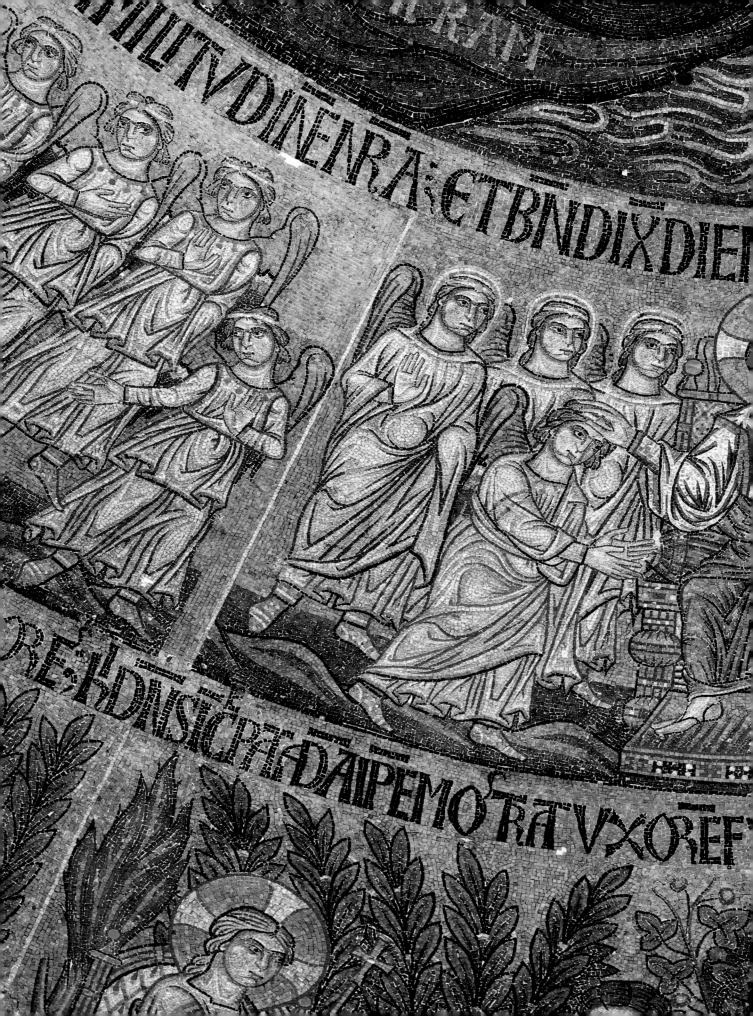

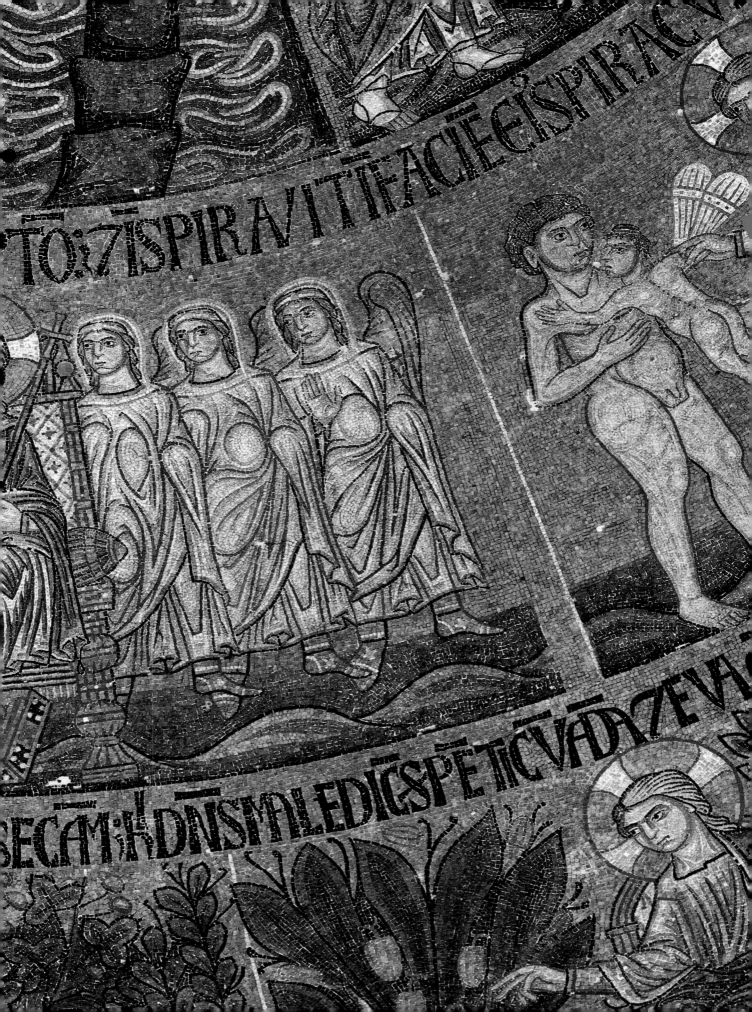

TO: 7 ISPIRAVIT II FACIE EIS PIRACV

SECAM: HDNS MALEDICS PETICVAD ZEVA

59 *preceding pages*

God Blessing the Seventh Day, **mosaic, west atrium, Dome of the Creation, 13th century**

60 *above*

Go Forth and Multiply, **mosaic, west atrium, Dome of the Creation, east lunette, 13th century**

This mosaic, by the early local workshop, is set above the Door of St. Clement.

61 *below*

Leaving the Ark, Scenes from the Story of Noah, **mosaic, west atrium, 13th century**

The image is completed and enclosed by a rainbow, a mark of the new pact of alliance between God and humanity.

62 *far right*

St. Mark in Ecstasy, **west atrium, semidome of the central portal**

Mosaic by Francesco and Valerio Zuccato, to a cartoon by Titian or Lorenzo Lotto (1545).

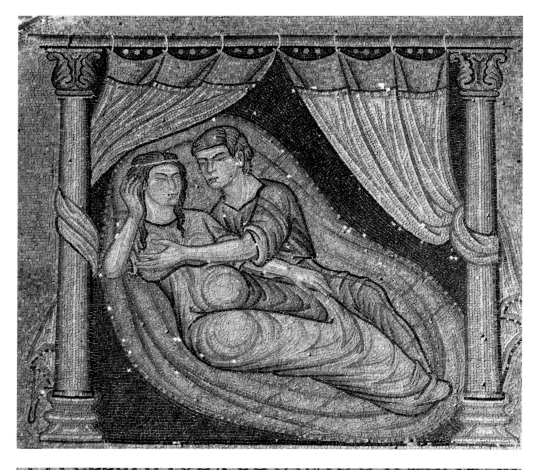

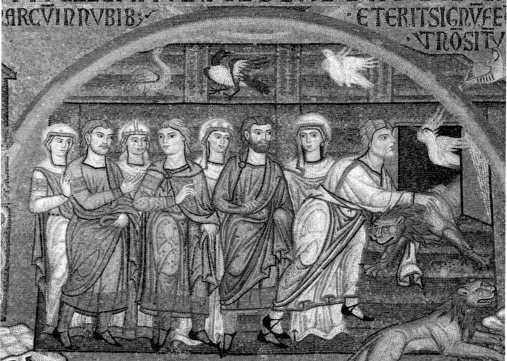

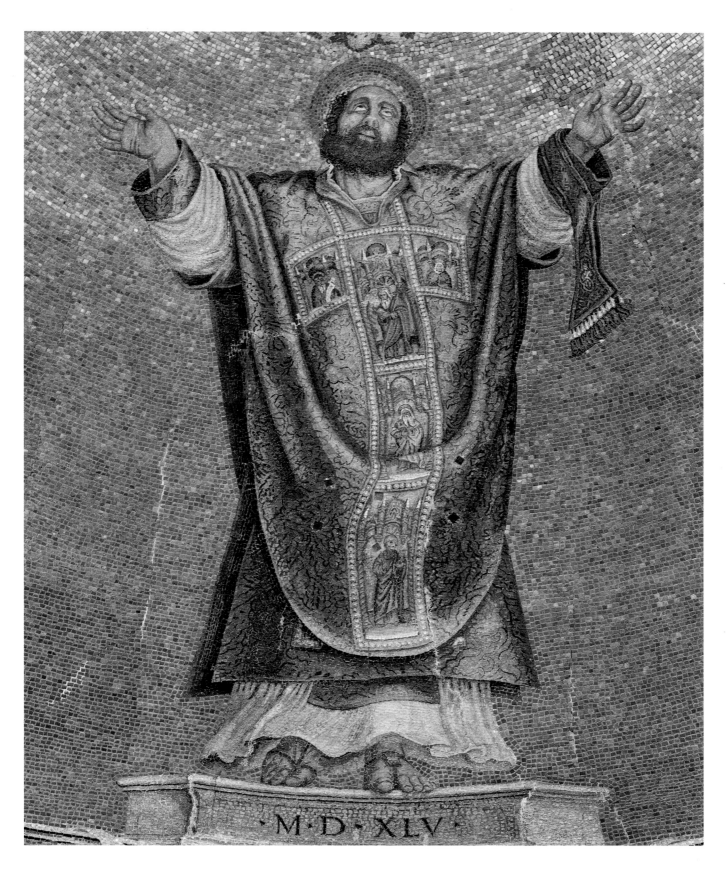

THE MOSAICS

Maria Da Villa Urbani

When Venice decided to renovate the structure that housed the precious relics of St. Mark, patron and protector of the city, the plan was to create a *magna giesia*, a great church, that would bear witness to the expansion of both the city and the state under the rule of Doge Domenico Contarini (1043-71), as well as to the growing economic, civil and political importance of the Serenissima. As we know, the model was found in Constantinople, in the church dating from the reign of Emperor Justinian (sixth century) known as the Church of the Holy Apostles. This was justified by the fact that – especially in the East – the evangelists Mark and Luke were traditionally included among the twelve apostles.

Five domes, one in each arm and one set above the central space of the crossing, supported by vaults that stand on angular piers with four feet, make up the magnificent Greek-cross structure of the basilica, which was designed from the start to be covered with mosaics on the upper part of the walls. While there were earlier precedents for such decoration in Italy (in Rome and in the basilicas of Ravenna), St. Mark's has to be considered of Byzantine derivation, owing to the evident reference to a precise figurative typology and to the documented presence of "Greek", i.e. from the Byzantine Empire, mosaicists who must have taught the art to the Venetians.

The mosaic decoration of St. Mark's, as we see it today, is a fascinating palimpsest, the product of a complex process covering the entire history of the church and spanning some eight centuries. The original nucleus of the mosaics, executed over the course of the twelfth century, follows the iconographic program drawn up by a Venetian theologian who was inspired by basic Byzantine models which he freely reinterpreted. The mosaics set out to convey the great message of Christian salvation, centering on the three domes in the nave, those of the Presbytery, the Ascension and the Pentecost, masterpieces by anonymous artists who, under the skin of gold tesserae, a traditional symbol of Heaven, created three precious symphonies of color representing prophets and apostles according to the canons of Eastern iconography. Around these are set lesser groups of mosaics with special ties to Venetian piety: the *Scenes from the Life of St. Mark* in the choirs at the sides of the main altar, the *Scenes from the Life of the Virgin* in the two transepts and the numerous figures of saints in the other two domes and the small vaults.

The decoration of the atrium was carried out over the course of the thirteenth century. In this extensive and varied group of mosaics modeled on early Christian miniatures and depicting scenes from the first five books of the Old Testament, it is possible to trace the

63 *right*

Dome of Abraham, mosaic, west atrium, 13th century

Like the other mosaics in the atrium, this dome has inscriptions explaining the scenes represented. The inscriptions are blended into the decoration to form a single design. The mosaics were executed by the early local workshop and date from the middle of the 13th century.

64 *below*

Detail of the inscriptions of a scene, Dome of Abraham, mosaic, 13th century

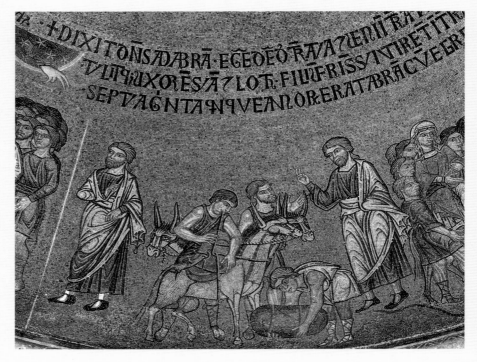

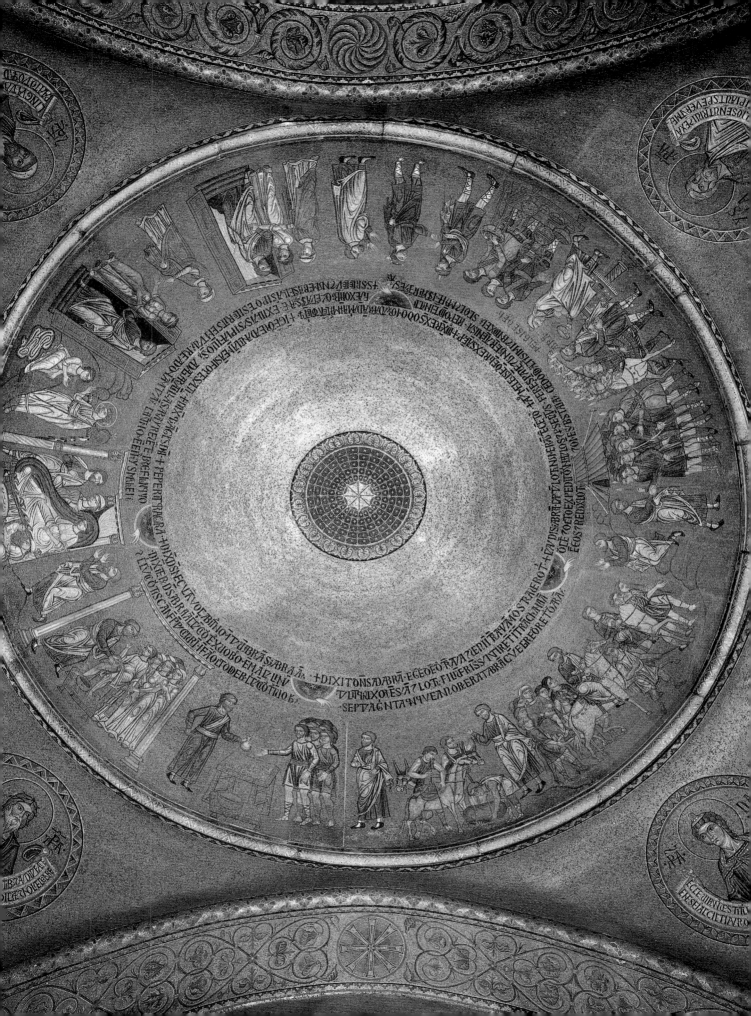

evolution and maturation of the language and style used by the mosaicists, who were now entirely Venetian. The figures no longer stand out in isolation against the gold ground, but are placed in natural or architectural settings of ever-increasing complexity. Beautiful thirteenth-century mosaics can also be seen inside the church itself (the tablets – pinakes – with prophets on the walls of the nave and the two large panels representing the Agony in the Garden and the Finding of the Body of St. Mark), as well as on the ceiling of the Zen Chapel, where they depict Scenes from the Life of St. Mark, and on the bowl-shaped vault of the Door of St. Alypius, on the façade, which represents the Placing of the Saint's Body in the Basilica. This last is the only thirteenth-century mosaic to have survived on the outside of the building.

The two major cycles of mosaics in the Baptistery and the Chapel of St. Isidore were commissioned by Doge Andrea Dandolo (1343-54). Here we find stylistic innovations of Western derivation – filtered through the work of Paolo Veneziano, the great founder of the Venetian school of painting – grafted on to the Byzantine tradition.

The mosaic decoration of the cappella nova, the Chapel of the Madonna, later known as the Mascoli Chapel after the confraternity that used to meet in prayer there from 1618 onward, dates from around the middle of the fifteenth century. The mosaics in this chapel, which present five Scenes from the Life of the Virgin drawn from the canonical and apocryphal Gospels, are an interesting testimony to the evolution of artistic taste and the development of the Renaissance style during this period.

The final contribution, dating from the early part of the sixteenth century, is the precious and absolutely original ceiling of the Sacristy, which was renovated to a

design by Giorgio Spavento, the proto, or director of works, of St. Mark's, between 1486 and 1493. We have documentary evidence for the involvement of Titian and his workshop in the design of the figures of prophets and apostles that encircle the great central cross, set against a tapestry of plant motifs in accordance with the canons of the High Renaissance.

It should be pointed out here that while the conception and execution of a mosaic had formerly been the work of a single person – who designed the figures based on fixed models, drew the sinopia (underdrawing) on the mortar that would form the support and then laid on the enamel tesserae – a division of the tasks had been introduced at some stage, perhaps at the beginning of the Quattrocento. From that time on, a painter was entrusted with the task of producing a cartoon, which was then translated into mosaic by a skilled craftsman, using the technique of pouncing. From the sixteenth century onward, all the great painters of the Venetian school (among them, Titian, Tintoretto, Veronese and Jacopo Palma il Giovane) worked on mosaics for St. Mark's. After the cycle in the Sacristy and the Tree of Jesse in the north transept, the many works executed over the course of the sixteenth, seventeenth and eighteenth centuries were all replacements of existing mosaics. Mosaics that crumbled away or were ruined by fires, earthquakes or other violent events could be remade, so long as certain precise and well-documented instructions were followed, at the behest of the high procurators of St. Mark's, the state magistracy responsible for the administration of the church. Although it was permissible to use a new and modern style, the mosaics had to represent the same scenes as before, so that they would fit into the original iconographic program,

and the same words had to be repeated in the inscriptions. The chosen painter was obliged to depict "the same scene and letters, that are there at present, without altering anything at all."

A clear example of this is provided by the vault located between the ancient Domes of the Presbytery and the Ascension (twelfth century), which have remained essentially intact in spite of many restorations. The original scenes recounting the beginning of Jesus's historical life (the Annunciation, Adoration of the Magi, Presentation in the Temple, Baptism of Christ and Transfiguration) were replaced between 1588 and 1589 by the same scenes to designs by Jacopo Tintoretto. He introduced the rich coloring and inventiveness of his many canvases of similar subjects to the mosaics, that were then executed by Giannantonio Marini.

65

Axonometric views of the three levels of mosaics in the basilica

The three drawings show the different levels of the mosaics in the basilica: the ones on the underside of the lower arches (above left), of the vaults (above right) and of the domes (below).

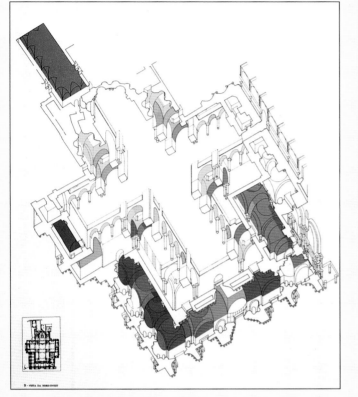

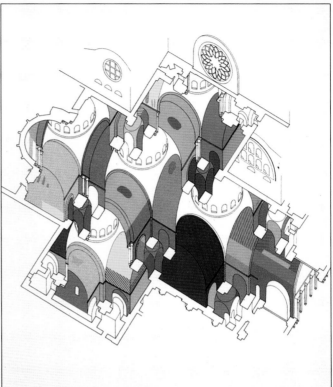

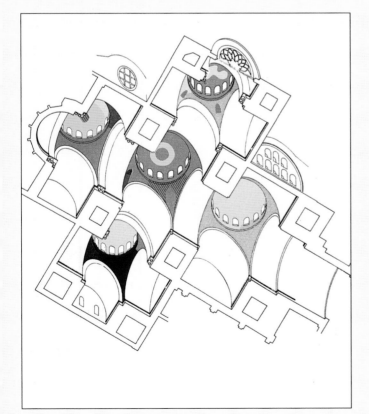

Key

The colors identify the age of the mosaics. Each century, from the 11th to the 19th, is represented by a substantial proportion of the mosaic decoration on the inside and outside of the basilica.

Gray	11th century
Light yellow	1st half of 12th century
Dark yellow	2nd half of 12th century
Orange	1st half of 13th century
Red	2nd half of 13th century
Dark green	14th century
Light green	15th century
Light blue	16th century
Dark blue	17th century
Brown	18th century
Purple	19th century

THE PORTA DA MAR

Ettore Vio

Since ancient times, it had been the custom for a seafaring people to arrive at their destination by water, leaving the boat, whether large or small, at the foot of a grassy bank or a landing with stone steps. The ancient ducal *castrum-castellum*, now the Ducal Palace, was surrounded by the waters of the lagoon and a broad canal: a sort of harbor-cum-canal on the western side, facing the basilica's south façade. It was therefore easy for Venetians to enter the church from the southern end of the atrium, through the door that had always been known as the Porta da Mar (Sea Door). It was used by humble fishermen, sailors and great naval commanders up until 1501, when it was walled up to accommodate Zen Chapel. It signalled the end of Venice's dominance of the sea as a result of the emergence of new trade routes to the

West following the discovery of America by Columbus in 1492. However, the root of the decline may have run deeper, as the ambition and drive of the Venetian society of the day were waning.

Originally an apsidal portal crowned by early Romanesque statues, it was enlarged by the addition of a deep tunnel vault. This was intended to serve as a support for the terrace when the façade was being renovated. Two lions bearing columns on their backs were carved to support the structure, but were never used owing to architectural modifications.

No pictures survive of the Porta da Mar. Even the perspective view by Jacopo de Barbari, dated MD (1500), in which the south front of the basilica is visible in the foreground, shows the large doorway already walled up, although this did not actually happen until 1501. However, the

lintel of the portal with statues representing the *Annunciation* can still be seen in the Treasury of St. Mark's.

66 *below*
Recess of the former Porta da Mar, apsidal semidome
The Virgin and Child stand at the center flanked by archangels paying homage to them. The mosaic was renovated in the second half of the 19th century, with extensive restoration to the two archangels.

67 *right*
View of the former Porta da Mar from the south
When arriving by water, the Venetians used to disembark next to the Ducal Palace and then pay their respects to St. Mark. The door was later walled up and converted into the Zen Chapel.

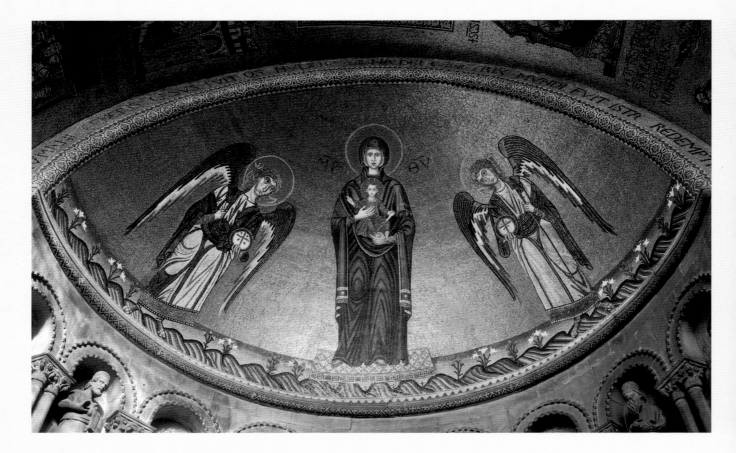

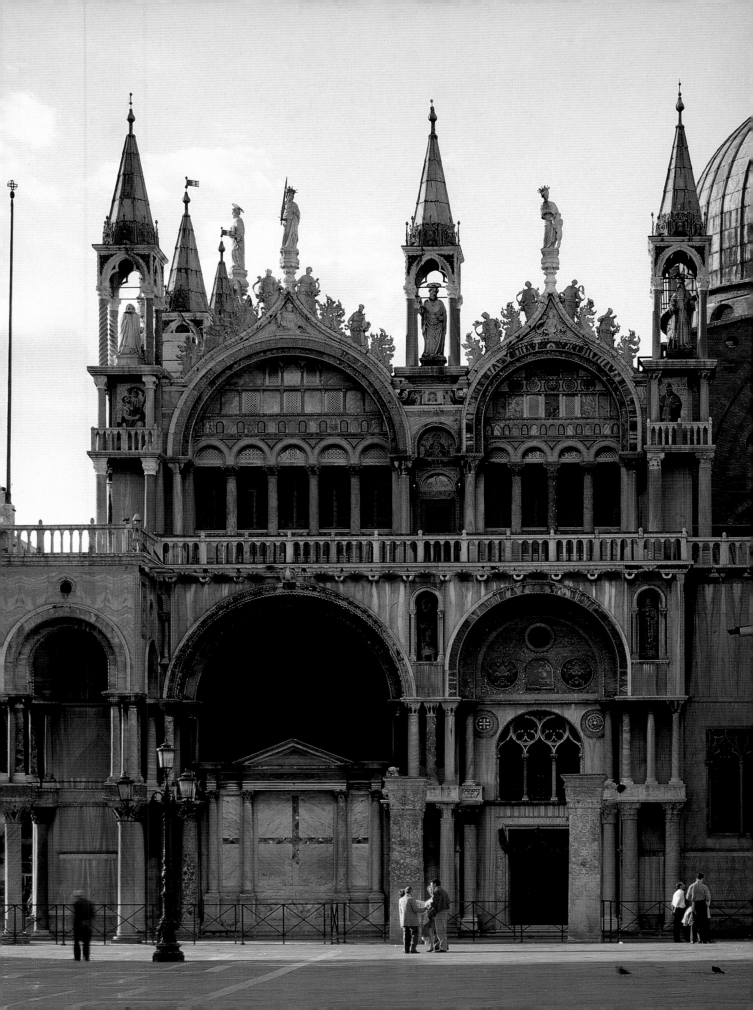

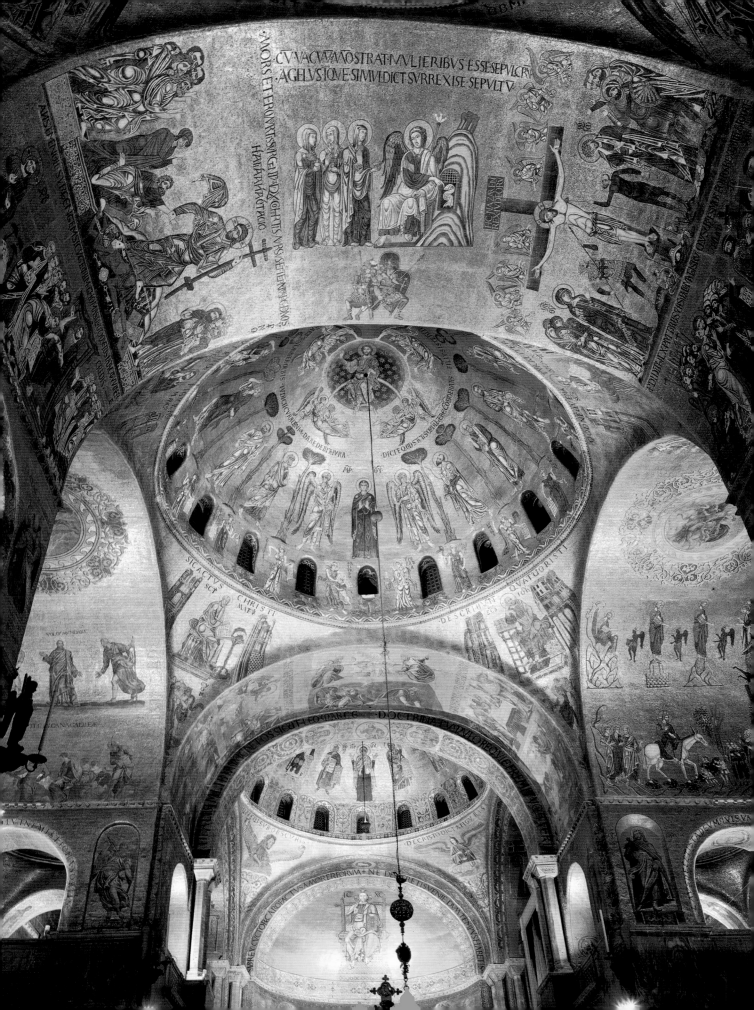

THE INTERIOR OF THE BASILICA

Ettore Vio

The impression that the basilica makes on anyone entering it for the first time is a profound one. The light glinting on the mosaics and the succession of arches, vaults and domes, forming a vista that draws the eye toward the main altar, requires a period of contemplation for the visitor to adjust to this almost unreal setting, made up of a blend of light and shade, of scintillating mosaics and precious marble. The first time, it is probably a good idea not to concentrate too much on the details but to let yourself be carried away by the atmosphere, since St. Mark's is worth many a repeat visit.

The basilica has a regular plan in the form of a Greek cross, with an elongated stem. The nave ends in a presbytery, which is raised by around sixty centimeters. The interior is roofed by five large domes resting on a system of semicircular vaults supported by enormous piers. Four of the domes are set above the arms of the cross, while the fifth is at the center. In fact the structural system of the basilica is based on the frame that supports each dome and which is repeated, with adjustments made to the surrounding architecture, five times. The same pattern can be found on a smaller scale in the structure of the piers: each is composed of four pillars linked together by vaults at two levels and topped by a cupola.

The eleventh-century church was not clad with marble and the Byzantine moldings that mark the beginning of the vaults and domes formed the lower limit of the basilica's earlier mosaic decoration. The rest was built out of unplastered brick on the inside as well as the outside, frugally adorned with columns, capitals, marble panels, and bas-reliefs set in the walls. It was only under Doge Vitale Michiel II (1156-72) that the marble facings began to be installed. Subsequently mosaics were set in the space between the Byzantine moldings and the marble. Each arm of the cross is divided into a nave and two aisles, with the aisles about half the width of the nave.

The columns and capitals are among the great glories of the architecture and decoration of St. Mark's. There are numerous Byzantine capitals, dating from between the sixth and eleventh century, in the shape of baskets or truncated pyramids, covered with floral motifs and decorated with figures of animals. Note the six gilded capitals with rams' heads in the nave and the ten with acanthus leaves set on the pillars of the transept.

The floor is in *opus sectile* and *opus tessellatum*. It is a twelfth-century work that has been recomposed many times,

adjusted and added to, with geometric designs and decorations with figures of animals. The floor, according to recent studies by Renato Polacco, presents an abstract version of the iconographic themes represented in the mosaics above. Below the central Dome of the Ascension, for example, the floor is made up of a large central panel of marble from Proconnesus, comprising twelve slabs, each measuring 1·5 by 4·5 meters, that together form a single block. They represent Christ as the *lapis angularis*, the cornerstone of his Church, the element that provides support through the twelve apostles and their successors.

Two levels can be distinguished in the church: the upper one of the mosaics, above the marble facing, and the lower one below it. From the crossing, we see the majestic iconostasis that separates the presbytery from the nave. It is an unashamedly precious piece of work from the late fourteenth century, a screen composed of fine Oriental marble and plutei made out of large slabs of equally valuable marble.

The presbytery, the basilica's sacred space, houses the high altar, under which is set the marble sarcophagus containing the mortal remains of St. Mark. Jacopo Sansovino, *proto* and architect of St. Mark's from 1529 to 1570, was responsible for important works of decoration within the presbytery.

The high altar is enclosed by a baldachin consisting of a groin vault encrusted with verd-antique marble and supported by four alabaster columns decorated with scenes.

The layout of the presbytery, apart from recent alterations made following the handover of the basilica to the patriarch of

68

Interior of the basilica

Here we can see the sequence of domes and vaults that characterize the nave and two aisles. Originally galleries, used by women attending services, were set above the columns that separate the nave from the aisles. As long ago as the 12th century, however, following the fire of 1145, many of the women's galleries were removed, leaving the walkway we see today. In the 13th century, after further fires, any remaining galleries were demolished. Their floors were made of wood and the part of the wall to which they were fixed is still clearly visible, as it was covered with slabs of red Verona marble, decorated with small sculptures. The parapets that line the walkway differ greatly in style and age. The ones facing on to the nave were made out of plutei dating from between the 6th and the 11th century, while the ones facing on to the aisles, constructed after the women's galleries had been removed, consist of small marble columns with no decoration.

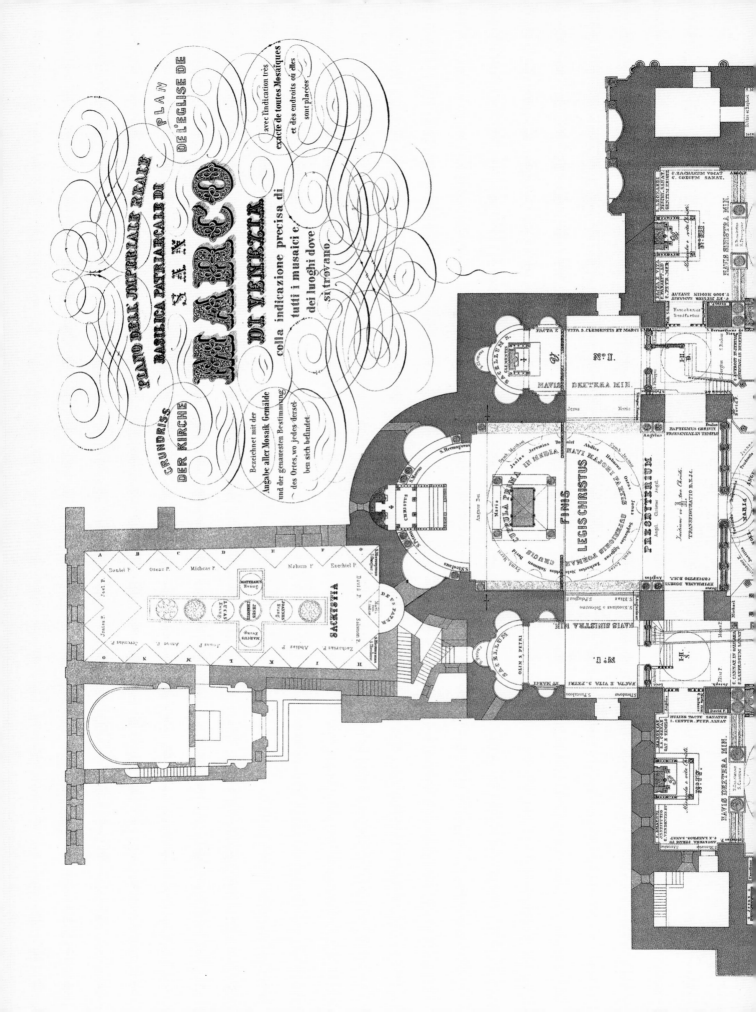

PIANO DELL' IMPERIALE REALE
BASILICA PATRIARCALE DI
SAN
MARCO
DI VENEZIA

PLAN
DE L'EGLISE DE

GRUNDRISS
DER KIRCHE

colla indicazione precisa di
tutti i mussaici e mussaici
dei luoghi dove
si trovano

avec l'indication très
exacte de toutes les Mosaïques
et des endroits où elles
sont placées

Bezeichnet mit der
Angabe aller Mosaik Gemälde
und der genauesten Bestimmung
des Ortes, wo jedes dersel-
ben sich befindet.

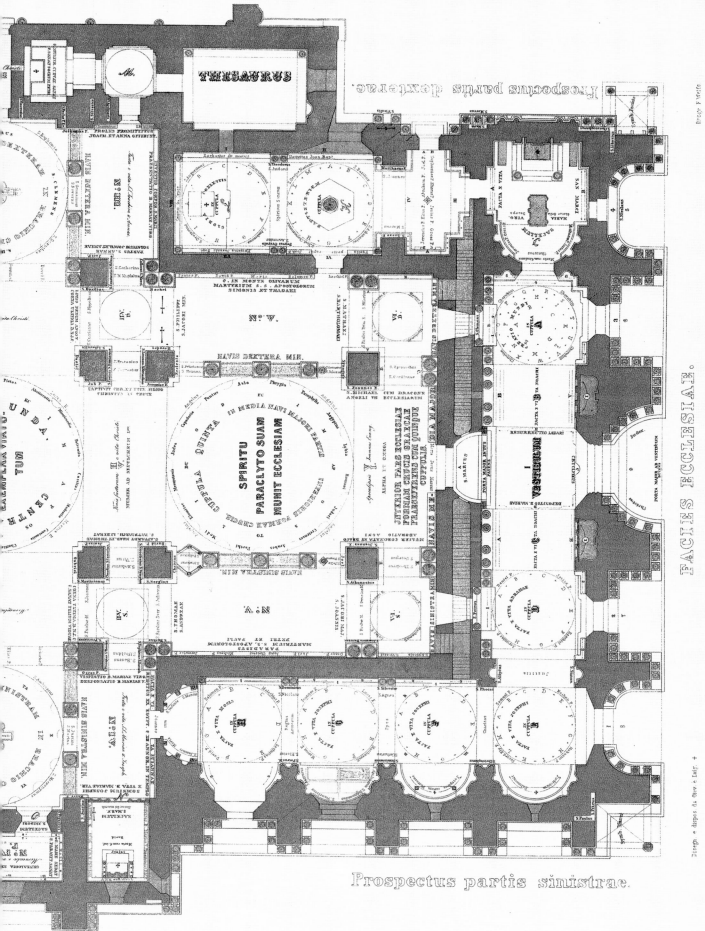

FACIES ECCLESIAE.

69 *preceding pages*

G. and L. Kreutz, *Plan of the Imperial Royal Patriarchal Basilica of St. Mark in Venice,* **lithograph by F. Weifs, Vienna, 1843**

The drawing shows where the various mosaic panels are located in the basilica, differentiating them on the basis of a careful analysis of the type of lettering used in the inscriptions, as well as according to their importance and height.

The entire surface of the walls above the marble facing is decorated with mosaics, covering a total of about 8600 square meters. They have grown steadily over the centuries, earning the church its nickname of the Golden Basilica.

The mosaics are the living compendium of an art form handed down by the Republic of Venice through its mosaicists, to ensure the respect of an iconography that has been assigned not only a religious but a political and social value too.

Many of the mosaics on the domes, the pendentives and the vaults that support them are of Byzantine origin. They were restored and added to during the Renaissance, replaced where they were threatening to disintegrate in the 16th and 17th centuries and underwent modest additions in the following century. Finally they have been subjected to extensive restorations from the 19th century onward.

The iconography

The iconography, based on a Greek model, emphasizes the particular functions assigned to the different parts of the church as well as the presence, role and duties of the doge, who occupied the right-hand side of the building, and of the *primicerius*, who carried out his activities on the left-hand side. The mosaics are also subdivided vertically.

Starting from the top, the godhead is represented in the domes, while facts connected with the events depicted in the respective domes are illustrated on the vaults that support them. The side walls narrate the history of the church and its major saints. In the mosaics applied to the undersides of the arches that used to support the women's galleries and to the vaults that connect the piers we find the everyday saints, those closest to the lives of ordinary believers to whom the ground level of the basilica is assigned.

All this emphasizes the profound interdependence of the Christian community on earth with that of the saints, the apostles and Christ.

Dome of the Presbytery

Starting nearest the high altar, the Dome of the Presbytery depicts God's promise to humanity that a Savior would be born of a Virgin. The prophets are distributed around the dome, together with the Virgin who will be the Mother of God. An idealized – as his identity is still unknown – and eternally youthful God is represented at the top. The pendentives contain the four Biblical symbols that will later be attributed to the evangelists: the lion, ox, angel and eagle.

Dome of the Ascension

In the central dome, we see Christ ascending to heaven after his resurrection. He is represented as a historical figure, as Man, and surrounded by the apostles. At their feet, between the windows of the dome, are set the Human Virtues, along with those deriving from Christ's teachings. The four evangelists who testified to Christ's presence on earth are portrayed in the pendentives.

The four vaults that support the dome are decorated with *Scenes from the Life of Christ*, from the *Nativity* to his *Baptism* (east vault), the *Wedding at Cana* (north vault), the *Temptations in the Wilderness*, the *Entry into Jerusalem*, the *Washing of the Feet* and the *Last Supper* (south vault), and finally from the *Betrayal of Judas* to the *Ecce Homo*, *Crucifixion*, *Women at the Tomb*, *Descent into Limbo* and the *Incredulity of Thomas* (west vault). Christ asks Thomas, who has touched his wounds, whether he believes at last, a question that is addressed to every Christian.

Dome of the Pentecost

At the center of the dome is set the throne with the open book of the Gospels and the Spirit of God, awaiting the return of Christ at the end of time. All around, the apostles are filled with the Holy Spirit and transfigured, before going out to take the message of salvation – the great news that we are the sons of God – to the peoples, who are represented below them, between the windows of the dome.

In the pendentives the archangels sing the *Sanctus Dominus* of praise for and gratitude toward this God who loves and saves. The iconographic scheme pervades the entire basilica and illustrates this hope for the future, which is a certainty for believers, accompanying and protecting them at every moment of their lives. If they raise their eyes, its harmonious repetition on the heavenly vaults reassures them of the love of God.

Sides of the high altar

The *Scenes from the Life of St. Mark* and the *Retrieval of St. Mark's Body from Alexandria* emphasize the fact that the church is dedicated to the evangelist and houses his mortal remains.

Doge's area, south transept

The fasts and prayers of the people, the clergy and the doge are depicted on the west wall, along with the *Finding of the Body of St. Mark*.

Dome of St. Leonard

Leonard, Blaise, Clement and Nicholas might all be called political saints for the role that they assume with respect to the doge. Leonard, a king who became a saint, stands for the kind of government that is based on the rectitude of the sovereign's treatment of his subjects. Nicholas, saint of the sea, linked Venice to the Adriatic and Aegean, where he was widely venerated. Clement, the third pope, indicates the attention and respect paid by the Signoria of Venice to the papacy. Blaise was one of the saints venerated in territories with which the Repubblica Serenissima maintained continuous ties. In the pendentives we find the female saints Erasma, Euphemia, Dorothea and Thecla.

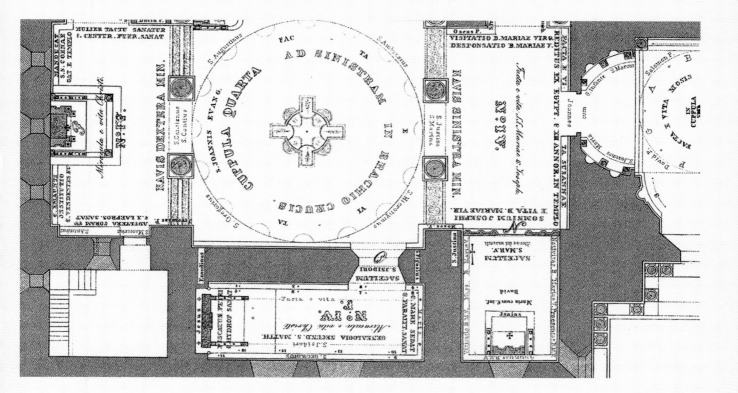

Dome of St. John the Evangelist

Here the mosaics represent *Scenes from the Life of St. John the Evangelist*, prototype of the priest. At the center a sort of wind rose indicates the cardinal points and superimposes on them the new reference points of the coming of Christ, who permeates and transforms everything. They are a splendid, concise and to some degree hermetic interpretation of the apotheosis of creation following the birth of Christ.

In the pendentives, we find the four Doctors of the Western Church: Jerome, Gregory, Augustine and Ambrose.

Walls of the transepts

Scenes from the Life of Christ are depicted on the eastern walls. At the center, in the semidome of the apse, we see the Pantocrator, a majestic figure reworked in 1506. On the western walls, facing the *Scenes from the Life of Christ*, are *Scenes from the Life of the Virgin*, partly drawn from the Apocryphal Gospels. She is the only human being worthy of this position at the same height opposite Christ. The lives of Jesus and the Virgin intersect at the promise made by God to Adam which has its root in Jesse. And on the north wall of the north transept we find the splendid representation of the *Tree of Jesse*, which has been described as "the Sistine Chapel of Venice." At its top is set a *Virgin and Child*, the work of Vincenzo Bianchini (1542-52), to a cartoon by Giuseppe Porta, known as Salviati.

Nave

Scenes from the lives of the apostles are depicted on the walls and vaults under the Dome of the Pentecost. In a masterly sequence executed by two or more mosaicists between 1214 and 1220, at the bottom on the southern side, we see Christ's *Agony in the Garden* with the *Betrayal of Judas* represented at the start of the vault, between the Dome of the Ascension and that of the Pentecost.

West vault of the Dome of the Pentecost

As we leave the basilica, the large Vault of the *Last Judgment* is preceded by *Scenes from Revelation* and completed, on the walls, by depictions of heaven and hell. At the exit, in the bowl-shaped vault of the central portal, the narrative returns to the theme of Christ the Judge flanked by his mother.

70

G. and L. Kreutz, *Plan of the Imperial Royal Patriarchal Basilica of St. Mark in Venice*, lithograph by F. Weifs, Vienna, 1843, detail of the north transept

This is the area currently set aside for prayer.

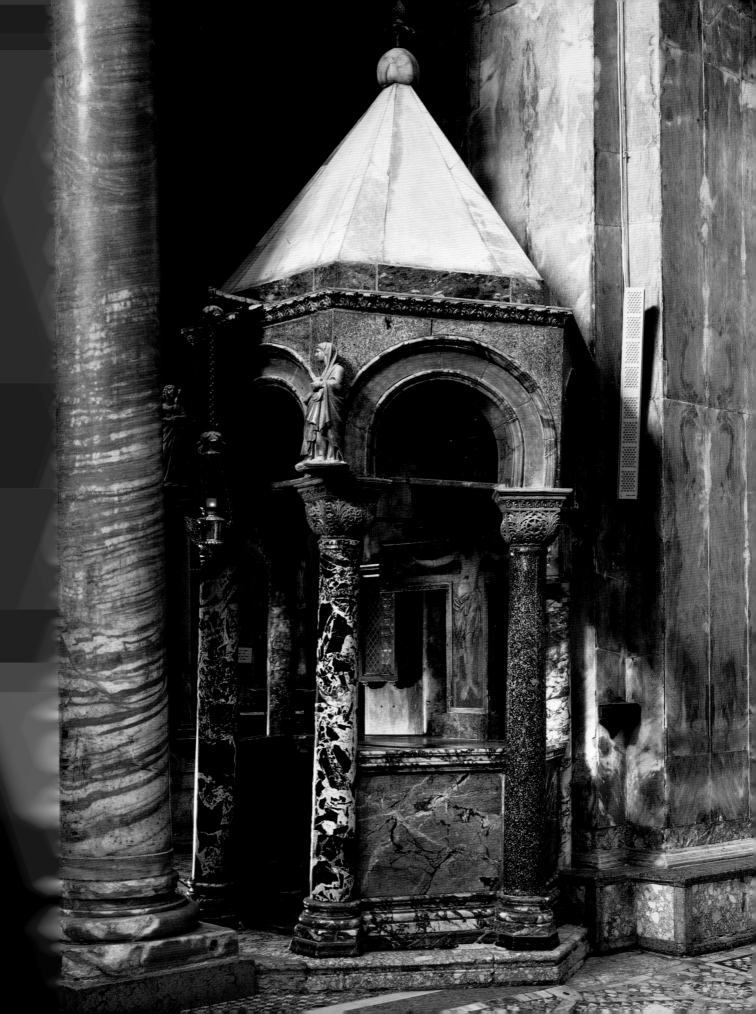

71

Altar of the Crucifix, nave, pier on the left before the crossing

The small altar is enclosed in an aedicule with a hexagonal base and a pointed roof, constructed out of precious marble, columns and capitals. It houses an ancient icon in the shape of a cross, with Christ painted on panel, which according to legend was brought to Venice prior to the booty of the Fourth Crusade. Allegedly a madman struck it several times with a dagger in the second half of the 13th century, and the image bled. The recent restoration carried out by Antonino Rusconi between 1972 and 1975 appears to confirm the presence of damage that could have been inflicted in such a manner. The altar is continually lit up by many votive candles.

72

Iconostasis, detail, 14th century

Above the trabeation, the large and recently restored Christ in embossed silver is hemmed in by statues of the apostles and by figures of the Virgin and St. John the Evangelist, who act as mediators between the congregation and the sacred area of the presbytery.

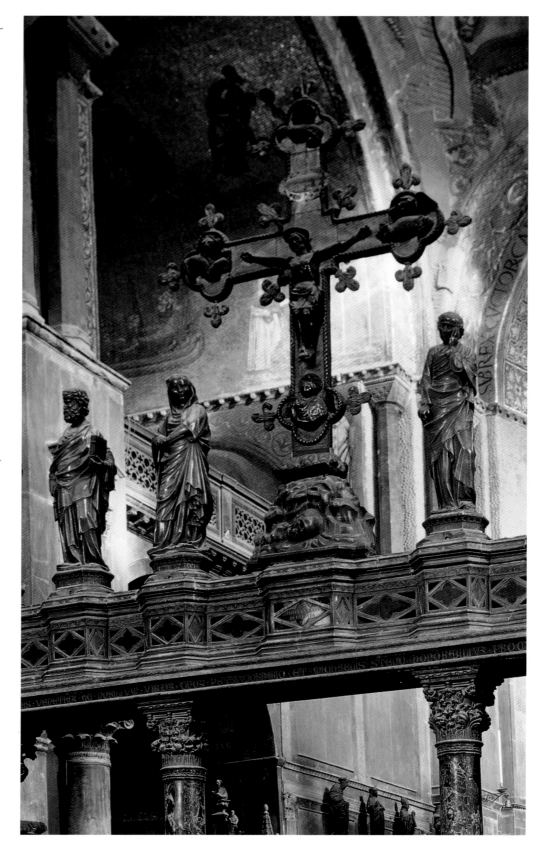

Venice in 1807, dates from the thirteenth century. The changes made in the first half of the nineteenth century were carried out for liturgical reasons. To the left of the presbytery we find the apsidal Chapel of St. Peter, screened like the corresponding Chapel of St. Clement on the right by a marble iconostasis. Above the architrave in the Chapel of St. Peter is set the *Virgin between Saints Mary Magdalen, Cecilia, Helen and Margaret*, a late fourteenth-century work attributed to the Dalle Masegne brothers. Above the altar of the chapel we see a marble bas-relief from the first half of the fourteenth century. Reassembled in the nineteenth century, it depicts *St. Peter Adored by Two Procurators*.

In the northwest corner of the north transept we find the Mascoli Chapel, dedicated since 1618 to the confraternity of the same name, which was founded in St. Mark's at the beginning of the twelfth century. They originally met in the crypt, then in the Chapel of St. John, now the Nicopeia Chapel, and finally in the Mascoli Chapel. At the outset it was simply called the *cappella nova* or new chapel. It dates from the mid-fifteenth century and is a splendid example of Venetian Gothic. The altar is adorned with statues of the *Virgin and Child between Saints Mark and John*, the work of Bartolomeo Bon.

Opposite the Altar of the Nicopeia stands the Porta della Madonna, the doorway between the north transept and the north arm of the atrium. The mosaic above the door represents *St. John the Evangelist* and dates from the fourteenth century. On the pier set at the corner with the nave we see the *Virgin of the Gun*, a nineteenth-century armorial bearing that may have been a votive offering from marines in the Venetian navy who had miraculously survived the Austrian shells that fell on Marghera on May 10, 1849.

73

Chapel of St. Clement, iconostasis, 14th century

A work attributed to the Dalle Masegne brothers that, together with the iconostasis in the Chapel of St. Peter, completes the splendid enclosure of the presbytery.

The work dates from the High Gothic period and is characterized by the quality and preciosity of the marble used. Five statues are set on top: the Virgin and Child in the middle, flanked by Saints Christine, Clare, Catherine and Agnes.

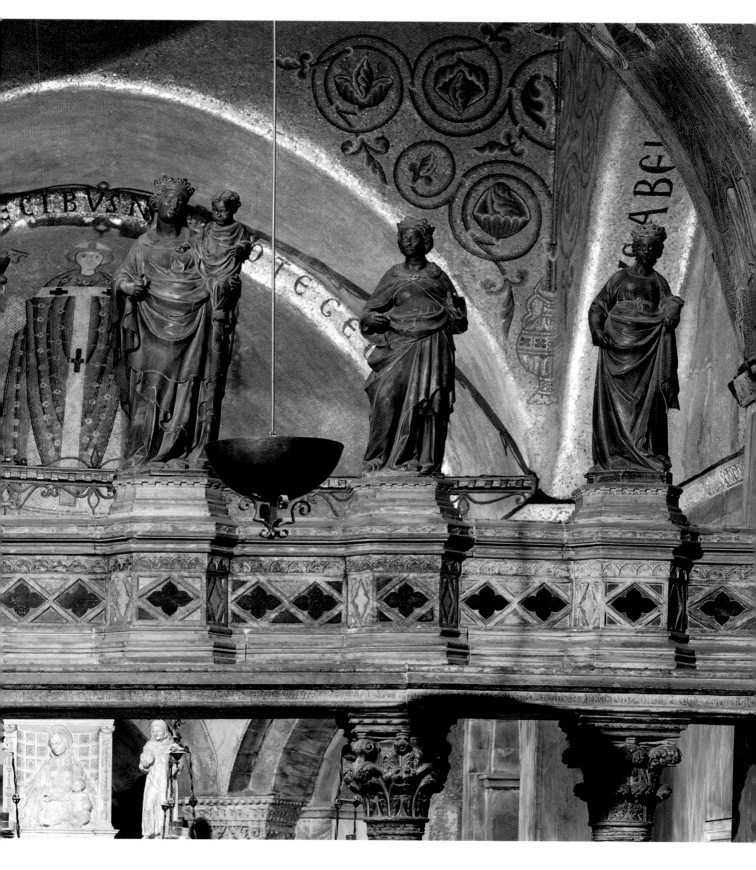

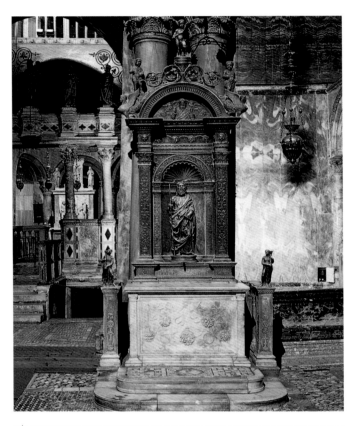

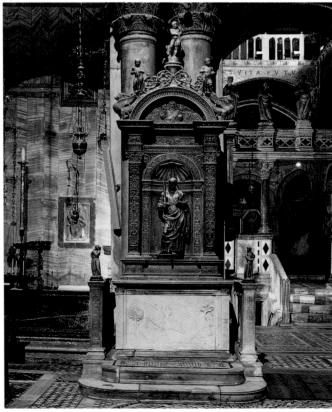

74 *above*

Small altar of St. Paul, south pier of the Altar of the Nicopeia

The work, dating from the Venetian Renaissance, is refined in its proportions and both the statues that adorn it and the bas-relief of the marble altar frontal are particularly fine. It was commissioned by Doge Cristoforo Moro (1462-71).

75 *below*

Small altar of St. James, north pier of the Altar of St. Leonard, formerly of the Holy Sacrament

The work, dating from the Venetian Renaissance, is refined in its proportions and both the statues that adorn it and the bas-relief of the marble altar frontal are particularly fine. It was commissioned by Doge Cristoforo Moro (1462-71).

76 *right*

Chapel of St. Peter

The chapel to the left of the presbytery, along with that of St. Clement to the right are worth a closer look, for they tell us about the history of the alterations that were made to the architecture of St. Mark's. The original ceilings of the two chapels, which were certainly part of the first church, have been removed. The height of what remains of the vaults above the floor of the crypt is consistent with hypothetical reconstructions of the first church, based on the position and size of the figures in the mosaic of the *Deposition from the Cross*, found on the southwest pier of the presbytery. All that remains of the ceiling decoration, in both the Chapel of St. Peter

and that of St. Clement, are the apsidal bowl-shaped vaults with figures of the saints to whom the chapels are dedicated. In that of St. Peter, four seraphim at the sides accompany the inscription: "This covered head represents the deity. The future life is our hope. The past and the fleeting present are barely known to us."

77 *following pages*

Prayer for the Discovery of the Body of St. Mark, mosaic, south transept, west wall, second quarter of 13th century

Here we find a detailed representation of the basilica's interior. Note the baldachin and the double ambo. The domes on top of the basilica are of the depressed – and therefore Byzantine – type, clad in lead. This mosaic is about fifty years older than the one on the outside, in the bowl-shaped vault of St. Alypius, where the domes appear as tall as they are today.

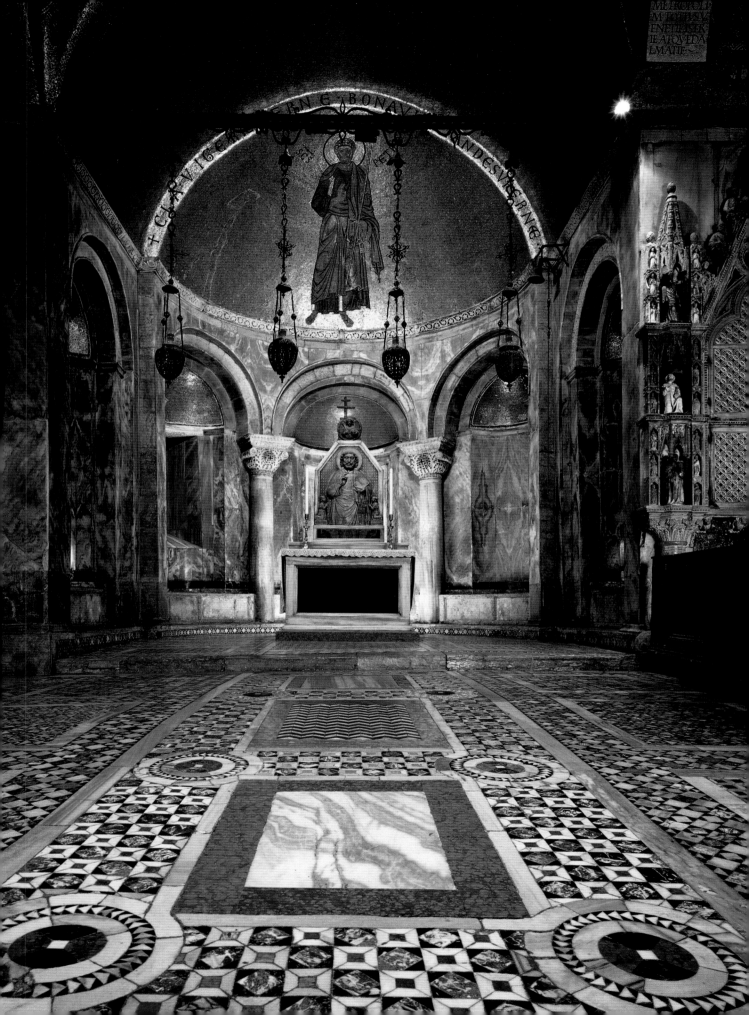

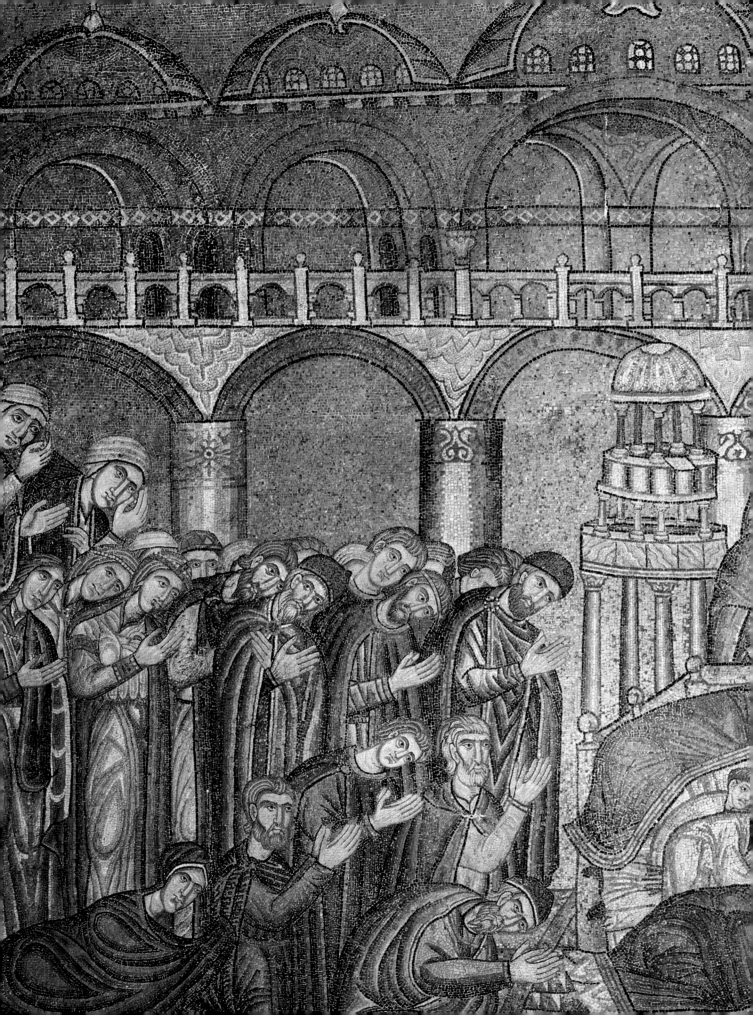

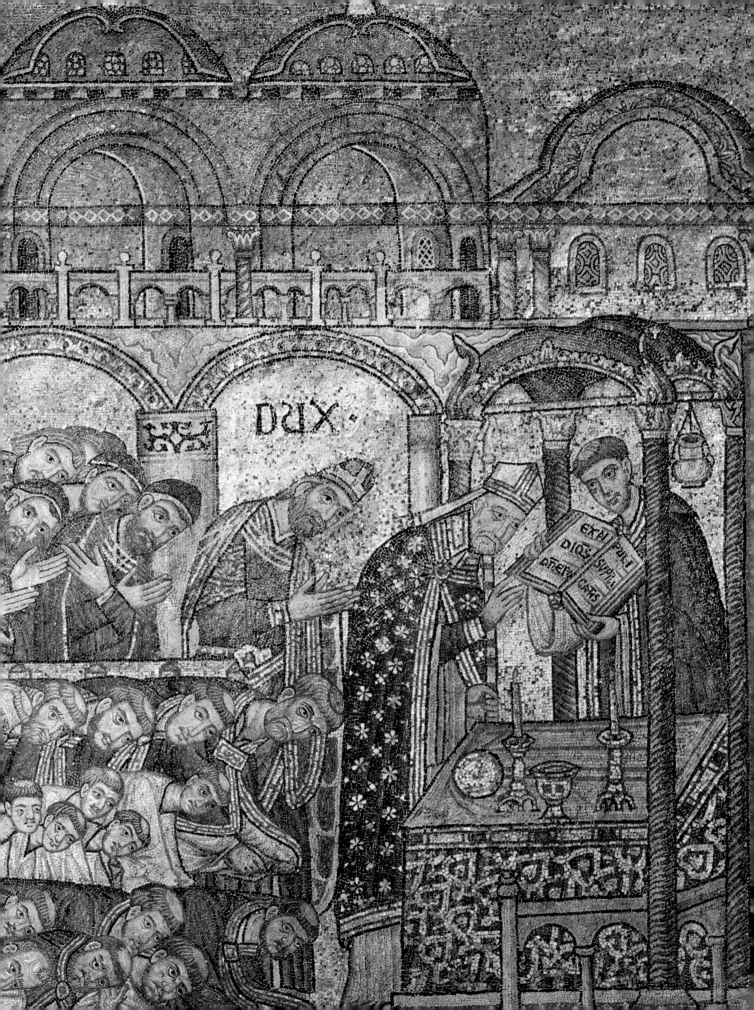

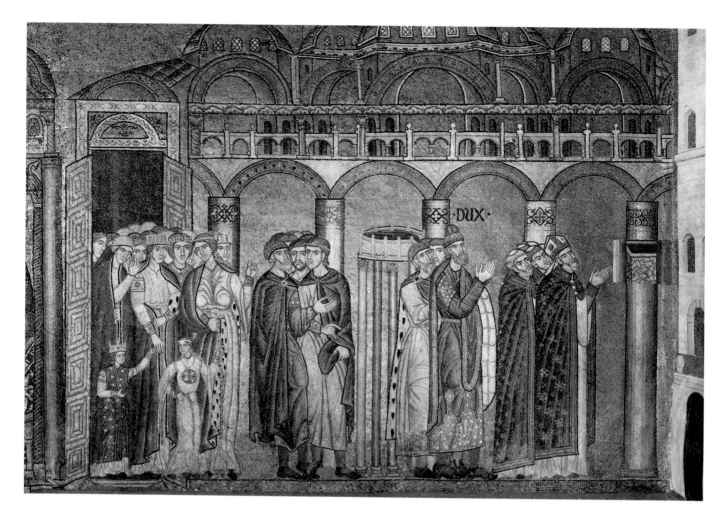

78

***Finding of the Body of
St. Mark,* mosaic, south
transept, west wall,
second quarter of
13th century**

This is a different, but equally
detailed, representation of the
interior of St. Mark's. Note the
doge's ambo and the large gilded
door at the entrance to the
church. Here, too, the domes
that roof the basilica are of the
flattened, Byzantine type.

79 *right*

**Icon of the *Blessed Virgin
Nicopeia,* Altar of the
Nicopeia, north transept**

After modifications were made by
Tommaso Contin, this icon in the
Byzantine style was placed on the
altar in 1617. Also called *Hodegetria*
(she who points the way), the
image was carried into battle at
the head of the army, as *Nicopeia*,
(bringer of victory). It is said to
date from the 10th century and
used to belong to the Monastery
of St. John the Theologian in
Constantinople.

It came to Venice with the
booty of the Fourth Crusade in
1204. The icon used to be covered
with votive jewelry but this was
removed after the burglary that
took place in 1970, though it
still has its original silver frame,
modified in the 17th century.

The icon was displayed on the
high altar on solemn feast days
and when Venice was under threat.
Along with the Altar of the
Crucifix, the icon of the *Blessed
Virgin Nicopeia* is the object of
constant devotion.

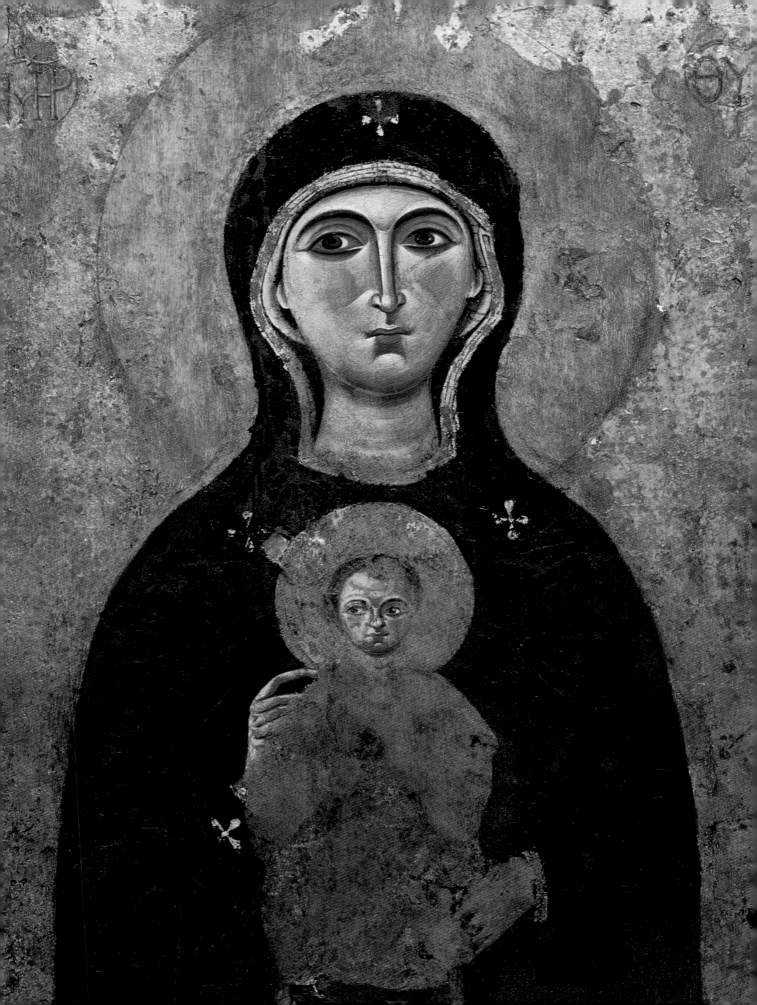

THE ICONOSTASIS OF THE DALLE MASEGNE BROTHERS
Guido Tigler

The presbytery is raised slightly above the crypt, the majority of which is located below ground and the visible façade of which is decorated with small arches carved in bas-relief at the end of the eleventh century. As early as 1094, a sort of iconostasis (or, rather, a *templon*) may have been set on top of these, and some fairly fanciful hypotheses have been put forward about it. However, it is likely that it consisted simply of an architrave supported by columns, like that of the Chapel of St. Peter on the left which is depicted in a scene of Paolo Veneziano's *Pala Feriale* (Weekday Altarpiece), dating from 1345, which is now in the Museum of St. Mark. The present late Gothic screen, which has essentially the same structure but is enriched with decorative details and adorned with statues, is similar in character to those in the chancel and in the two side Chapels of St. Peter and St. Clement. The precious antique marble of the panels at the bottom, the clouded red Verona marble of the columns and the once-vivid colors of the statues, now blackened by the smoke of candles, make it a feast for the eyes.

It is a masterpiece of Venetian architecture and sculpture, which was dominated in the last two decades of the fourteenth century by the two brothers who signed the iconostasis: Jacobello and Pier Paolo Dalle Masegne. Wolfgang Wolters assigns the statues of the central part (the mourners to either side of the cross and the apostles) to Jacobello, owing to their affinities with some of the figures in the altarpiece of San Francesco in Bologna, begun in 1386. This central section bears the inscription-cum-signature of the two brothers, referring to the work as a whole, and the date 1394. The metal crucifix in the middle, on the other hand, is signed, again in 1394, by a certain "Jacobus M(a)g(ist)ri Ma(r)ci Benato." The figures

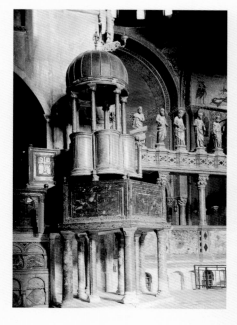

of the lateral iconostases (the Madonna, represented twice, and female saints), dated 1397, can be attributed to Pier Paolo. The Dalle Masegne are also believed to have been responsible for the elegant structures of the two shrines, documented in 1388, but the small figures they contain are the work of assistants.

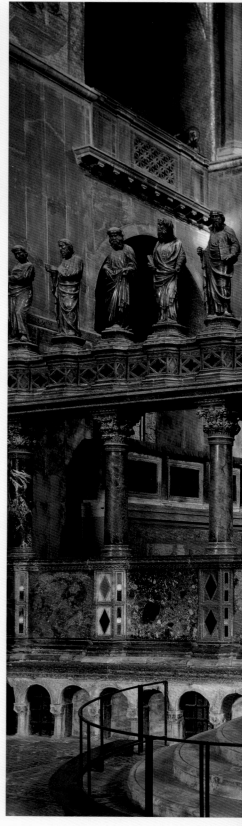

80 *above*

The left-hand ambo of the iconostasis
Ancient 13th-century walls from the East were reassembled to form a double ambo. The Epistle is read from the lower level and the Gospel from the upper level.

81 *right*

View of the iconostasis
On top, we find statues of the twelve apostles, with the Virgin and St. John the Evangelist at the foot of the central cross, in gilded bronze with Christ in embossed silver. The sculptures are the work of Pier Paolo and Jacobello Dalle Masegne (1394). Christ and the figures that adorn the cross are by Jacopo di Marco Benato.

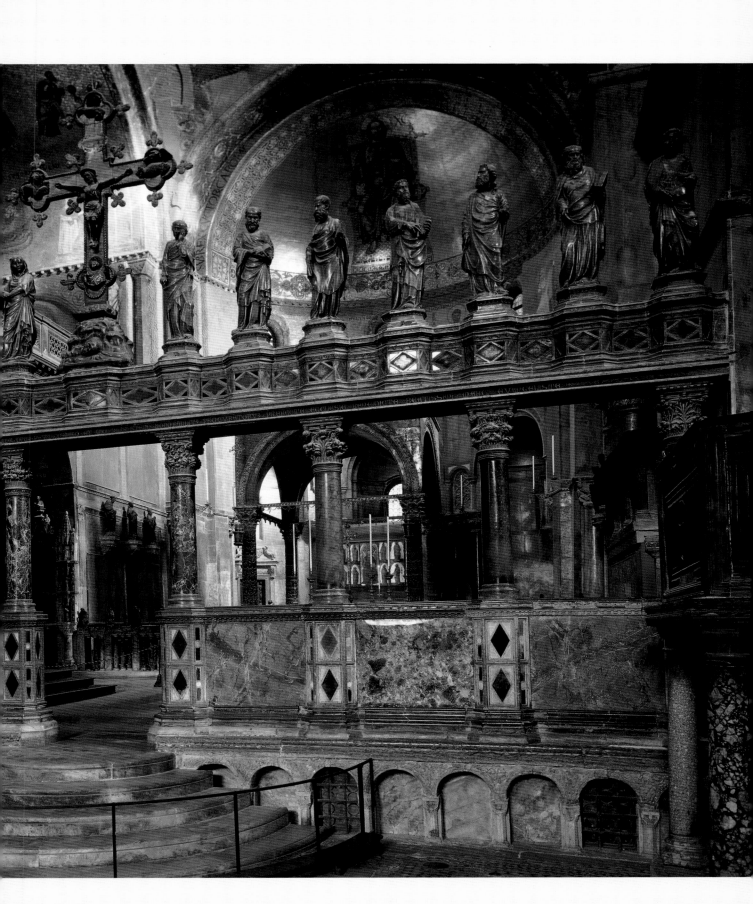

THE BALDACHIN
Ettore Vio

The baldachin, or ciborium, supported by four columns of alabaster from the East, is the most precious feature of the presbytery. The block, carved into two intersecting tunnel vaults and covered in its entirety with slabs of verd-antique, rests on twelfth-century capitals. In a print made in the first half of the eighteenth century, Antonio Visentini shows it surmounted by a cupola of gilded wood. Statues of Christ between St. Mark and St. John are set on the side facing the congregation, while the Redeemer (1751) between St. Mark and St. Luke (thirteenth century) are placed at the back, facing the apse. The central figure of Christ at the front has been attributed to the great sculptor Tullio Lombardo by Anne Markham Schulz.

The debate over the baldachin has focused primarily on the date and provenance of the four columns. The bas-reliefs that adorn them, while differing slightly – such as in the form of the small arches that enclose the scenes, in the type of lettering and in the style of the clothing – are basically alike and must come from a single center of production, even if executed by sculptors of varying talent.

In the first half of the twentieth century, scholars like P. Toesca and S. Bettini argued that the style of the columns was similar to that of Syrian and Egyptian ivories from the fifth and sixth century, as well as to Coptic sculptures. After the Second World War, however, Lucchesi Palli used analogies with Western iconographies and models to claim that that they were more likely to have been produced by a thirteenth-century Venetian workshop.

According to tradition, the columns came from Santa Maria in Canneto and were brought to Venice by Doge Pietro Orseolo II (991-1008) after an expedition to Dalmatia. An authoritative German scholar, Thomas Weigel, has now confirmed their ancient origins. Among the evidence

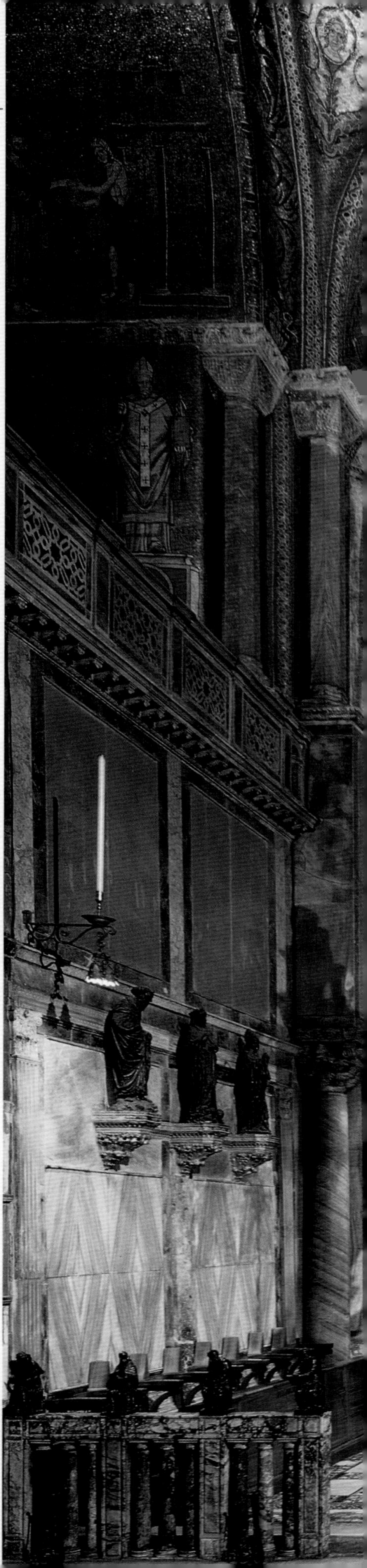

82

View of the baldachin

The most sacred place in the basilica encloses the high altar that has been left open on its longer sides so that the marble sarcophagus housing the body of St. Mark can be seen. In the background, the Pala d'Oro, facing the congregation, echoes the splendor of the columns with its repetitive series of small arches containing *cloisonné* enamels. Above, a mosaic of the Pantocrator in the semidome of the apse is signed "1506 Petrus."

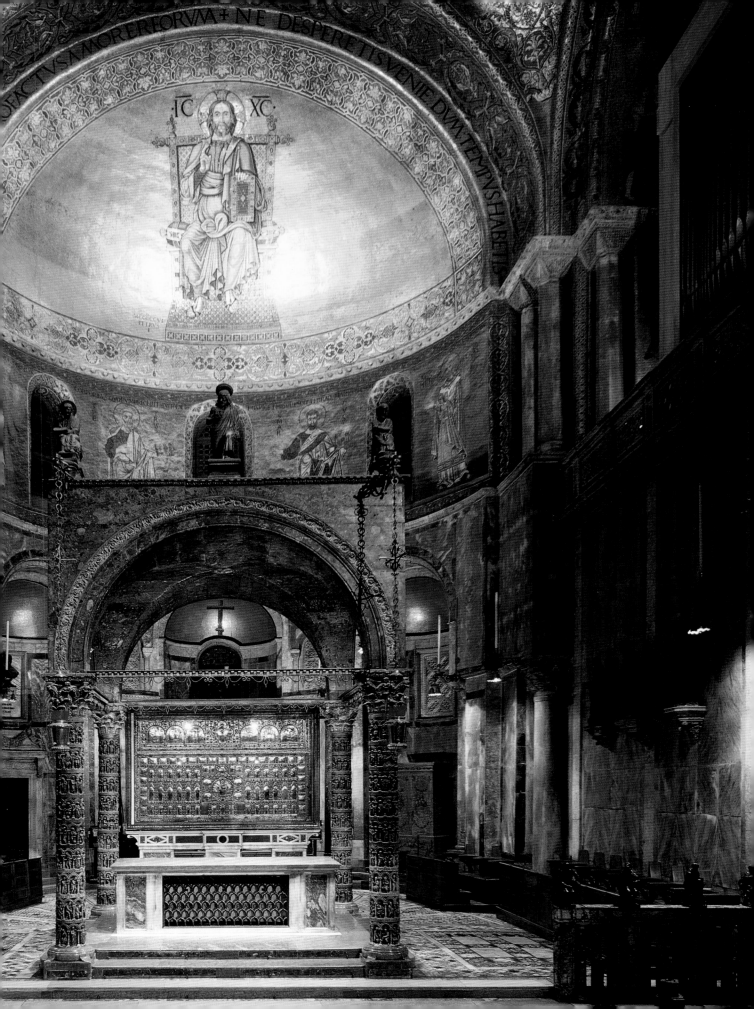

for this and for their transportation to St. Mark's are the iconography of the crucifixion – where the figure of Christ is replaced by the symbol of the Mystic Lamb – and the fractures visible on the upper and lower shafts, which were caused by the columns being moved and having to adapt to a new location. Gaps in the inscriptions caused by these fractures have been filled in.

As for the iconography, Weigel cites the decision, taken at the Trullan Council held in Constantinople in AD 692, forbidding the use of the Mystic Lamb in the place of Christ, owing to the incapacity of the majority of believers to grasp its purely symbolic value. This did not prevent the Venetians from using the ancient columns, whereas it would certainly have stopped them from carving new ones with an iconography that had been banished from the artistic repertory of the time.

The baldachin is the heart of the basilica and assumes maximum significance, as the hub of the basilica's message as well as of its history and values, on feast days in honor of the saint. In celebration, the gratings around the sarcophagus and its relics are removed and covered with red roses, while the Pala d'Oro gleams in splendor, facing the congregation.

83

Baldachin, detail of the carving on one of the four alabaster columns that support the vault

Recent studies have dated the columns, which were used for another purpose before being installed in St. Mark's, to the 7th century. They are decorated with ninety scenes, each accompanied by an inscription engraved on the band that separates one panel from the next. The rear column on the left has *Scenes from the Life of the Virgin*, from her birth to marriage, and the front left depicts *Scenes from the Lives of the Virgin and Christ*. Both the rear and front columns on the right show episodes from the *Life of Christ*, from the entry into Jerusalem to his glorification in heaven.

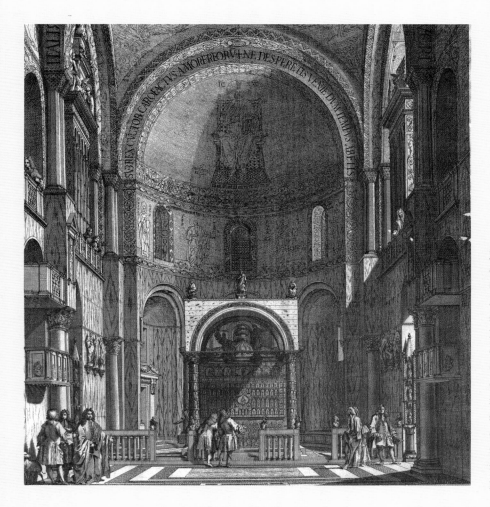

84

Antonio Visentini, *View of St. Mark's Basilica*, engraving, early 18th century

At the center we see the presbytery surmounted by a gilded dome that no longer exists. To the right and left, the organs that predated the ones made by Callido in 1766 face one another in the choirs. In the only surviving record of these instruments, the 15th-century organ is shown on the right, the 16th-century one on the left. A section of the wooden tribunes, used by the choristers, is visible in the foreground, between the north and south piers of the presbytery.

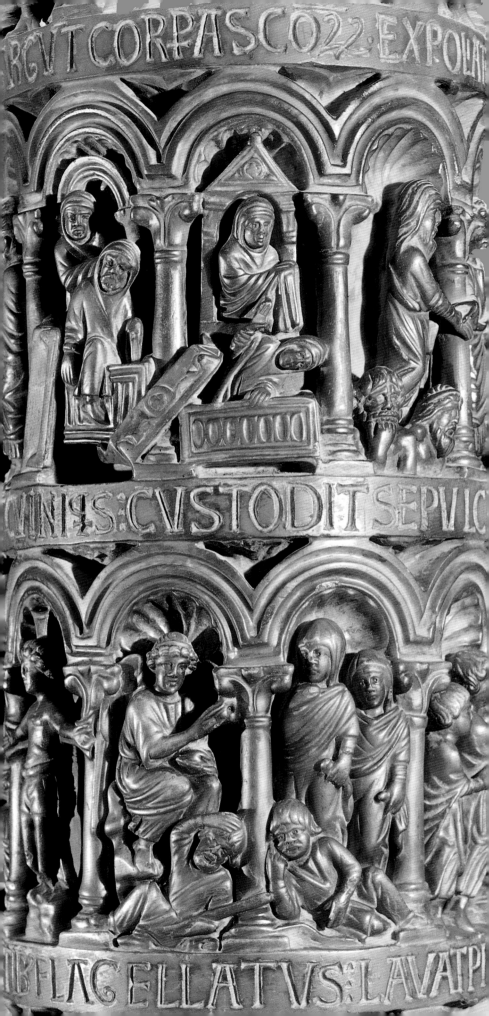

... RCVT CORPAS CO22 EXPOLIAT ...

... CINI‡S:CVSTODIT SEPVIC ...

... ‡BF‡AGELLATVS:LAVA‡ ...

of Common Prayer, a vast
ated missal, bound with
of parchment" was just
elling images used by
book *The Stones of*
n effort to convey his
Mark's, that splendid
h and civilization in
ity he loved most in
en reading this "vast
" we should follow the
me drawn up for its
a medieval theologian
tury: the story of
n.

er an explanation of
at accompany each
es and amplify their
The majority of these
the Latin tongue and
n in abbreviated
re based on the
Old and New Testament
nmentary on each scene.
are also numerous
ations, in typically
orm (leonine rhyme),
rches, semidomes and
addressed to St. Mark, it
were composed
enetian church.

ple, we shall examine
ntral portal leading from
e church itself. Four
doorway contain figures
elists in the canonical
Mark, Luke and John. They
be some of the church's
ting from the end of the
A hemistich runs along
each niche: *Ecclesiae*
quattuor isti / quorum
t et movet undique
are sentinels of Christ's
t song rings out and
s everywhere).

Above, a smaller register of niches contains the images of eight apostles, also very old mosaics, around that of the Virgin. It is to the latter that the inscription running horizontally between the two registers refers, associating her with the Church in accordance with ancient patristic tradition: *Sponsa Deo gigno natos ex virgine virgo / quos fragiles firmo fortes super ethera mitto* (Bride of God, ever virgin, she gave birth to children whom she strengthened in their weakness and sent to Heaven). The prayer on the front of the large semidome above the portal is addressed directly to Mark, the evangelist and patron saint of the city. *St. Mark in Ecstasy*, a sixteenth-century mosaic, shows the saint dressed as a bishop and welcoming the faithful to his church: *Alapis Marce delicta precantibus arce / ut surgant per te factore suo miserante* (O Mark, drive away sin from those who join their hands in prayer to you, may they be saved through your intercession and the mercy of God).

Above the portal itself, on the inside of the church, a lunette contains a thirteenth-century mosaic, a Deesis depicting the Virgin Mary and St. Mark interceding on behalf of humanity with Christ, represented as Pantocrator, lord and judge of the universe. However, it is the words from the Gospel according to John, clearly visible on the book, that give us the key we need to interpret the figure of Christ, as he says of himself: *Ego sum ostium, si quis per*

85

Dome of the Presbytery

This mosaic from the first half of the 12th century was executed by Byzantine craftsmen. It marks the beginning of the iconographic sequence, with the Virgin depicted among the prophets, reminding us of God's promise of the salvation of humanity. It is also known as the Dome of Emmanuel.

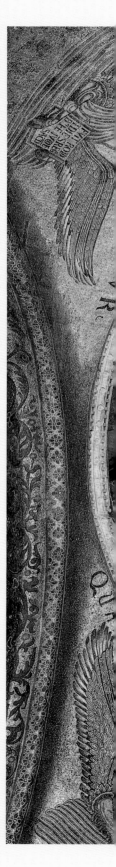

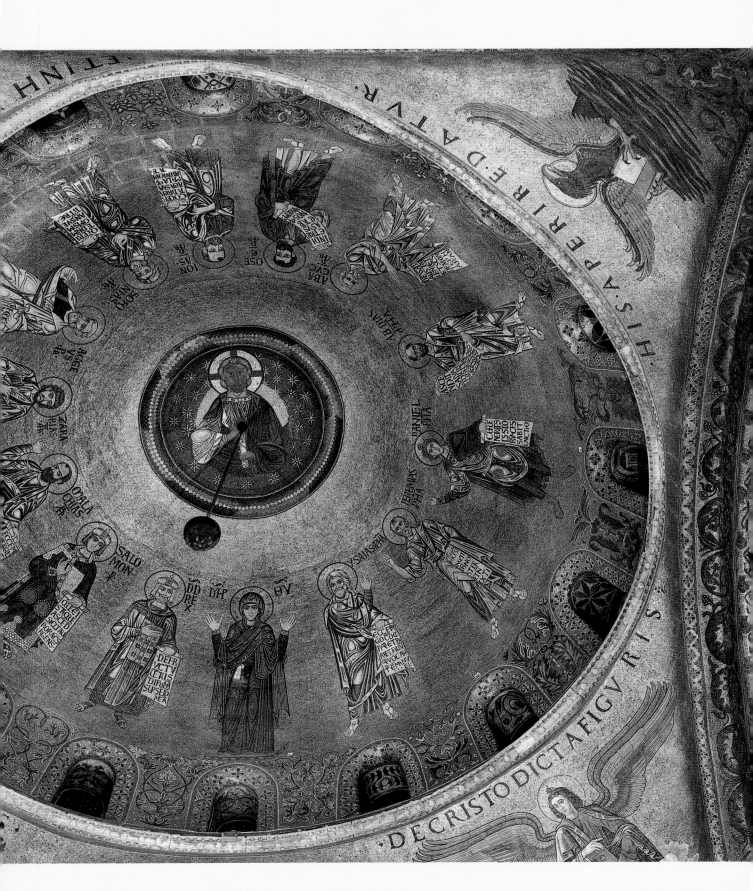

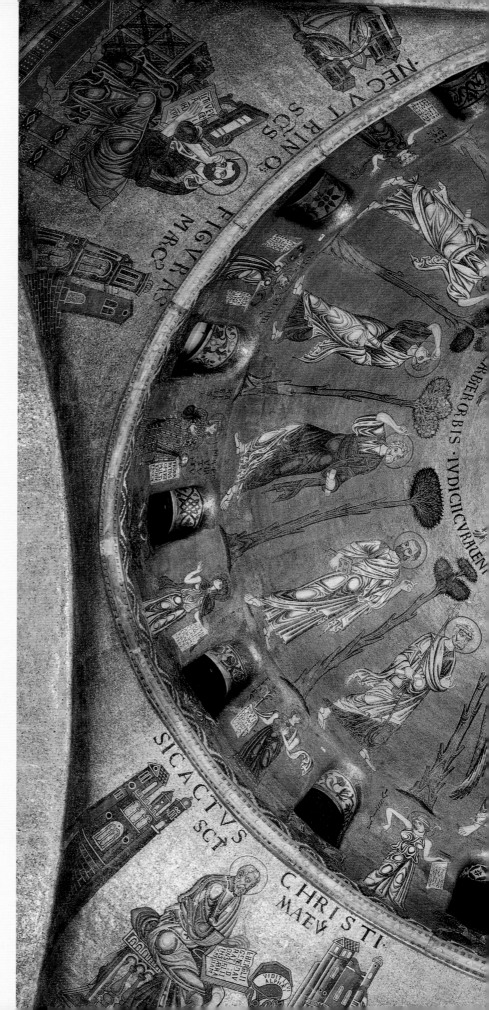

me introierit salvabitur et pasqua inveniet
(I am the door: by me if any man enter in,
he shall be saved, and shall go in and out,
and find pasture). As the portal through
which people entered the church, it
became a clear symbol of the door
to the kingdom of God, the figure of
Christ himself.

Finally, looking at the numerous figures
of prophets, apostles and saints that
throng the undersides of arches, the walls
at all heights and the piers of the great
vaults, we see that each is accompanied
by an inscription bearing the figure's name.
This practice is typical of Eastern icons
painted on wood, where the name is an
essential part of the picture. Nevertheless,
as has already been pointed out, the
inscriptions are in Latin, showing that
Venice, however strongly influenced by
Byzantium, lay fully within the sphere of
Western culture.

It is only for Jesus Christ and his mother
Mary that monograms in Greek are used,
as if to emphasize their superiority.

86

Dome of the Ascension

This mosaic from the last quarter of the
12th century was executed by Byzantine
craftsmen. At the center, angels support Christ
in a starry heaven. Around him, on the ground,
the apostles look on, with the trees that
separate the figures representing the new
life. At the base of the dome, between the
windows, the Virtues point out the path of
the Christian. The mosaic is considered one
of the finest examples of Byzantine art in Italy.

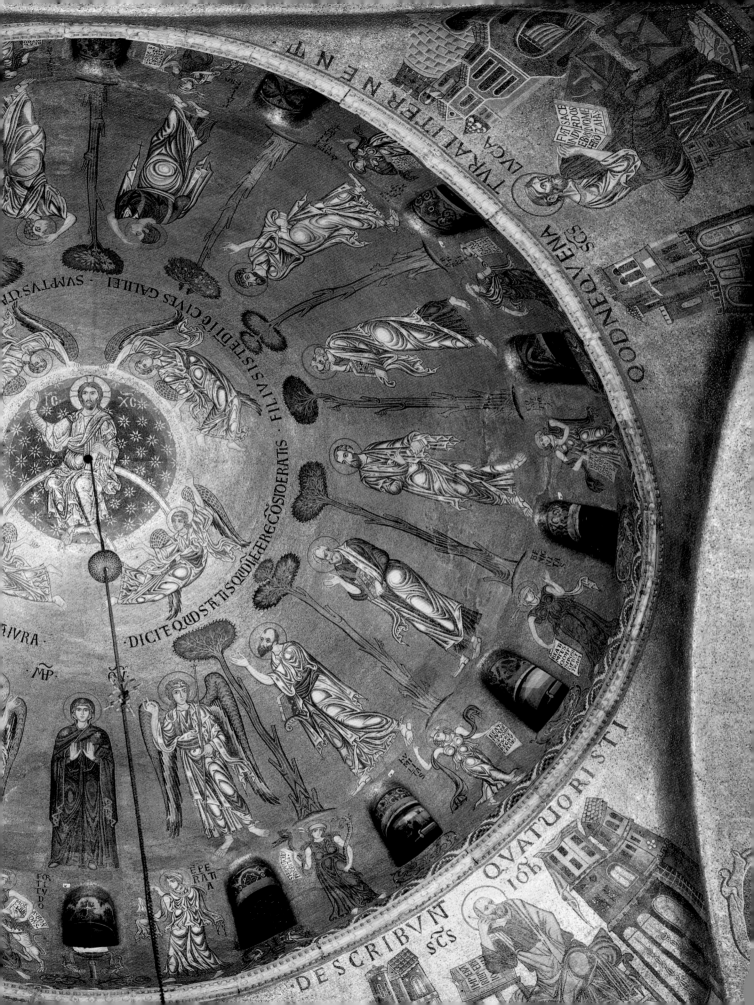

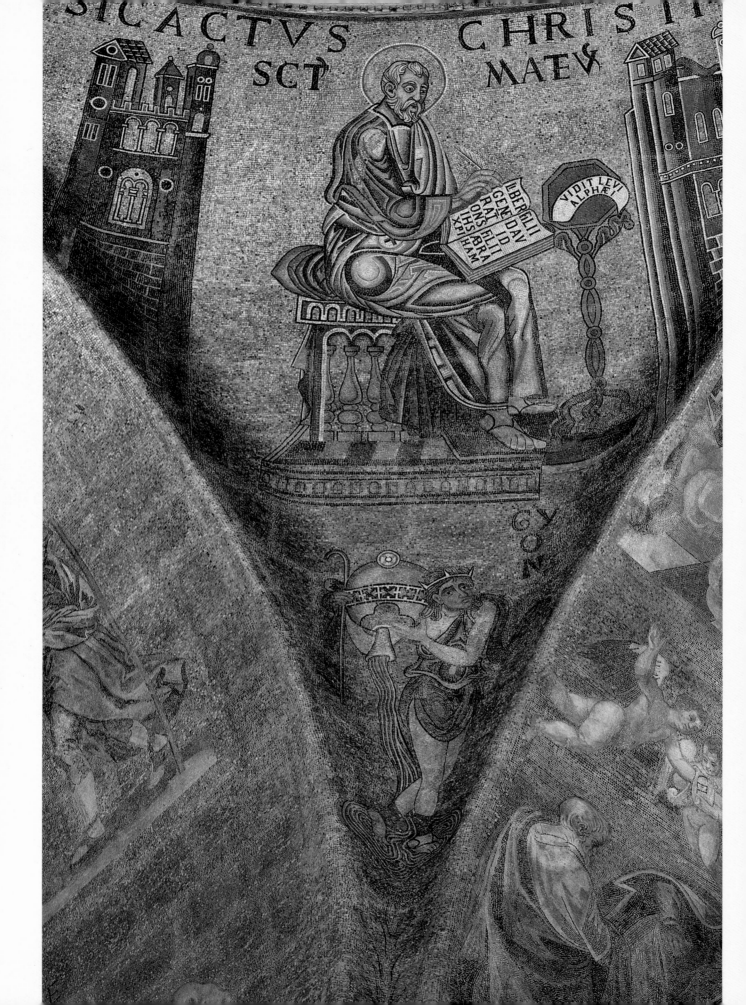

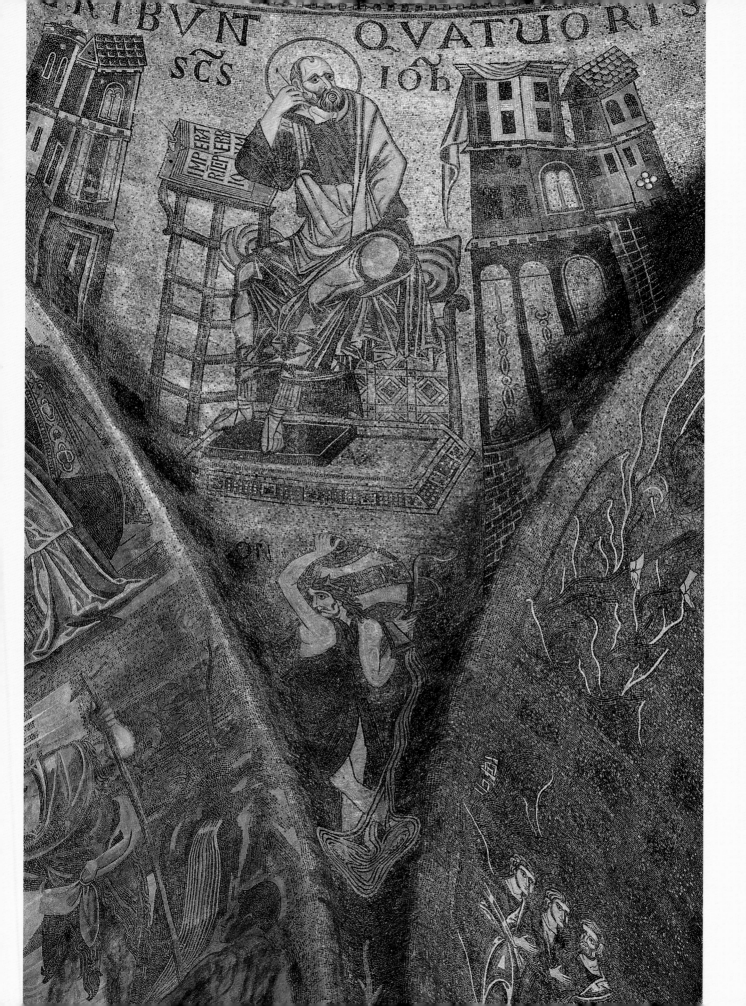

87 *on page 118*

St. Matthew the Evangelist Writing His Gospel, mosaic, Dome of the Ascension, northeast pendentive, last quarter of the 12th century

The mosaic is the work of Byzantine craftsmen. In the background, the buildings allude to places with which the saint is associated. The Biblical River Gyon symbolizes the water of new life that is to be found in the Gospels.

88 *on page 119*

St. John the Evangelist Writing His Gospel, mosaic, Dome of the Ascension, southeast pendentive, last quarter of the 12th century

The mosaic is the work of Byzantine craftsmen. In the background, the buildings allude to places with which the saint is associated. The Biblical River Phison symbolizes the water of new life that is to be found in the Gospels.

89 *above*

St. Luke the Evangelist Writing His Gospel, mosaic, Dome of the Ascension, southwest pendentive, last quarter of the 12th century

The mosaic is the work of Byzantine craftsmen. In the background, the buildings allude to places associated with the saint.

90 *below*

St. Mark the Evangelist Writing His Gospel, mosaic, Dome of the Ascension, northwest pendentive, last quarter of the 12th century

The mosaic is the work of Byzantine craftsmen. In the background, the buildings allude to places associated with the saint.

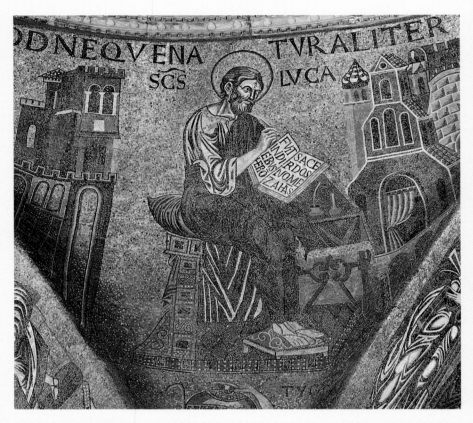

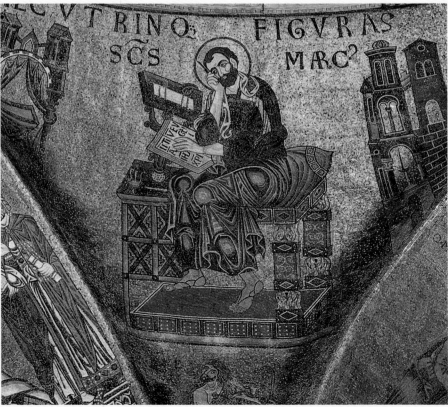

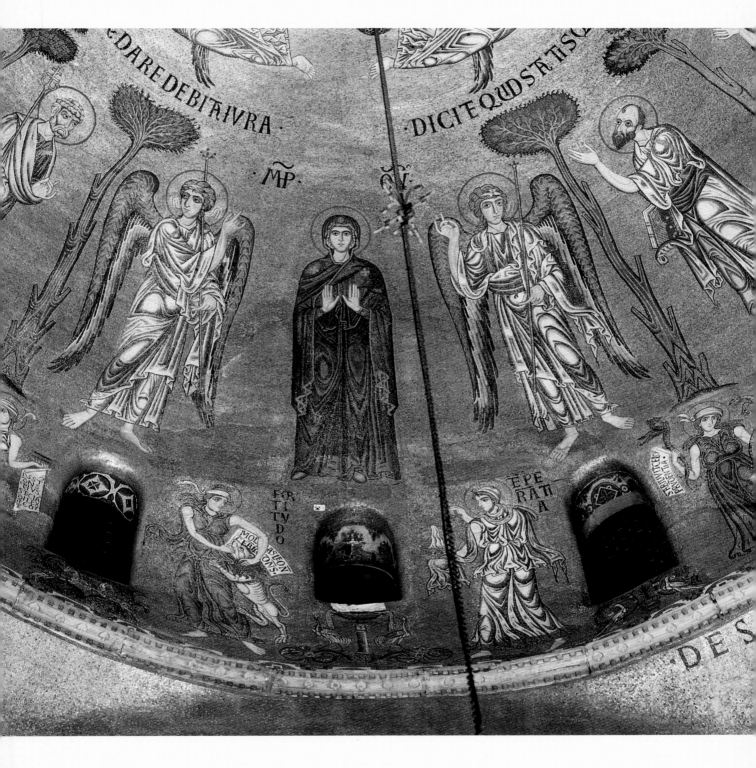

91

**Dome of the Ascension,
mosaic, detail, last quarter
of the 12th century**

The work of Byzantine craftsmen, the detail
shows the segment of the bowl-shaped vault
with the Virgin flanked by the apostles, with
the Virtues underneath.

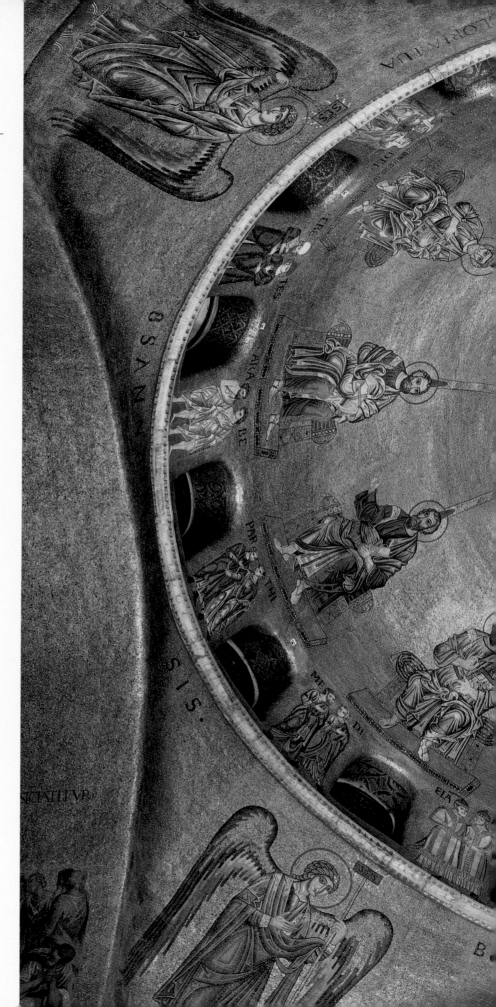

92

Dome of the Pentecost

This mosaic from the first half of the 12th century was executed by Byzantine craftsmen. Numerous restorations were carried out in the western part between the 15th and the 18th centuries.

At the center, we see the *Hetoimasia*, or throne of judgment, and the dove of the Holy Spirit. Around them, the Byzantine series of twelve apostles includes the four evangelists and St. Paul. The evangelists are identifiable by the book that they hold. The expressions of the figures are imbued with a new Spirit. Underneath, between the windows, we find the peoples who listened to their preaching, as listed in the Acts of the Apostles.

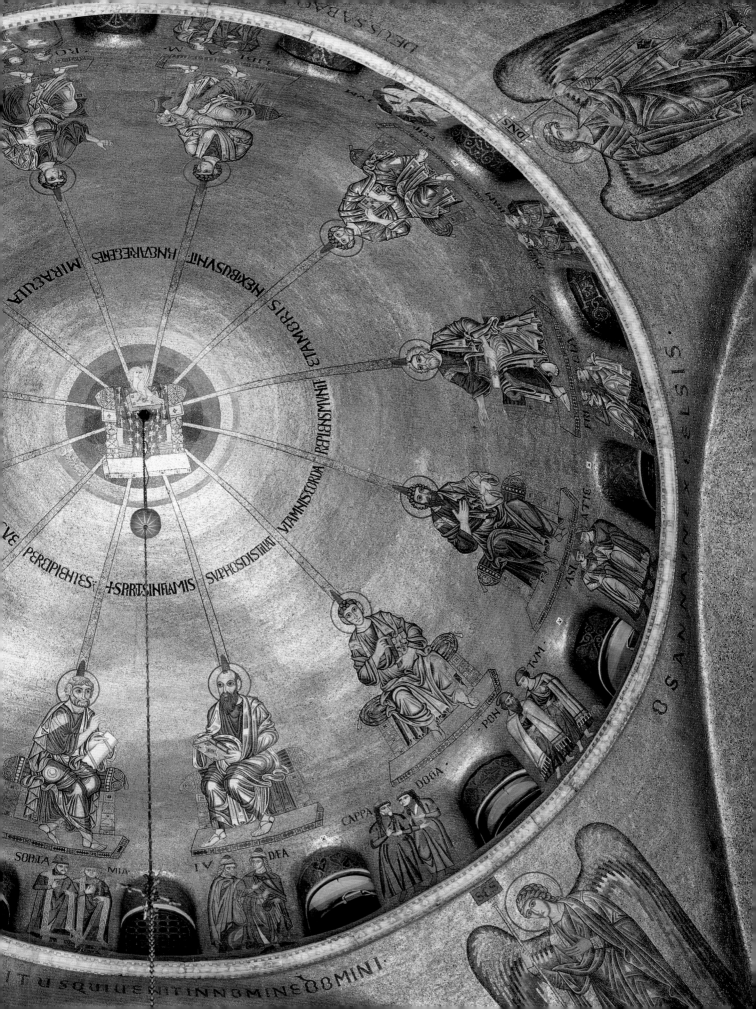

93 *right*

Dome of the Pentecost, mosaic, detail, first half of 12th century

In a pendentive, an archangel sings the *Sanctus Dominus* of praise for and gratitude toward God for the salvation of humanity, an image which is repeated in the other pendentives.

94 *far right*

Vault between the Dome of the Ascension and the Dome of the Pentecost, late 12th century

The work of the Master of the Crucifixion, the decoration of the vault is of exceptional artistic quality. Otto Demus cites them as some of the best mosaics in the basilica. From south to north, we see the *Betrayal of Judas*, the *Ecce Homo*, the *Crucifixion*, and the *Women at the Tomb* (remade in the 15th century) at the center; then the *Descent into Limbo* and finally the *Incredulity of Thomas*.

95 *following pages*

Betrayal of Judas and Ecce Homo, mosaic, vault between the Dome of the Ascension and the Dome of Pentecost, detail, 12th century

Otto Demus considers these to be among the finest mosaics in the basilica.

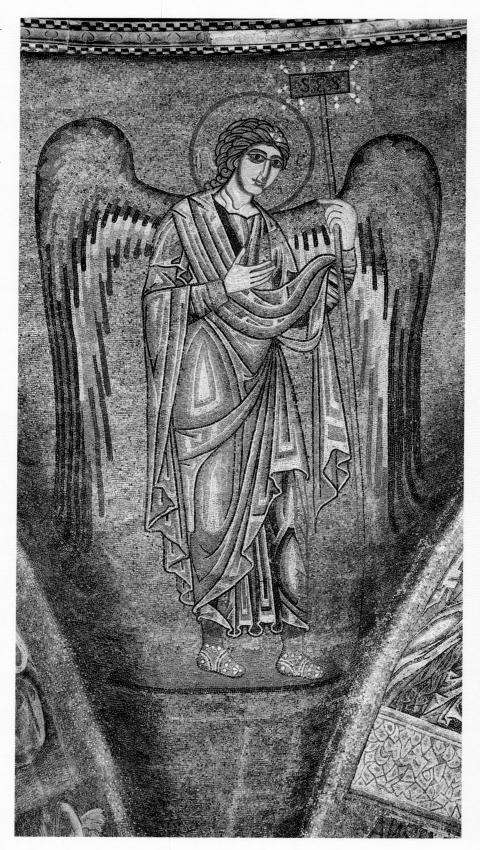

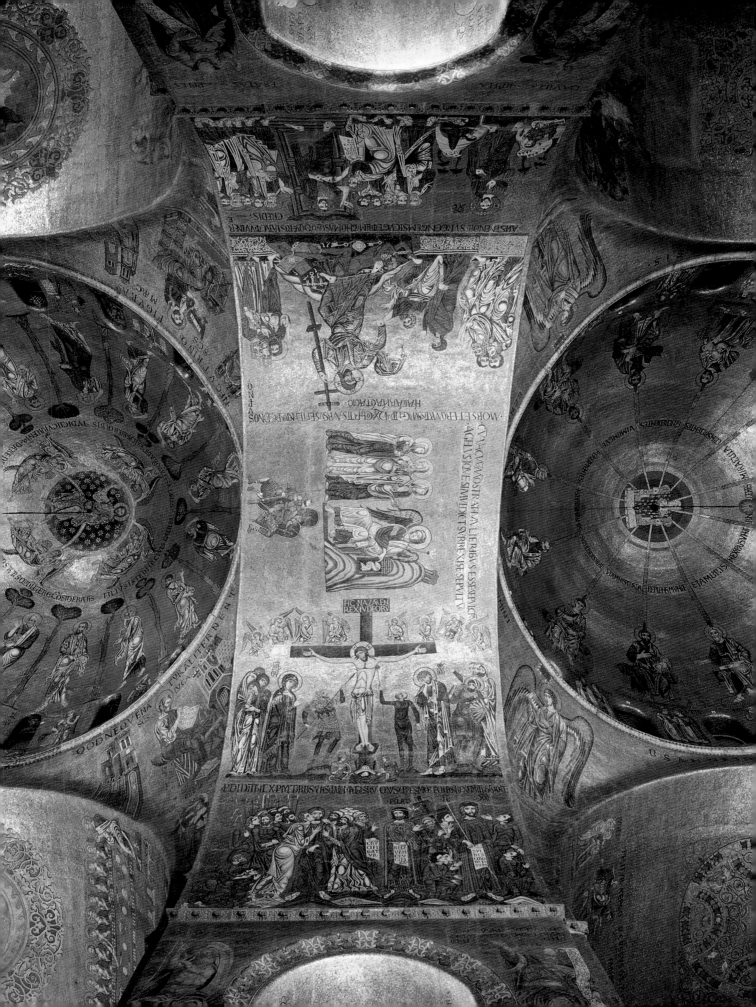

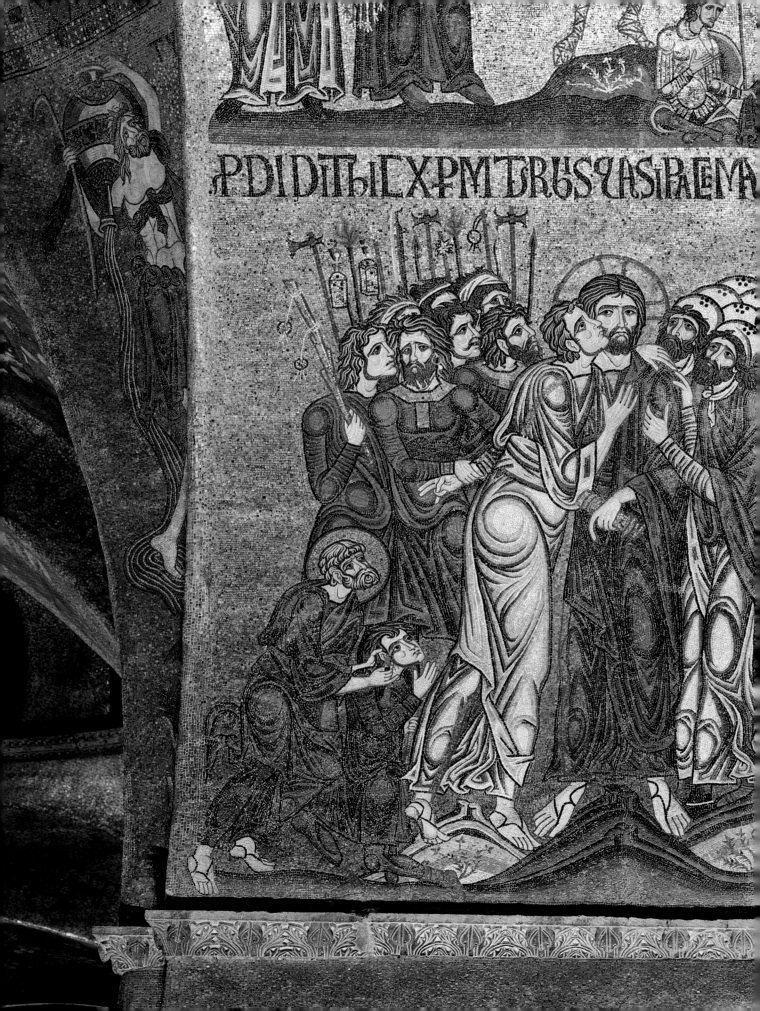

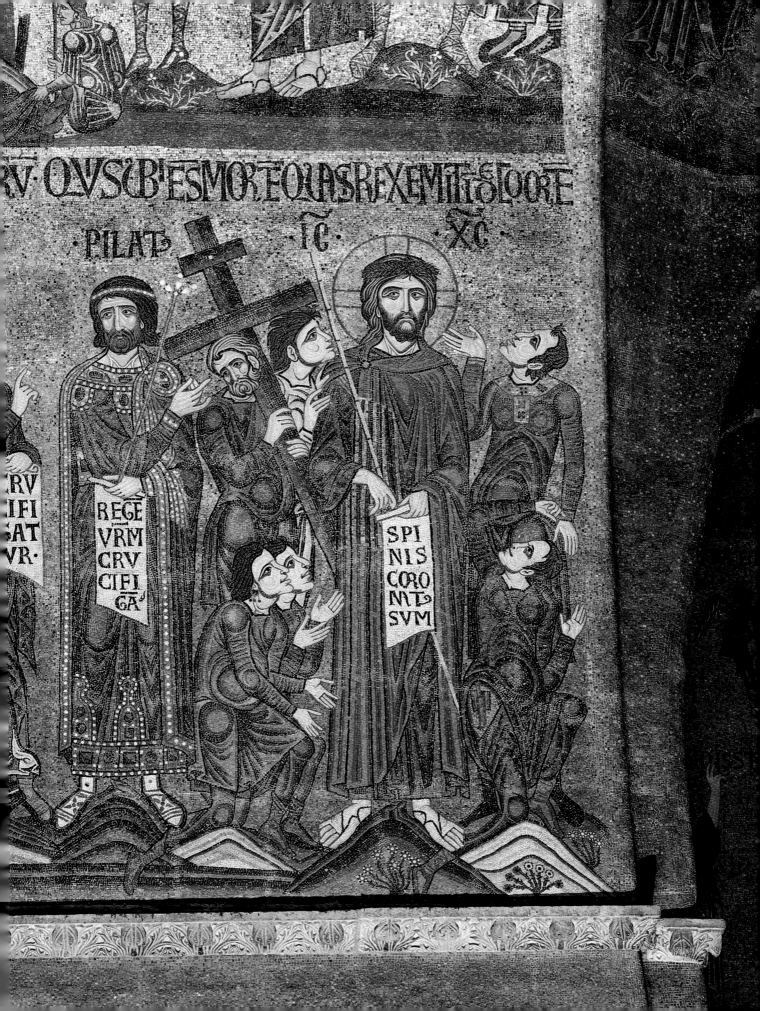

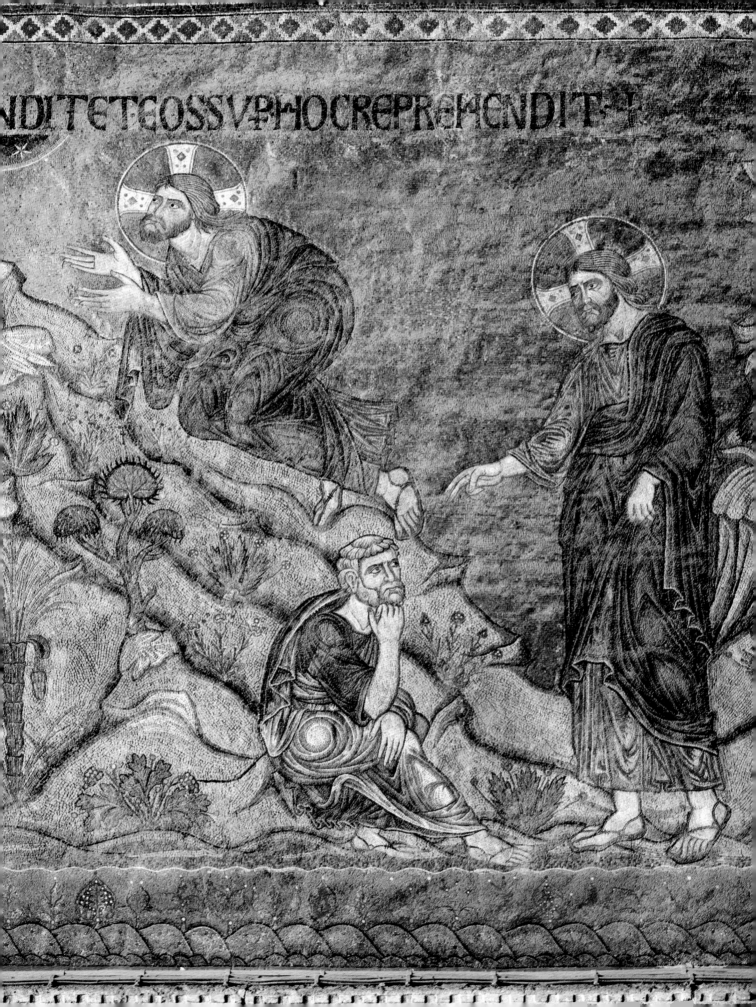

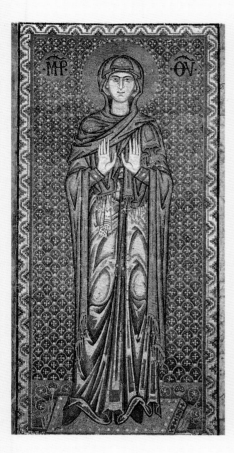

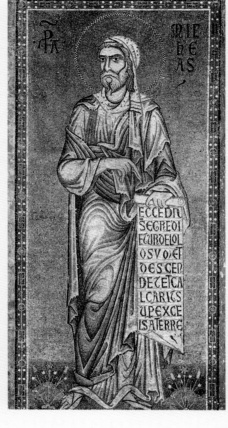

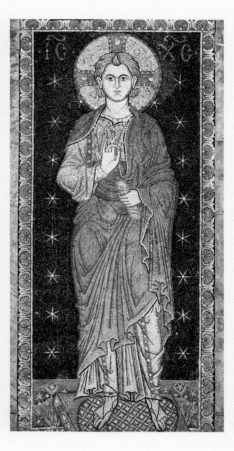

97

***The Virgin Mary*, mosaic, south wall of the nave, *pinakes*, 13th century**

The *pinakes* are panels of mosaic inserted in the marble facing. They repeat the iconography of the Dome of the Presbytery at a lower level, making it easier to see for the congregation in the nave. They represent the prophets, the Virgin and future Mother of God, and the Promised God, the Emmanuel, in the guise of a young man.

They were executed by the Master of the Prophets in the *Pinakes* in the third decade of the 13th century.

96 *left*

***Agony in the Garden*, mosaic, south wall of the nave, detail**

This work of several mosaicists dates from around 1214–20. The central part shows the figure of Christ at different moments during the *Agony in the Garden*.

98

***The Prophet Micah*, mosaic, north wall of the nave, *pinakes*, 13th century**

99

***The Promised God, the Emmanuel*, mosaic, north wall of the nave, *pinakes*, 13th century**

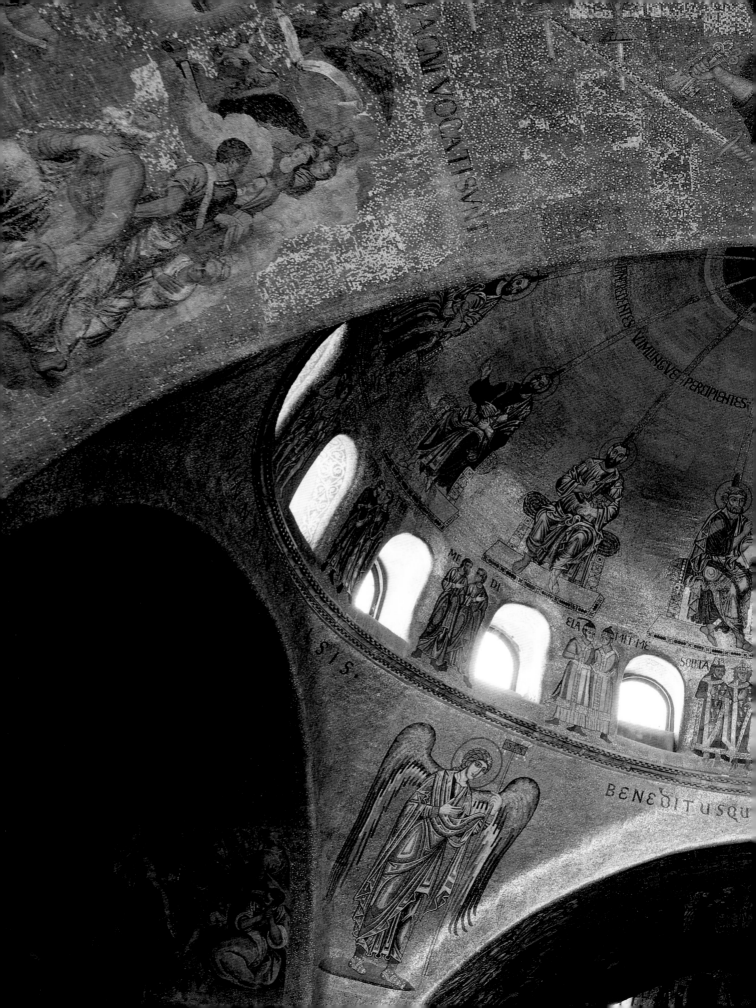

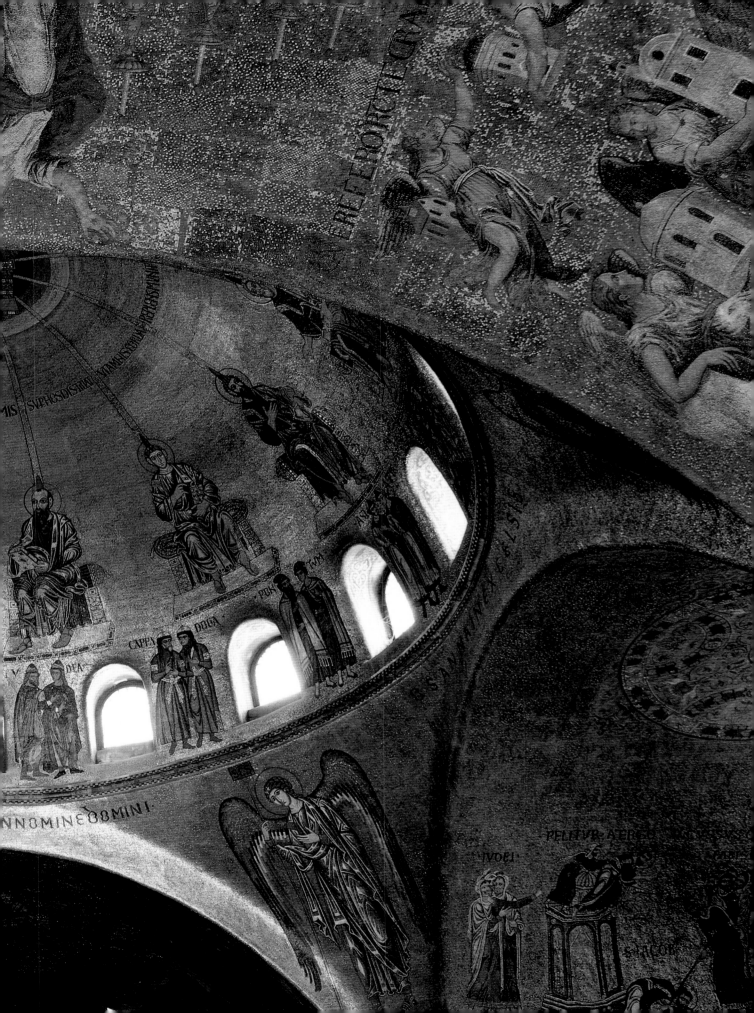

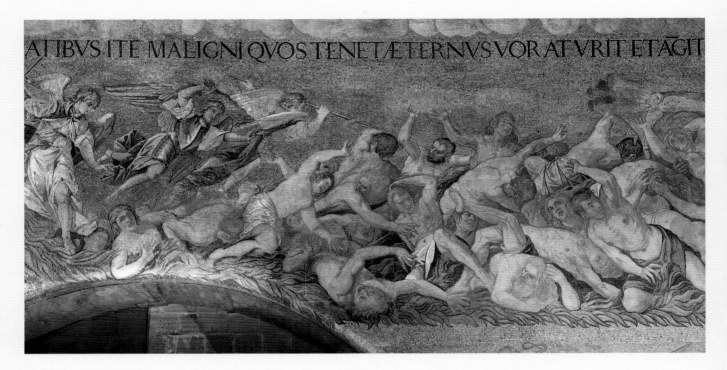

100 *preceding pages*

Vaults of the Apocalypse and of the *Last Judgment*

The mosaic that used to be set on the vertical wall closing off the sacred space before the construction of the large vault has suffered from the structural deterioration of the vault. Ever since the middle of the 19th century attempts have been made to renovate it, following interventions to consolidate the structure. The mosaicist Giovanni Moro made drawings of the 16th-century mosaic, but he ran into legal problems and the board of trustees was forced to dismiss him and use cartoons by the director of the Accademia di Belle Arti at the time, the Austrian Karl von Blaas, who received the commission directly from the government. This was in the years 1860-61, when Austria started to make an annual contribution to the upkeep of the basilica. The trustee Pietro Saccardo's more sensitive attitude prevailed and Blaas's mosaics were never executed. Instead a decision was taken to go back to the designs and skills of Giovanni Moro, as soon as Venice was annexed to the kingdom of Italy in October 1866.

101 *above*

Hell, mosaic, Vault of the *Last Judgment*, north base

Executed to a design by Maffeo da Verona (17th century), it is a splendid representation of the souls of the damned. The large cartoon – in practice a painted canvas – by Maffeo da Verona has survived.

102 *right*

Martyrdom of St. John, mosaic, Baptistery, north lunette at the base of the Dome of the Angels, detail

The mosaic was executed by the Venetian workshop of the 14th century (1345-54). The detail shows Salome with the head of St. John the Baptist.

The immediacy of the scene is highly dramatic. There is a feeling of terror at what has happened and Salome seems to be frozen to the spot.

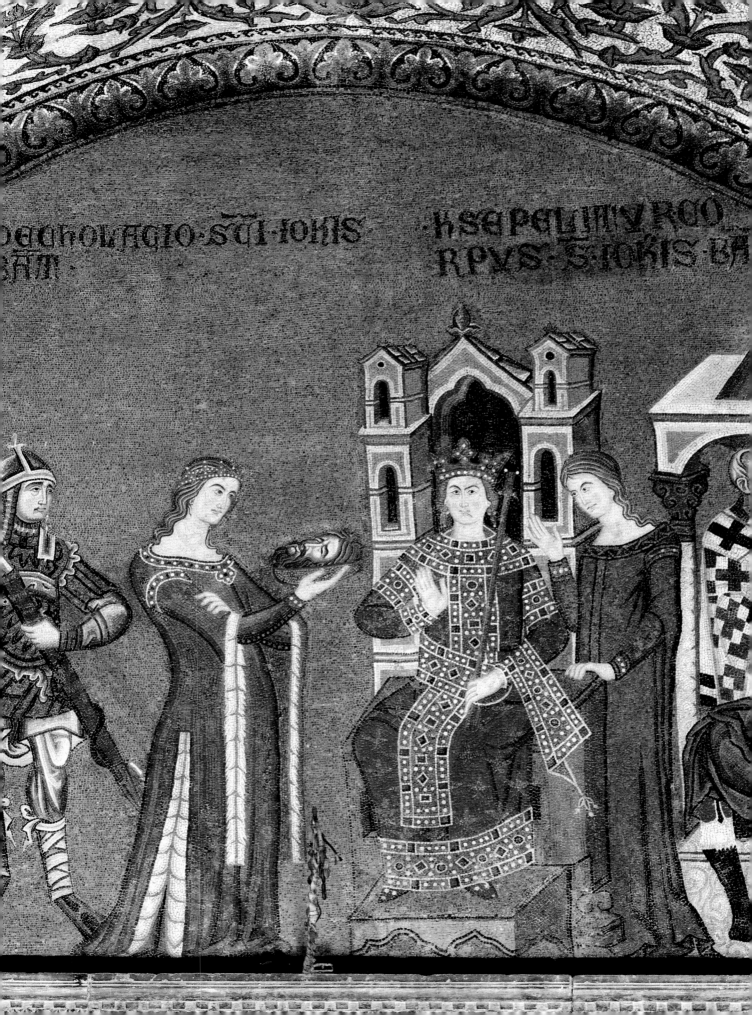

THE TESSELLATED FLOOR OF ST. MARK'S

Renato Polacco

The structural and iconographic modifications that had to be made to the basilica – in order to keep the evangelist's tomb in its original, ninth-century location and to suit the use of the building as a state chapel – mean that there are differences between it and the Church of the Holy Apostles in Constantinople, which the Venetians had used as a model. Nevertheless, St. Mark's retains all the basic features of Byzantine ecclesiastical architecture. In addition to the Greek-cross plan and five domes, the essential dichotomy between the earthly zone (wall and floors) and the heavenly part (vaults and domes) has been respected. Their contrasting purposes and functions are underlined by the use of different facing materials, or rather by the spatial effects created through suitable decoration of the walls. The upper part of the building assumes exclusively and evidently celestial connotations, which are therefore metaphysical, thanks to the reflected light from the tesserae. Made of glass and covered with gold leaf or painted a variety of colors, the tesserae were intended to symbolize the light of Paradise and to carry the richness and brightness of the individual figures to the limits of the intelligible. The lower part of the church, on the other hand, is given a more mundane feel by the solidity of the marble on the walls (even though this is richly colored, but in duller shades, and covered with geometric designs) and by the tessellated floor, made by techniques known as *opus sectile* and *opus tessellatum*. The overall impression is one of veiled luminosity, a pale reflection on earth of the light of Paradise and a schematic adumbration of the vision of Heaven presented in the mosaics of the domes and ceilings above.

In the mosaic floor of St. Mark's we find *opus sectile* (where the patterns are

103

Floor of the nave, executed in *opus tessellatum*

The technique involved preparing individual pieces of marble of the appropriate size and color to create frames around floor areas that correspond to particular structures and elements of the basilica's roof above. These frames had angular shapes, rhomboid or polygonal. They were often used to enclose slabs of marble, as in the case of the enormous area underneath the crossing known as the sea, made up of twelve large slabs of Proconnesus marble.

104

Antonio Visentini, *Floor of the Basilica*, original drawing, 1725-30

The drawing is made on a scale of about 1:100 in pen and sepia ink and constitutes the earliest detailed representation of the floor of the basilica. Visentini made two attempts to prepare the copperplate for printing, but was unable to finish the work owing to technical difficulties. Other representations followed, including a whole collection of drawings tinted with watercolor by Antonio Pellanda, the technician supervising work on the basilica in the middle of the 19th century. Another drawing was made in 1881, on a scale of 1:50, by the architect Nicolò Moretti and printed in several plates. The drawings differ from one another in a number of details, which suggests successive modifications.

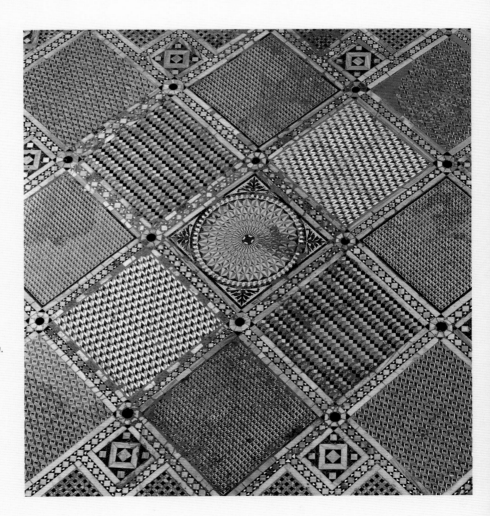

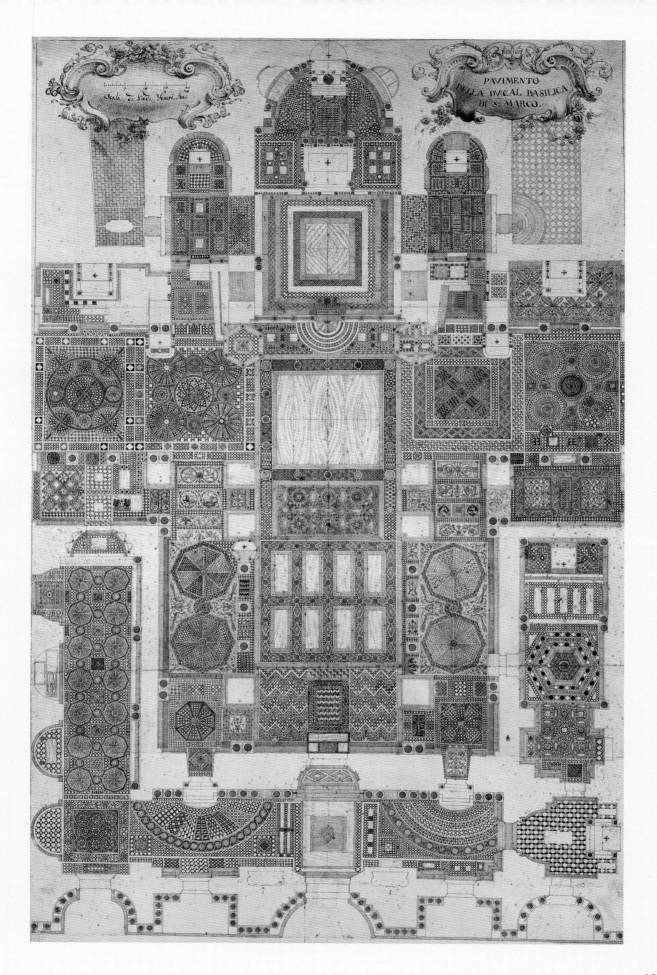

composed from different colored pieces of marble cut into shapes) as well as *opus tessellatum* (where tiny pieces of marble or enamel, obtained by tapping the material with a chip hammer, are used to create floral or animal figures), though the former is used much more widely than the latter. Both techniques originated in ancient times, as documented in Varro, Vitruvius and Pliny, and *opus tessellatum* was extensively employed in the early Christian and early medieval buildings of the Adriatic region. The early and mid-Byzantine period showed a preference for *opus sectile*, as is evident in churches like Hagia Sophia in Constantinople, in the Greek monastery of Hosios Loukas, near Delphi, and in the Nea Moni on the island of Chios.

The use of both techniques in St. Mark's testifies to the ample resources of the duchy. They were able not only to afford the huge amount of precious marble, indispensable because of its qualities of hardness and color, required to lay a flooring that covers a total of 2099 square meters, but also to hire skilled craftsmen

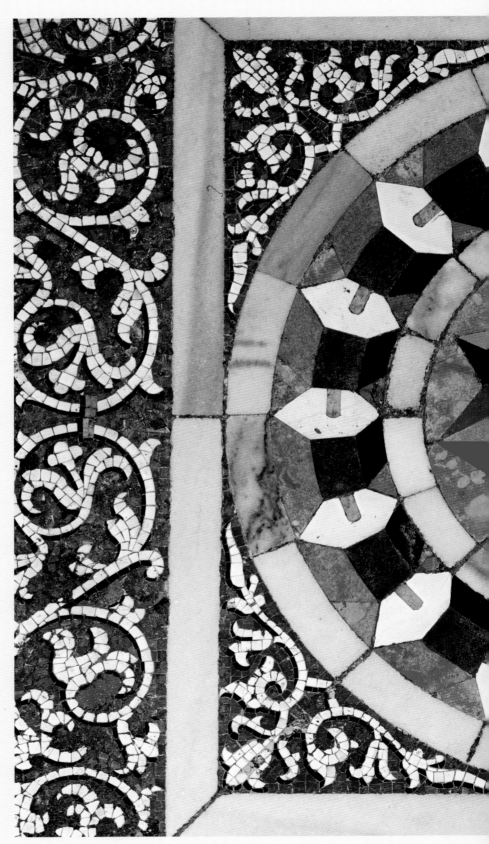

105

Floor at the entrance to the basilica known as the Door of St. Peter, executed in *opus sectile*, detail
The design, representing an icosahedron, is attributed to Paolo Uccello, who was active in the basilica between 1425 and 1433.

106 *following pages*

Floor, southern aisle, detail
Octagons linked by circles adorn the southern (original) and northern (relaid in the second half of the 19th century) aisles. The decoration is embellished with two pairs of peacocks, a Christian symbol of the Resurrection.

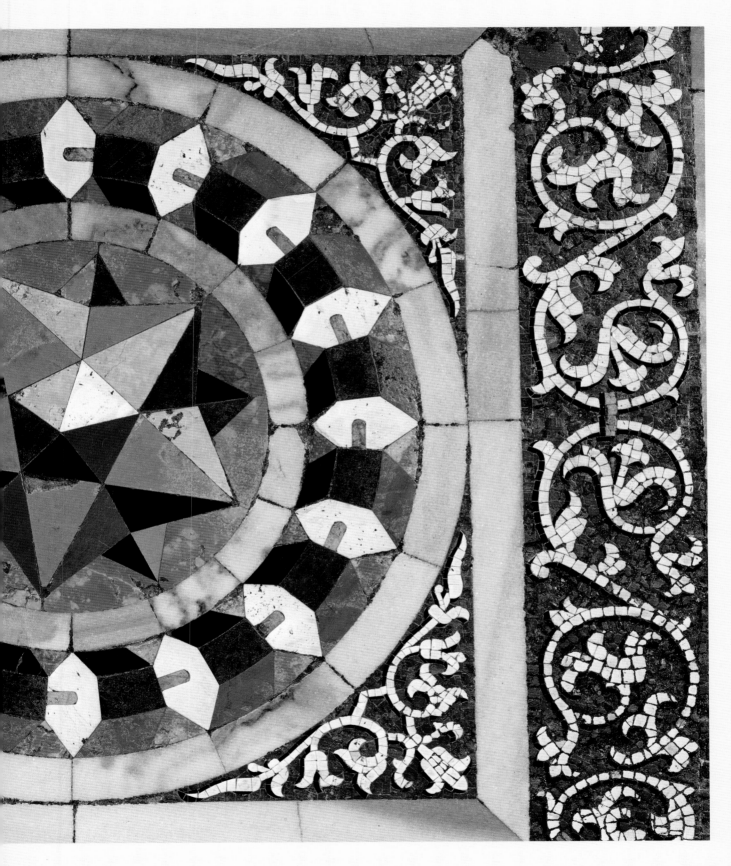

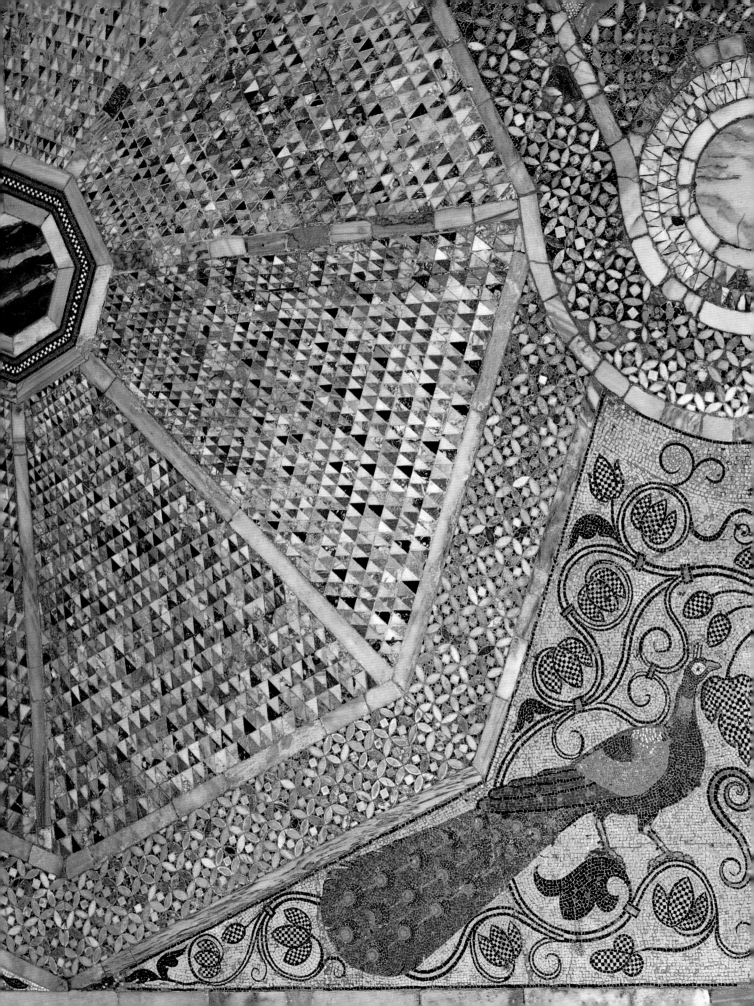

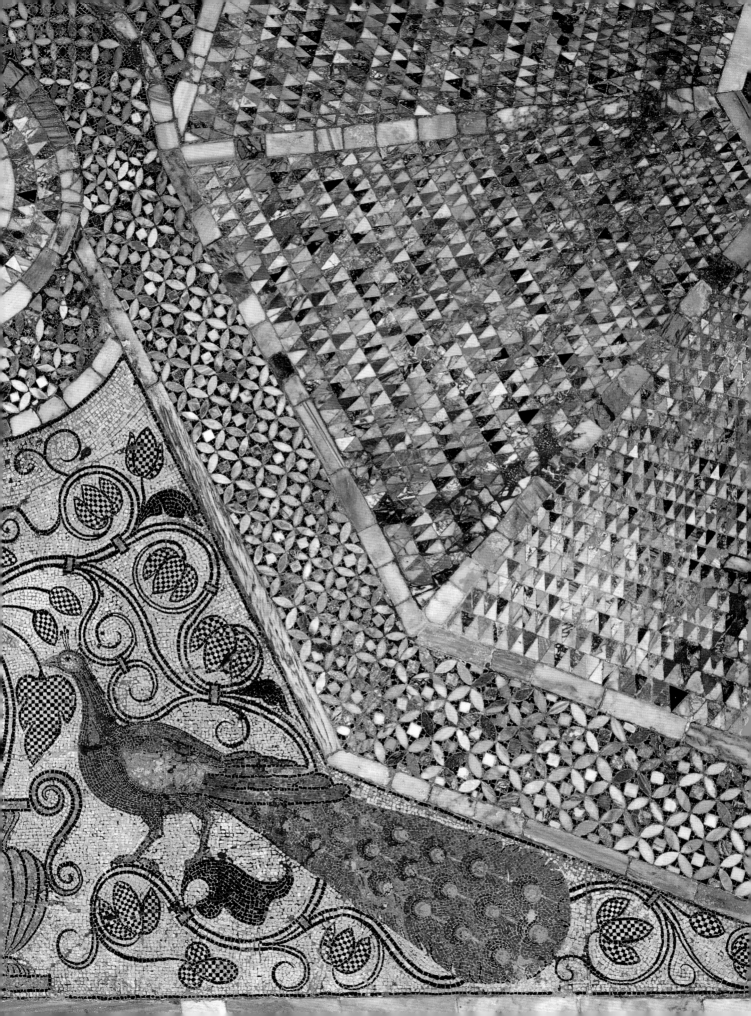

who, in all probability, like the architects and mosaicists, were brought to Venice from Constantinople or from Byzantine Greece.

The floor is made up of panels of different sizes, decorated with geometric or figurative motifs. Some of the more brightly lit areas, such as under the Dome of the Pentecost and that of the Ascension, are covered by large slabs of Proconnesus marble.

The patterns are laid out in a regular manner and wherever possible adhere to the principles of symmetry. The nave is decorated with a series of fairly linear designs. Near the entrance, we find a large rectangle adorned with a herringbone pattern and incorporating a smaller rectangle with a similar design. Moving east, two rows of four large rectangular slabs of Proconnesus marble are set inside elegant frames of diamonds and circles with red borders. This is followed, as we head toward the presbytery, by a large rectangle with two rows of polychrome rhombuses and wheels, separated by four squares alternating with three rhombuses. Then, under the Dome of the Ascension, we come to the sea of large slabs of Proconnesus marble.

Each arm of the transept contains two large squares. The ones in the northern arm are both decorated with a quincunx of five large Byzantine wheels, separated from one another by four smaller ones. In the southern arm, a pattern of diamonds surrounded by a frame also made up of diamonds is followed, further to the south, by a quincunx of four wheels.

The aisles to the north and south of the nave are each decorated with a square incorporating an octagon, followed to the east by a pair of similar patterns. The spaces in between are filled with two pairs of peacocks flanking a two-handled drinking cup, from which elegant shoots

of vegetation emerge. The peacocks in the southern aisle stand out for the brilliant colors of the enamel tesserae and for the refinement of their execution, an effect enhanced by the fact that they have survived almost intact.

The floor of the presbytery is enriched by a central marble panel that opens like a book and is surrounded by seven motifs, by two rectangles subdivided to form crosses at the sides of the altar and, behind the Pala d'Oro, by a large rectangle framed by bordered bands and flanked by two sunburst patterns that stretch as far as the semicircle of the walls.

In the northern atrium, an elongated rectangle inscribed with two rows of seven octagons linked by braided ribbon is preceded by a square with three rows of three circles each. The western arm of the atrium features geometric marble patterns at the center (the one in the middle allegedly marks the point where Pope Alexander III and Frederick Barbarossa met to draw up the treaty of Venice in 1177), flanked by two semicircles. The Baptistery is dominated by a large hexagon, with the font at its center, while the floor to the west is covered with eight circles arranged around a square.

Into this rigorously geometric scheme are inserted symbolic birds and animals and floral elements, enriching and completing a carpet of mosaics that seems to lead us through its allegories as if we were on a pilgrimage of faith. The various stages of that journey are defined by an iconographic program that we now find extremely complicated, but which would have been much more readily understood by the people of the Middle Ages.

While there are numerous examples of mosaic floors with geometric designs in the upper Adriatic region – Aquileia (*tessellatum*), Grado (*tessellatum*), Torcello (*tessellatum* and *sectile*), Murano (*sectile*

and *tessellatum*), Pomposa and Ravenna – that of St. Mark's stands out for the magnificence, preciosity and rarity of its marble, imported from the East, the West and even North Africa; for the splendor of the enamel tesserae; and for the variety of the scenes (funerals of foxes, peacocks and other animals), either derived from medieval symbolism and literature or inspired by Eastern and Western fabric designs.

107

Floor at the junction between the north transept and nave, executed in *opus sectile* made out of red porphyry and green serpentine

The wheel motifs are executed with particular skill. The large one at the center is attributed to the mosaicist Giacomo Pasterini, who took ten years to complete the task in the first half of the 17th century. An interesting feature of the pieces of marble is the shape that they take on with wear. With metamorphic marbles this happens faster at the edges, producing a convex surface, while in the sedimentary ones most of the wear occurs at the center, resulting in a concave surface.

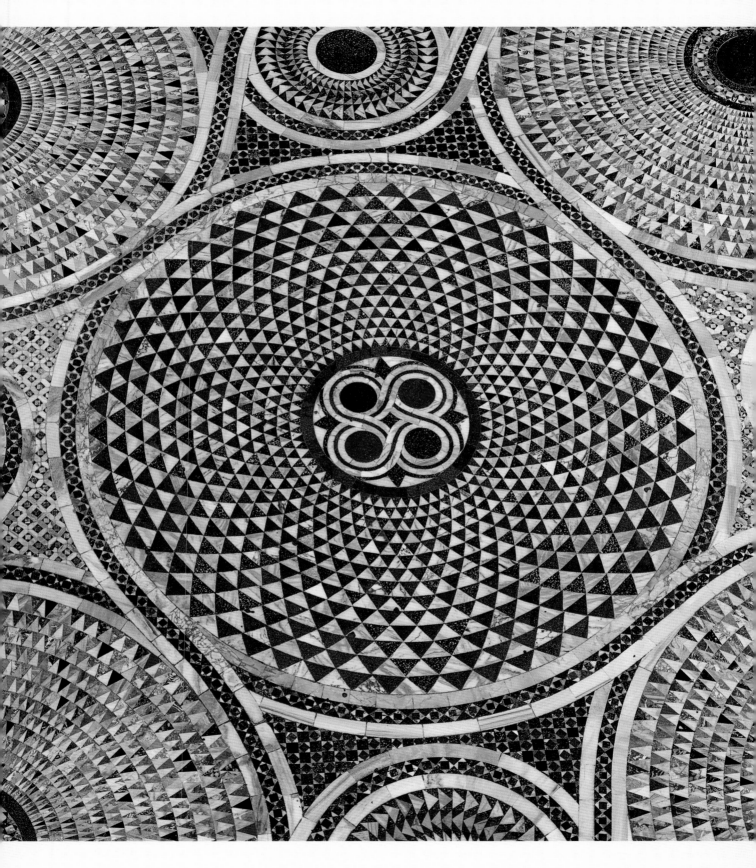

THE CRYPT

Ettore Vio

Underneath the presbytery lies the crypt. Divided into a nave and two aisles, each with an apse, the crypt is where the body of St. Mark was kept for centuries. The nave is located under the presbytery, while the southern aisle lies beneath the Chapel of St. Clement and the northern one under the Chapel of St. Peter.

You descend to the crypt by means of one of the two staircases located to the left and right of the presbytery, next to the ones leading to the two side chapels. To the west of the crypt lies the retrocrypt, located about midway underneath the area of the crossing of the main basilica; its height does not exceed 1·75 m. The floor of the crypt, laid to a design by Giovanni Battista Meduna at the time of the restoration in 1870, is 36 cm higher than that of the retrocrypt. The former is 20 cm below sea level, and the latter 56 cm.

The crypt is roofed with tunnel vaults built out of intersecting bricks of the Roman type, reaching a maximum height of 2·45 m. They are supported by fifty-six small columns with Veneto-Byzantine capitals that have been dated to the eleventh century. Six of these, of finer workmanship, encircle the mortuary chapel that used to house the body of St. Mark. The mortuary chapel consists of a massive slab of Verona marble, about 40 cm thick and with sides measuring 2·5 m, supported at the corners by four columns of Greek cipolin marble, with simple rough-hewn capitals of Egyptian green marble. The area around the mortuary chapel is decorated with Veneto-Byzantine plutei, also from the eleventh century. Inside the mortuary chapel, we find a finely worked altar frontal in the

place where the faithful used to come to lay objects and pieces of cloth next to the tomb of their patron saint and then take them away as mementos of their visit. The various calamities that have struck the basilica, such as earthquakes and fires, have not left the crypt unscathed. Some of the capitals and a few of the altar frontals have had to be replaced.

A marble altarpiece carved with five figures in high relief was placed against the west front of the mortuary chapel of St. Mark in 1494. It represents the *Virgin and Child Flanked by Saints Peter, Mark, Catherine and Ursula*. The recent restoration work, carried out to clear the mortuary chapel completely, has meant that the altarpiece has been moved into the left-hand aisle.

From the twelfth century onward, the crypt was the seat of the confraternity of the Mascoli.

In 1563, the Venetians, concerned about the rising sea level and the bradyseism that was causing the city to sink, attempted to raise the floor by 30 cm. However, the continual rise in the sea level extinguished all hope of being able to continue using this ancient part of the basilica, where the mortal remains of St. Mark were kept. In 1580 the entrances to the crypt were walled up, and it remained closed for almost three centuries.

Two investigations were carried out, one in the seventeenth century and one in the eighteenth. In both cases, the water level at high tide had risen by about 40 cm and anything that had not been considered worth saving at the time the crypt was walled up was then removed. It was only after Napoleon's handover of the basilica to the patriarch of Venice in 1807 that serious thought was given

to redressing the situation. Patriarch Gamboni, followed by his successor Pirker, devoted study and effort to the problem of recovering St. Mark's body. In 1825 Leonardo Manin published two volumes on the survey that was carried out, describing the marble sarcophagus and the body of the saint. A small box was found alongside the wooden coffin housing the holy remains: among other things, it contained the date – October 8, 1094 – on which the body had been placed in the sarcophagus, inscribed on a sheet of lead. The description was accompanied by several drawings, illustrating other objects that had also been found. It was Patriarch Pirker who had the sarcophagus removed and positioned immediately above its earlier location, under the high altar but at a level where it was safe from flooding. But it was not until Venice was annexed to the kingdom of Italy in 1868 that work began on reclaiming the crypt itself.

Success was immediate and the recovery of the crypt – strongly supported by the new state, the kingdom of Italy, through the collaboration of Prefect Torelli and Patriarch Trevisanato – was greeted with enthusiasm by the young people of the city and by all those who had placed their hopes for the preservation and appreciation of the history, faith and deeds of the ancient Venetians in the restoration of the basilica.

In 1890-91 the new *proto* Pietro Saccardo decided to use what was considered the best binding material of the time, Portland cement, and the retrocrypt was reopened. The work proved effective and succeeded in keeping the crypt dry throughout the first half of the twentieth century. After the

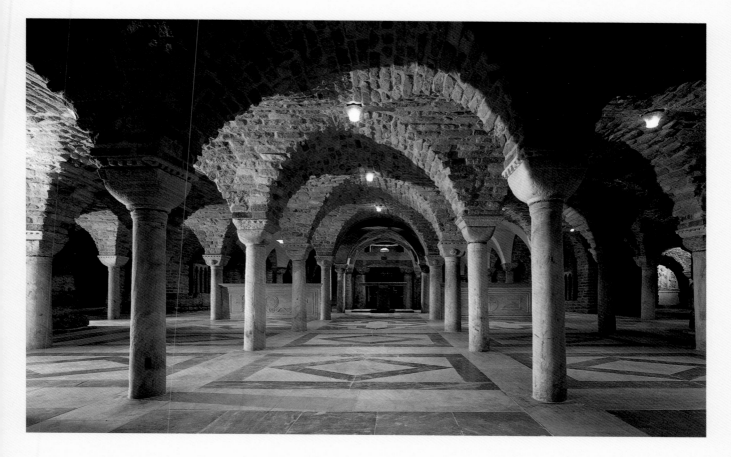

Second World War, an acceleration in the rate of subsidence of the ground as well as the rise in sea level led to water infiltrating both the floor and the walls. The process peaked with the flood of November 4, 1966.

As well as permitting examination of the line where the vaults were broken to carry out the foundation work on the main basilica in 1063, the restoration has also allowed an evaluation of the modifications that were made to the vaulting system as a result of those foundations. The date of the first intervention, that of the mortuary chapel, corresponds to the construction of the church in 829-32. Work on the foundations of the present basilica commenced in 1063. As the vaults were built between these two dates – in fact they partially destroyed the columns of

the mortuary chapel which were then modified to insert the new foundations – they can only have been constructed on the one occasion of historical importance for the basilica, the burning of the church during a revolt against Doge Pietro Candiano IV in 976. During the reconstruction, a fireproof cavity was installed to protect the body of the saint: the outside of it is visible as the vault built out of 40 cm-thick bricks.

The present level of the retrocrypt is the same as that of the crypt before it was raised in 1563. It was only with the construction of the existing basilica that the space, which originally opened freely on to the church and was then reduced to a sub-confessio opening on to the nave in the reconstruction after the fire of 976, became a true crypt.

Now reclaimed and fitted with new lighting and ventilation systems, the crypt can be visited on request and is used for special religious functions.

108

View of the crypt, the mortuary chapel that contained the body of St. Mark until 1811

Note the ancient supporting columns of the mortuary chapel, the characteristic roof with tunnel vaults in brick and the enclosure of the central area, built out of Veneto–Byzantine marble altar frontals, many of which have been replaced.

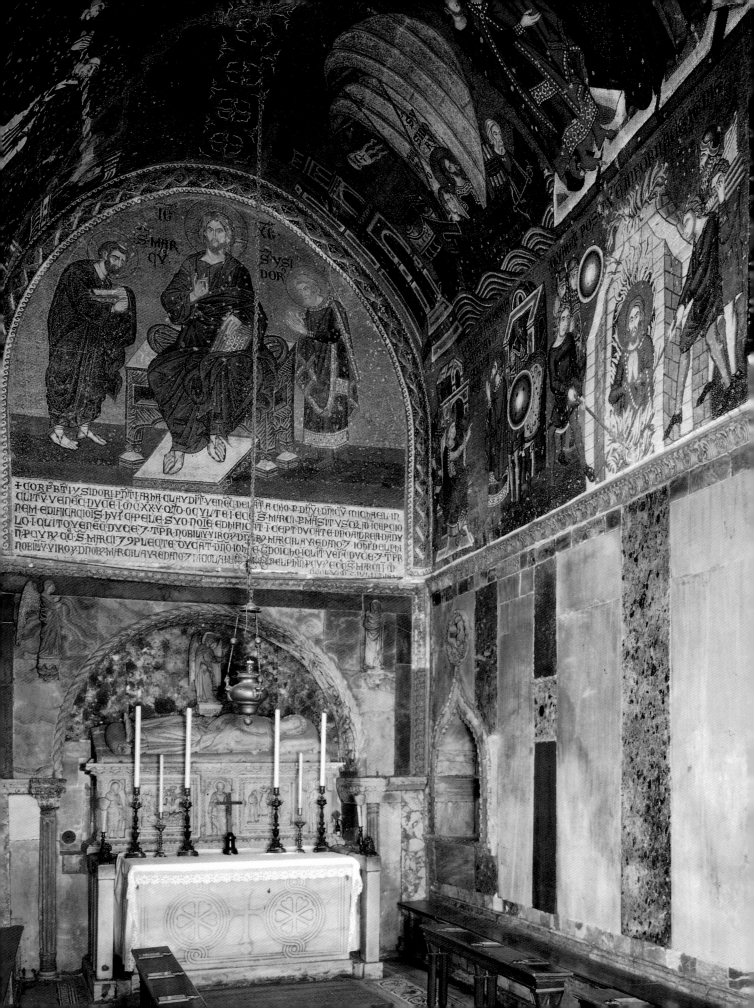

IC S MAR QV XC S VSI DOR

+ CORP BTI YSIDORI P NT T RA QLAV DIT VENEC DELAT A CHO P DNV MICHAEL IN
QLITV VENEC DVCE T OC XXV QLO OCVLT EI EOC S MARCI P MASIT VSQ AD ICEPCIO
NEM EDIFICACIOIS HVI APELE SVO NOIE EDHIA CIT I CEPT DVOATE DPO ALREN DADY
LO I QLITO VENEC DVCE 7 TPR NOBILV VIRO V DI T R MARCI LA REDM O7 IOH P DELPHI
N P QV R QO S MARCI 7 P LE QTE DVGAT DNO IOH A E DO I CHO IGLIT VEN DVGE 7 TPR
NOBILV VIRO V DNOR MARCI LA REDMO 7 NIQOLAN E DELPHIO P QV V EOC MRON P

THE CHAPELS

Ettore Vio

Particular significance is attached to the spaces at the sides of the main structure of the basilica, which are used as votive and subsidiary chapels.

At the far end of the north transept, a wooden door faced with bronze and fitted with arched gratings is thought to date from the fourth century. It leads into the Chapel of St. Isidore, a simple but impressive space that is richly adorned with marble facings on the walls. In a lunette above the altar is set the sarcophagus containing the mortal remains of the Roman soldier, St. Isidore, brought to Venice from Chios in 1125.

The architecture of the chapel dates from considerably later, from the fourteenth century. The ceiling is covered entirely with mosaics, including the soffits of the windows. They represent scenes from the saint's life and martyrdom. An image of *Christ Between St. Mark and St. Isidore* is set above the altar. The long inscription underneath recounts the saint's body being transported from Chios to Venice by Doge Domenico Michiel, and the construction of the chapel as the saint's tomb, begun by Doge Andrea Dandolo and finished by Doge Giovanni Gradenigo in 1355.

What is now the Baptistery was created from what used to be the portico decorated with a fresco of the *Ascension* (the feast day was formally celebrated in Venice from AD 990 onward) in the *giesia dei putti* (or Church of the Putti), the original place for baptism. It was completed in its present form by Doge Giovanni Soranzo (1312-28). The mosaic decoration (1343-54) was carried out by a local workshop and is one of the most significant surviving examples of the Venetian school of mosaics. On the walls we see the cycle of the *Life of St. John the Baptist* from his birth to his decapitation, while the *Story of Salvation* is represented on the vault of the entrance and the two domes, in an analogous cycle to that in the large domes of the central nave of the basilica. The prophets who foresaw the coming of Christ are depicted on the vault of the Baptistery, with *Christ Sends the Apostles to Baptize the Peoples of the World* in the central dome over the font installed by Jacopo Sansovino, and *Christ in Glory among Angels* in the Dome of the Angels above the altar. Among the mosaics, it is worth singling out the *Baptism of Christ*, showing the first meeting between St. John the Baptist and Christ, the *Dance of Salome* at Herod's banquet and the splendid *Crucifixion* on the eastern wall, above the altar, in which we see not only St. Mark, the

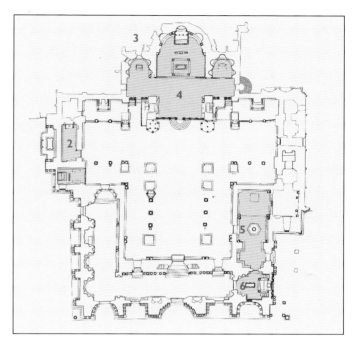

109
Chapel of St. Isidore, view of the altar with the sarcophagus of the saint
The chapel was built in the 14th century during the rule of Doge Andrea Dandolo, in the years of the great plague that swept across Europe, killing up to half of the population. The chapel, probably the right-hand aisle of the ancient church of San Teodoro, is adorned with a cycle of mosaics covering the entire ceiling. It has a highly unitary character and, along with the Baptistery and the Mascoli Chapel, constitutes one of the three Gothic gems in the originally Byzantine basilica. In the years 1885-86, the *proto* Pietro Saccardo brought it back into use, restoring the splendid mosaics and sculptures.

It is now reserved exclusively for prayer. It is used to house the Communion bread and wine and Mass is celebrated there on weekday mornings.

110
Plan of the basilica showing the location of the chapels
1. Mascoli Chapel
2. Chapel of St. Isidore
3. Sacristy
4. area of the crypt (under the presbytery)
5. Baptistery
6. Zen Chapel

111

St. Athanasius, mosaic, Baptistery, northwest pendentive of the central dome

Forming part of the iconography of the Baptistery, the mosaics in the pendentives represent the Doctors of the Church, those of the East – Athanasius, John Chrysostom, Gregory of Nazianzus and Basil – and those of the West – Ambrose, Gregory, Augustine and Jerome. The central dome has been partially restored, with the replacement of some of the heads of the apostles and of the people being baptized. The line which divides the old mosaics from those that were remade in the second half of the 19th century passes through the base of the dome, in the southwest corner. The mosaic of *St. Athanasius* is completely original.

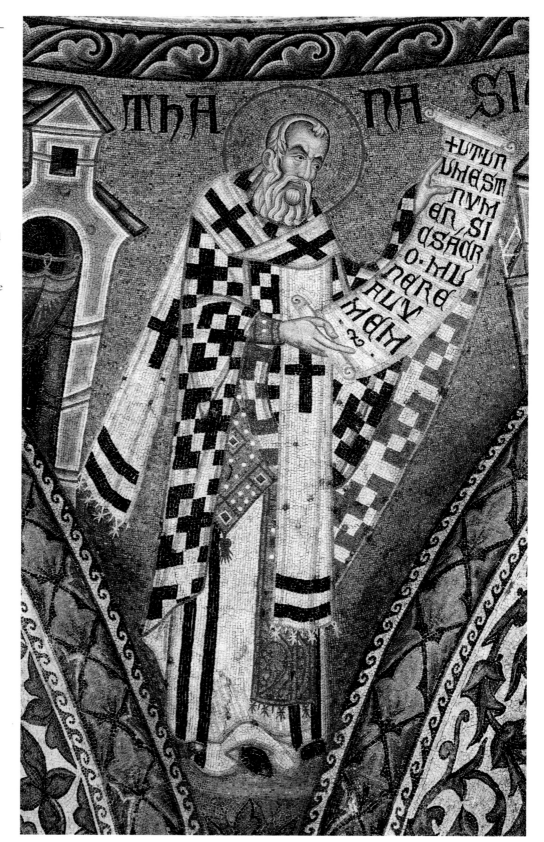

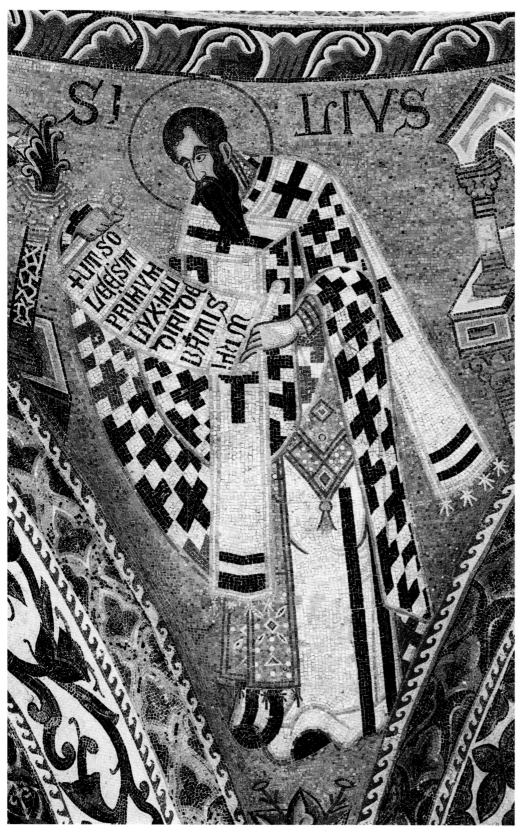

St. Basil, mosaic, Baptistery, southwest pendentive of the central dome

The mosaic of *St. Basil* has been completely reconstructed. Notice the marked difference in style and quality between *St. Basil* and the original *St. Athanasius*.

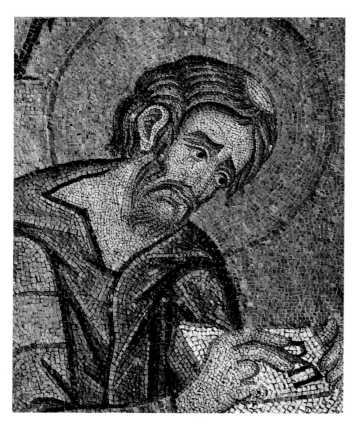

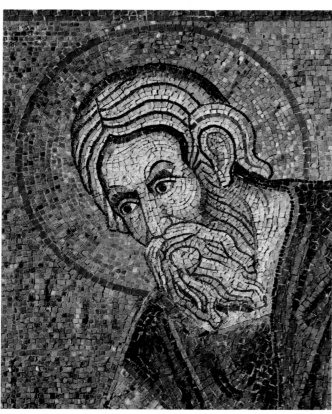

113-114 *left*

**St. Luke (above) and
St. Matthew (below), mosaics,
Baptistery, west supporting
arch of the central dome,
14th and 19th century**

The arch is decorated with the
figures of the four evangelists.
Half of the arch underwent
considerable alterations during
the restoration of 1865-75. The
mosaics in the southern part were
completely replaced.
A comparison of the heads
of St. Luke (1345–54) and
St. Matthew (1875), at the
north and south base of the arch
respectively, reveals the difference
in quality between the original
and the replacement mosaics.

115 *right*

View of the Baptistery

The Baptistery, once the *giesia dei
putti*, is a special area of the basilica,
that right from the outset was
separate from the rest of the
church with its own entrance
from the outside. In its present
form, given to it by Doges
Giovanni Soranzo († 1328) and
Andrea Dandolo († 1354), it
comprises an antebaptistery,
enclosed by a vault, and the
baptistery proper with the font
at the center and the altar in
the eastern part. There are two
domes, one over the area of
the font and one over the altar.
The iconography of the mosaics
develops two main themes: *Scenes
from the Life of St. John the Baptist*
on the walls and *Scenes from the Life
of Christ* on the vault and domes.

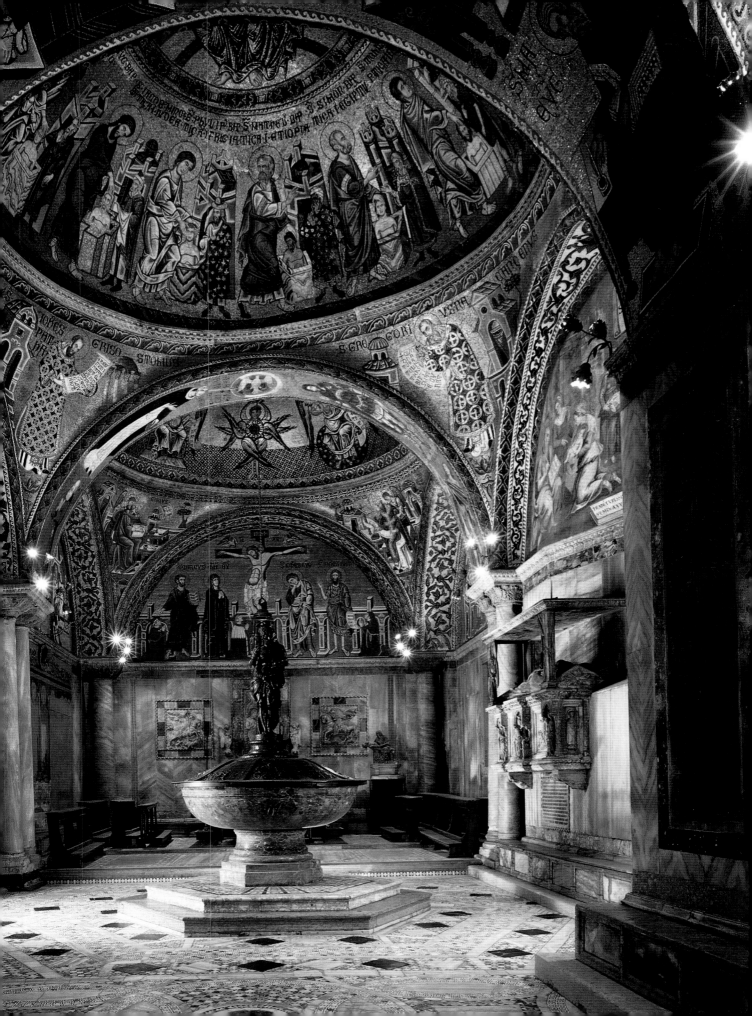

Virgin, St. John the Evangelist and St. John the Baptist, but also Doge Dandolo, who promoted the work, and the State Chancellor Rafaino Caresini.

The Baptistery contains a number of other elements, such as the tombs of Doge Giovanni Soranzo (1328) and Doge Andrea Dandolo (1354). The altar is set on top of a block of granite and has an inscription that has never been translated. Tradition has it that this was the stone from which Christ gave the Sermon on the Mount, brought here from Tyre by the Venetians. Recent restoration work on the base of this mighty mass, with sides measuring 2·5 m and 60 cm thick, has revealed a system of drains. They probably served to collect water from a tub used for baptism by immersion.

The Sacristy of St. Mark's now consists of two large spaces. The first is the sacristy proper, which was almost doubled in size by the *proto* Giorgio Spavento in the years following 1486, to stretch as far as the Rio di Palazzo, the canal to the east of the basilica. The other space is the ancient church of San Teodoro, entered through a doorway of modest proportions, in which religious services are still held today.

Between 1500 and 1530 the ceiling of the Sacristy was adorned with a mosaic that is considered the last example of the traditional type, in which gold is still the primary component of the decoration. Typologically, the image belongs to the Renaissance, with ancient Roman motifs set alongside a large cross bearing the figure of Christ and saints. The mosaics in the lunettes on the walls, located above the marble facing, represent apostles, prophets and saints to designs by the young Titian, who took a completely new approach here with respect to the mosaics on the ceiling. Each figure has a lunette to itself and stands out against the gold ground without blending into it. In so doing, a new sense of depth is created in a type of decoration that had previously been confined to expressing itself in two dimensions. A *Virgin and Child* to a design attributed to Lorenzo Lotto is placed above the entrance.

The altar frontals and inlaid cabinets in the eastern part of the Sacristy, made by the Antonio and Paolo Mola brothers from Mantua, are of great importance. There are twenty-one altar frontals and fifteen cabinet doors with themes that display a new formal style in the representation of urban architecture and depict the principal objects used by scientists, priests and musicians at the time. The altar frontals in the second part of

the Sacristy are designed by Jacopo Sansovino and have a simple structure, decorated with pilaster strips and topped by architraves of classical proportions.

The Zen Chapel was built to house the tomb of Cardinal Zen, in accordance with the terms of his last will and testament, which left a substantial legacy to the Republic on condition that he be buried in St. Mark's. The Zen Chapel is formed out of the recess that contained the door known as the Porta da Mar. On the arch of the recess are a Virgin and Child and prophets with Christ Emmanuel, while the vault, added at a later date, is adorned with mosaics depicting *Scenes from the Life of St. Mark* up until his martyrdom. In 1501, the outer end was closed by a marble screen wall, with a window above it, that forms a backdrop to an altar with bronze columns, called the Madonna of the Shoe. Representing St. Peter and St. John the Baptist as well, the altar is the work of Antonio Lombardo. The cardinal's sarcophagus is also made from bronze and has the figure of the deceased sculpted in high relief on the lid. The chapel was restored at the beginning of 1980 and can be entered from the atrium and from the Baptistery. Both the large gate with late Roman gratings and the bronze door leading to the Baptistery have been restored recently.

116

Zen Chapel

The former Porta da Mar, or Sea Door, closed up by the construction of an external screen wall out of panels of Greek marble and a large upper window, now houses the Madonna of the Shoe, carved by Antonio Lombardo. The figure of the Virgin is flanked by St. Peter and St. John the Baptist and enclosed by a baldachin with columns whose bases are made out of Parian marble with shafts of bronze. The baldachin itself is made of bronze over a wooden structure and has a relief depicting the Eternal Father and the Holy Spirit on its ceiling. At the center of the chapel stands the sarcophagus of Cardinal Giovanni Battista Zen, complete with a sculpture in full relief of the deceased dressed in his cardinal's robes. The engraver and sculptor Paolo Savin collaborated with Antonio Lombardo and took over from him to complete the work. The bronzes were cast by Pietro Campanato.

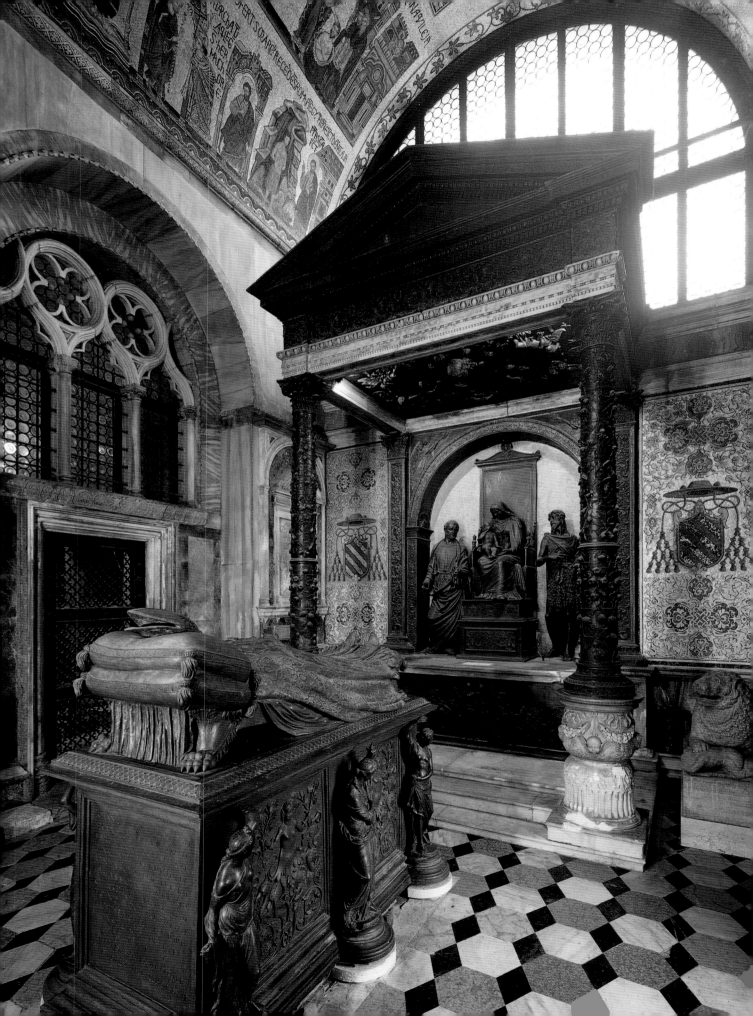

THE INLAID CABINETS IN THE SACRISTY

Umberto Daniele

The wooden inlaid work in the Sacristy constitutes one of the most remarkable late fifteenth-century cycles of images to have survived in Venice, very close to the dreamlike visions of Carpaccio. Three of the cabinets, set against the walls that back on to the Rio di Palazzo, are decorated with fifteen still lifes, located inside a *trompe-l'oeil* closet with open doors. Above them a tall architectural structure encloses twenty-one urban views. Some of them have a scene or miracle from the life of St. Mark in the foreground and they constitute the earliest representations of the hagiography of St. Mark in the modern era, drawing on the basilica's *Legendary* (twelfth-fifteenth century). The other views depict an ideal city, framed by a triumphal arch, in which the most recent sacred and profane works of architecture in Venice (the façades of Santa Maria dei Miracoli and San Zaccaria, and the Scala del Bovolo) are presented as emblems of the *renovatio urbis* promoted by Doge Agostino Barbarigo. Likewise, the still lifes do not represent just the conventional church vestments and ornaments, but also musical instruments, fountains and other Neoplatonic symbols of the harmony of the cosmos.

Many famous inlayers, such as the Canozi brothers from Lendinara and the Olivetan monk Sebastiano da Rovigno, have been suggested by historians as authors of the work. In reality the precious carvings (*c.* 1493-96) are probably by the Florentine Tommaso Astorio, while the majority of the inlays (*c.* 1497-1500) are the signed work of the Mantuan brothers Antonio and Paolo Mola, who were also responsible for the inlays in the chancel of the Certosa in Pavia (1489) and Isabella d'Este's Grotto in Mantua (1506). In 1523, the cycle was completed by the Olivetan Vincenzo da Verona, with the assistance of

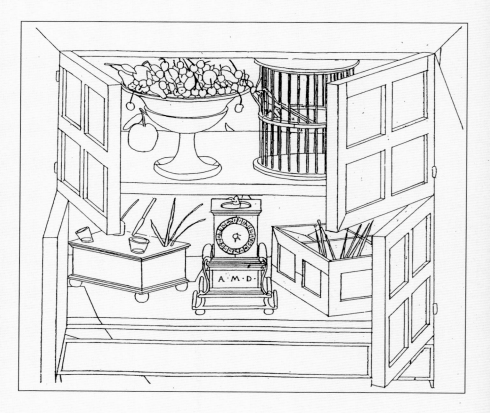

the Jesuit Pietro da Padova. Originally it also included the inlays of a large bench, used to close off the area of the cabinets, that is now lost.

117

Design of one of the doors of the cabinets under the altar frontals in the Sacristy

When the fifteen doors are open they reveal representations of articles used for scientific, religious and musical purposes by the learned and refined men of the Renaissance.

118

Inlay of an altar frontal in the Sacristy

The work of the brothers Antonio and Paolo Mola of Mantua (1496–1506), the twenty-one altar frontals represent views of cities. Genuine proposals of urban design, based on the new canons and models of Renaissance architecture, they depict, by means of a perspective view placed inside an arched frame, an imaginary window, through which to enjoy the inlaid scene. Here, we see the lagoon with a type of cargo vessel armed for defense, known as a Venetian carrack, represented at an angle that emphasizes the urban scene. Many of the inlays depict miracles performed by St. Mark.

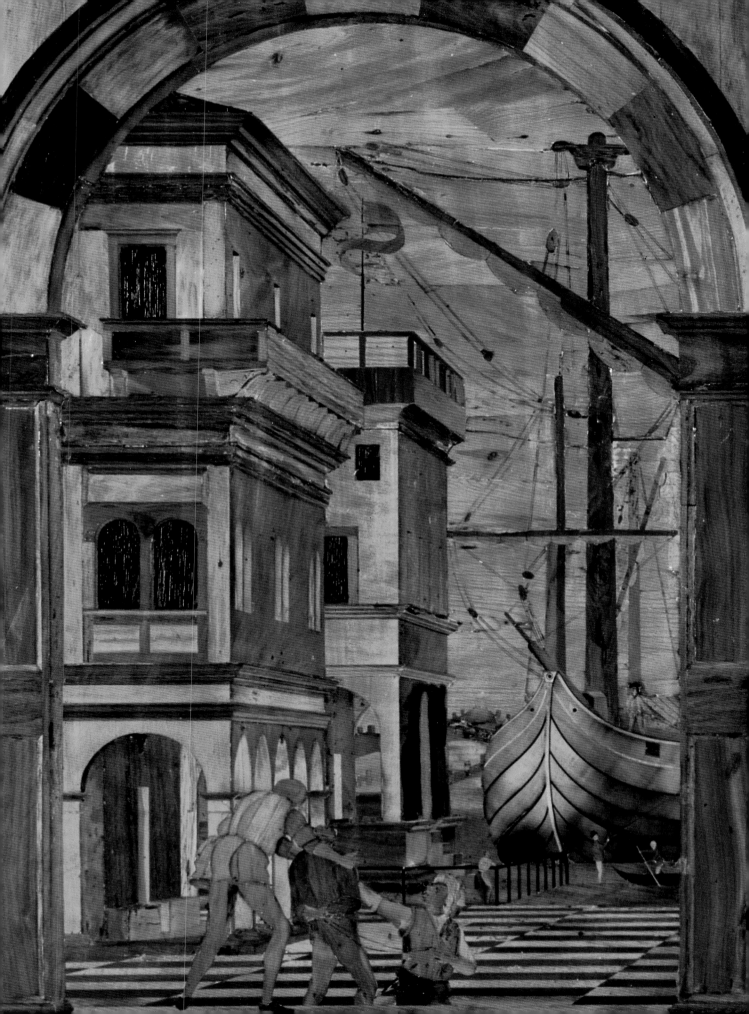

THE ANGELS IN THE BAPTISTERY

Antonio Niero

The dome above the altar is split into three concentric circles. In the central one, Christ is shown blessing, flanked by two six-winged seraphim as described in the book of Isaiah (6, 1-2). The second circle is supported by nine angels, each holding a torch, a succinct reference to the nine hosts or choirs of angels of which Christ is the Lord, according to the doctrine of the New Testament.

In the third circle, nearest the base of the dome, we see nine angelic choirs, in keeping with the specific doctrine put forward in the thirty-fourth homily of Pope Gregory the Great (540-604). This in turn harks back to Dionysius the Areopagite's fifth-century *The Celestial Hierarchy*, one of the fullest treatments of the subject. Each choir is represented by a single angel in the role of choirmaster. The iconographic interpretation of the nine choirs can be read either from the ninth to the first (from bottom to top), as we suggest to the visitor, or in the opposite direction. The point of reference is provided by the seraphim, the highest choir, located near the cross of the altar below.

We begin at the opposite side of the dome, with the angels and archangels, who are holding the souls of the righteous, swathed like mummies. Those held by the angels have their heads covered, while the heads of those held by the archangels are bare, perhaps to indicate that they are people of greater authority, since archangels would be expected to be given more prestigious charges. They are followed in an anticlockwise direction by the virtues, with a corpse near a stream of water flowing from some rock and a devilish figure in the background on the top of a pillar of fire. Next come the powers, with the choirmaster binding a demon, and the principalities with the

choirmaster brandishing a sword, seated on a throne.

At this point it is necessary to go back to the angels at the bottom again and, moving in a clockwise direction this time, look first at the dominions, where the choirmaster is weighing a soul in the form of a naked youth. He is struggling with a demon who is trying to gain possession of the soul by adding heavy stones to make the pan of the scales tip in his direction. Continuing clockwise around the circle we discover the last triad of angelic choirs: the thrones with their leader seated on the celestial globe, wearing a royal crown and holding a lilied scepter; the ten-winged cherub, around whom runs the inscription *sciencie plenitudo* (fullness of knowledge); and the seraphim with their choirmaster seated on a throne.

Before attempting an iconographic interpretation of the whole, it should be said that the program for these figures seems to have been drawn up by Doge Andrea Dandolo (1343-54), who intended the Baptistery to serve as his mortuary chapel. In fact, the iconography of the angels, or rather of the archangels, recalls the offertory of the Mass said for the souls of the dead, in use since the ninth century. In this, God is asked to let the archangel Michael lead the souls into the holy light, after Christ has freed them by raising them from their sufferings in the deep lake, shown here in the cave beneath the angels and archangels where a number of souls are waiting to be set free. The images relating to the choir of the virtues summarize their function, that of working miracles. This explains the allusion to the corpse they are protecting and the water flowing from the rock, a reference to the miracle wrought at Mont Saint-Michel off the coast of Brittany, as well as to salvation from Hell (devil amidst the flames). Among the powers, the devil about to be bound

with a long chain takes its inspiration directly from the text of Revelation (20, 1-3). Although this speaks only of a generic angel, it is intended as a reminder of the holy choir's function of restraining the forces of evil in their assault upon Christian believers. The fact that the principalities are seated on a throne is meant to show that they are the chiefs (*principes*) of the lesser angels who ensure that divine orders are promptly executed. The image of the weighing of the soul and the struggle with the demon in the dominions underlines the strength that they impart to the faithful through their participation in divine decrees, although the scene of St. Michael as the weigher of souls was common in medieval iconography. The thrones seated on the starry globe symbolize their mission of supporting the throne of God and of keeping human beings on the righteous path. The fullness of the knowledge of God represented in the cherubim serves to enlighten our ignorance. The inscription *sciencie plenitudo* is taken straight from the aforementioned thirty-fourth homily of St. Gregory the Great. He points out that fullness of knowledge, according to St. Paul, is fullness of Love, and the ten wings of the cherub therefore allude to the perfect number ten, or rather to the Ten Commandments which epitomize the love of God and our fellow human beings. The seraphim with their classic six wings, set at the very top of the ranks, are burning with love for God, with the aim of inflaming human hearts as well.

Dandolo may have drawn this iconography directly from St. Gregory's long homily, though he must have taken the episode of the virtues with the water flowing from the rock from the *Golden Legend* of Jacobus de Voragine (1208-98). St. Gregory presents the choirs of angels in the following order: angels, archangels, virtues, powers, principalities (represented in exactly the same sequence in the mosaic, but we then have to cross to the opposite side of the dome to continue the hierarchy), dominions, thrones, cherubim and seraphim. Support for Dandolo's preference for St. Gregory's text is provided by the representation of the saint in the pendentive beneath the seraphim.

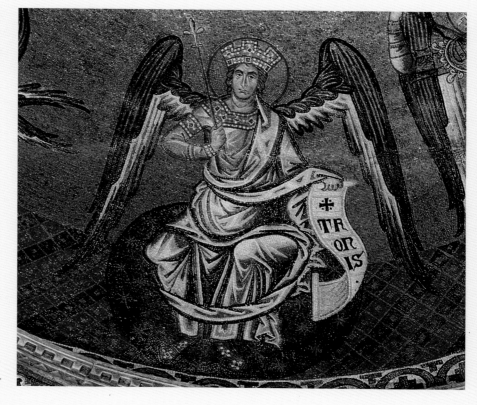

119 *above*

Detail of the thrones, Baptistery, Dome of the Angels

The angel that denotes the choir of the thrones is represented with a crown on his head and holding a scepter to indicate his power. He is seated on a throne of stars.

120 *below*

Detail of the angels and archangels, Baptistery, Dome of the Angels

This unique and delightful image shows the two figures facing one another, taking a direct interest in the lives of human beings.

121 *following pages*

Baptistery, Dome of the Angels

One of the few complete representations of the angelic hierarchy. In an anticlockwise sequence, we find personifications, accompanied by their principal functions, of the angels that watch over the soul during its earthly existence, the archangels that present the soul of the deceased to God, the virtues, the powers, the principalities, the seraphim, the cherubim (portrayed with ten wings and the inscription *sciencie plenitudo*), the thrones and the dominions. The mosaic is original and dates from 1343–54.

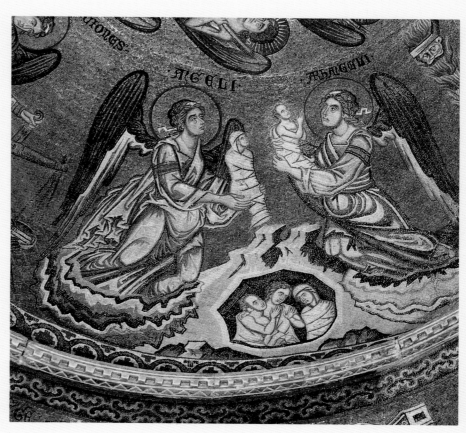

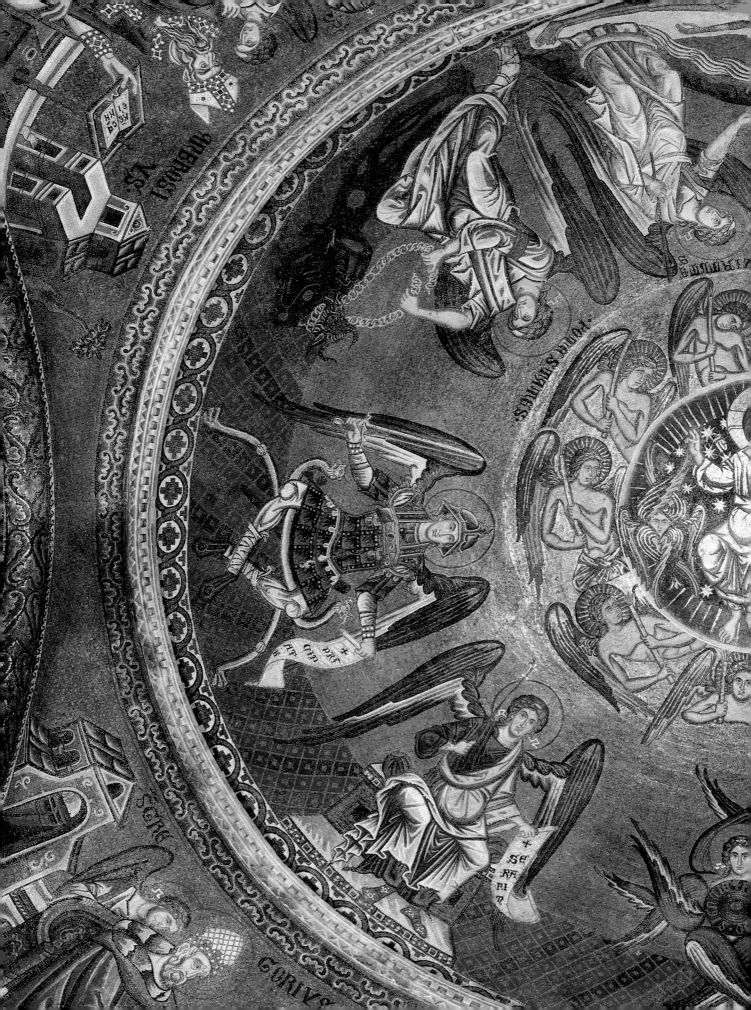

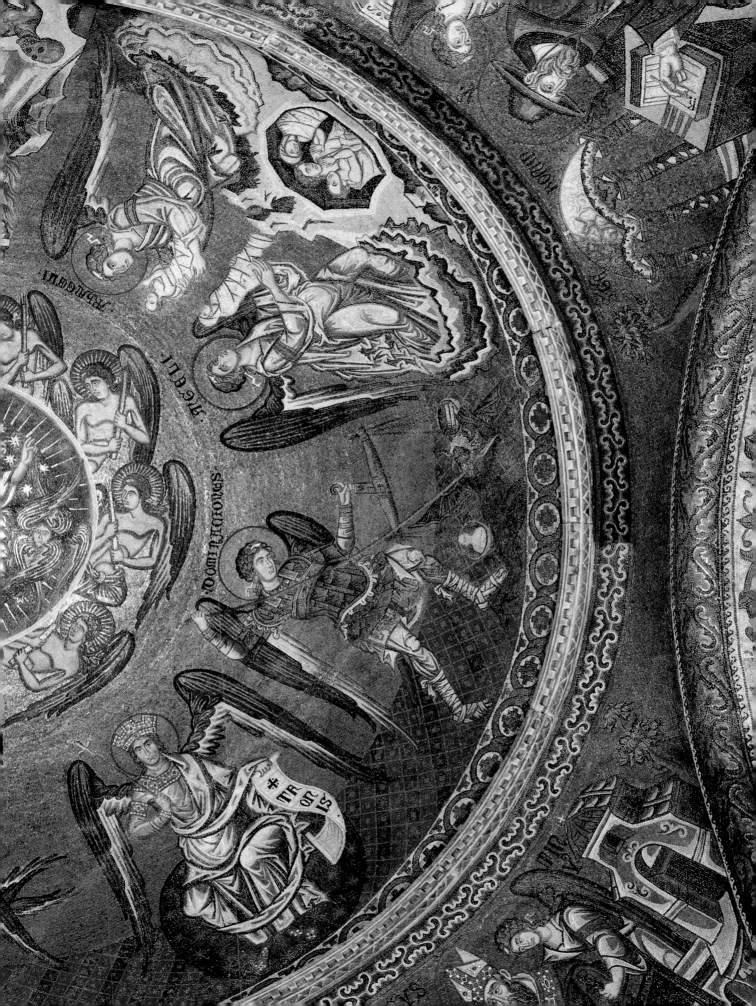

THE MOSAICS OF THE MASCOLI CHAPEL

Maria Da Villa Urbani

The *cappella nova* of the Madonna, also called the Mascoli Chapel, was built at the behest of Doge Francesco Foscari in 1430, as a mark of his gratitude to the Virgin for having survived an attempt on his life by political opponents. The name by which it is most commonly known derives from the ancient confraternity of the Mascoli, whose first seat had been in the crypt. When this became impracticable in the second half of the sixteenth century, the confraternity moved to the Chapel of St. John in the north transept. Then, in 1618, when the image of the Madonna known as the *Nicopeia* was given a definitive home there on a sumptuous baroque altar, the confraternity was assigned the small Chapel of the Madonna by Doge Antonio Priuli.

In 1430, Doge Foscari, to fulfil his vow, decided to restructure this space, originally the vestibule to the neighboring Chapel of St. Isidore, with which it communicated through a door that, although still visible, is now walled up. The room, which is small in size (7·11 x 4·21 m and 7·95 m high), is completely open on the side facing the church and has an altar set against the back wall. The marble altar frontal is decorated with two angels kneeling at the sides of the cross, holding censers. The altarpiece, in pale marble with traces of gilding, consists of three narrow shell-shaped niches surmounted by inflected arches adorned with foliage. Inside the niches, separated by spiral columns terminating in tall polygonal spires, are set three splendid examples of Gothic sculpture that display Venetian innovations as well as Tuscan influences. They represent the *Virgin and Child*, *St. Mark* and *St. John the Evangelist*, in an echo of the iconography of the mosaic in the bowl-shaped vault over the nearby door, the Porta della Madonna, leading from the atrium to the Dome of

St. John the Evangelist in the north transept. St. John is traditionally associated with the figure of the Madonna, who was entrusted to him by the dying Jesus on the cross, according to the account in his Gospel (19, 26-7).

The mosaic decoration of the Mascoli Chapel's tunnel vault and rear wall, executed around the middle of the fifteenth century, depicts five episodes from the *Life of the Virgin* drawn from the canonical Gospels of Matthew and Luke and from the apocryphal Gospels. As the basilica's overall iconographic program already comprised a Marian cycle, located in the small western vaults of the two transepts, the scenes in the new chapel amount to a sort of appendix.

At the top of the vault, a rectangular section decorated with shoots of flowering acanthus contains three tondi: the *Virgin and Child*, *David* and *Isaiah*. The figure of Mary is presented here as the link between the Old Testament, represented by the two prophets, and the New Testament, embodied in the figure of the Christ Child, whom she is holding in her arms and showing to humanity as its Redeemer. David and Isaiah, with their prophecies of the Messiah, appear alongside Mary several times in the basilica. The best-known examples are at the center of the Dome of the Presbytery and on the south wall of the western arm of the nave, where they are set in precious thirteenth-century *pinakes*.

The sequence of the five scenes begins on the left (west wall) with the *Birth of the Virgin,* located inside a house depicted in the Venetian Gothic style. Her mother Anna is shown lying on a bed in the background, while two midwives bathe the newborn child under the affectionate gaze of her father Joachim. The scene is completed by a woman spinning on the

122
View of the Mascoli Chapel

The chapel is a perfect example of Gothic Renaissance architecture and decoration. On the splendid vault adorned with the most delicate mosaics in the basilica (made with tesserae as small as three millimeters a side), the Venetian school of Michele Giambono – with the *Birth of the Virgin* and the *Presentation in the Temple* – confronts the Tuscan one of Andrea del Castagno, with the *Visitation* and the *Death of the Virgin*. The former have architectural backdrops in the Gothic style, the latter in the Renaissance style.

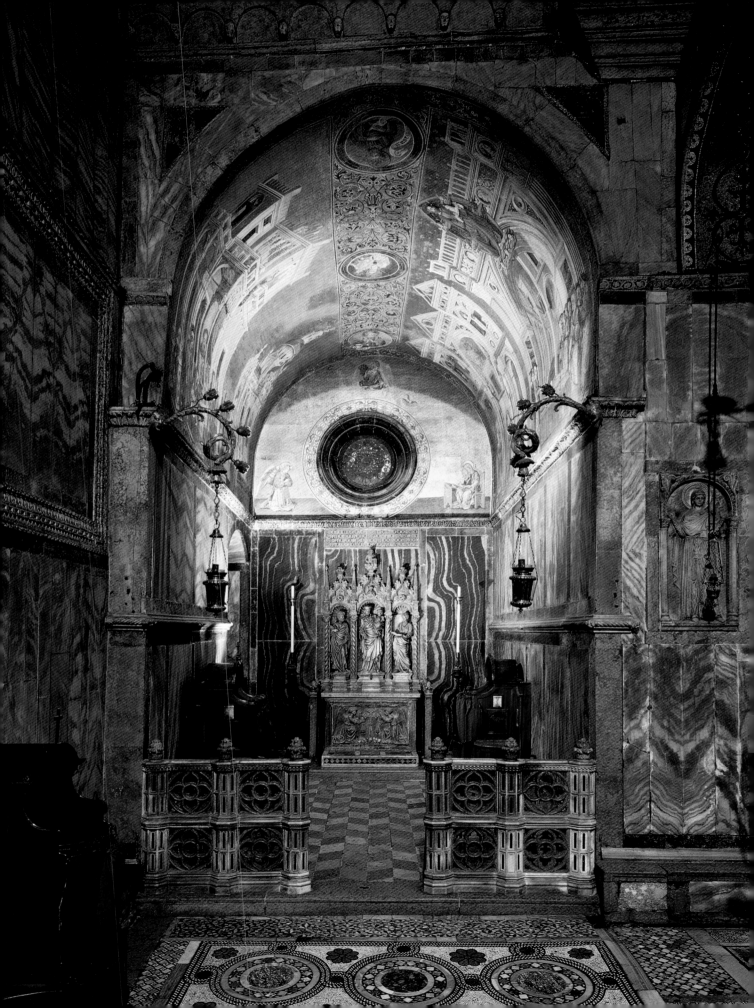

left and by two more women arriving to visit from the right. A large peacock is perched prominently on a balcony above, symbolizing resurrection and immortality.

Mary's *Presentation in the Temple*, in the second scene, is set on the threshold of a centrally planned domed building, again in the Venetian Gothic style. This has already been turned into a Christian church, as crosses are clearly recognizable on top of the small cupolas at the sides. An old priest greets the girl, who hands him a lighted candle. She is accompanied by her elderly parents and two women, one of whom is holding two white doves in her half-hidden hands, a traditional sacrificial offering.

In the lunette on the back wall, pierced by a richly decorated and highly symbolic circular window, the only source of light in the chapel, we see the *Annunciation* to Mary of the birth of her son Jesus, a light that will never set for humanity. Gabriel is kneeling on the left, while Mary is seated at a desk on the right, busy reading the Scriptures. The expression on her face and the gesture of her hand conveys her surprise at the events. In the middle, above the eye of light provided by the window, God the Father is sending his Spirit down to Mary in the customary guise of a dove.

Moving on to the right-hand (eastern) half of the tunnel vault, the novelty of the magnificent Renaissance architecture that frames the two last scenes is immediately apparent. The stylistic difference between the two sides of the vault has led to long debate over the reason why Michele Giambono, who signed the scenes on the left-hand side, failed to complete the work, and over the hypothetical influence on the right-hand side of a Tuscan artist, such as Andrea del Castagno, who was present in Venice during that period. Consequently,

the small chapel has come to be seen as a melting pot, bringing together the stimuli and ideas of both Venetian artists and *foresti* (literally, artists from outside). The right-hand half of the vault can be considered almost as a manifesto of the imminent architectural rebirth of the city.

The first of the two right-hand scenes is the *Visitation* of Mary to Elizabeth, her elderly cousin who is expecting a son, the future John the Baptist. The embrace of the two women, standing by themselves at the center, powerfully expresses the intense feelings that prompted Mary to pronounce the *Magnificat*, the hymn of praise to God for the great things that he had done to her, as we read in the Gospel according to Luke (1, 46-55).

The Death of the Virgin, finally, in the presence of the twelve apostles, is taken from the Apocrypha. For centuries, the story has formed the basis of this well-known iconography, in which the Virgin's death is associated with the idea of her immediate assumption into Heaven, where she is greeted by her son Jesus, depicted in a mandorla of glory.

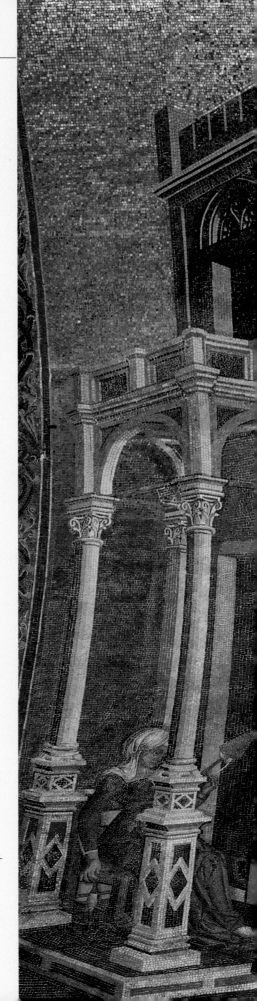

123

***Birth of the Virgin*, mosaic, Mascoli Chapel, detail**
The detail shows the Gothic architecture of the mosaic; the typology of the transennas is characteristic.

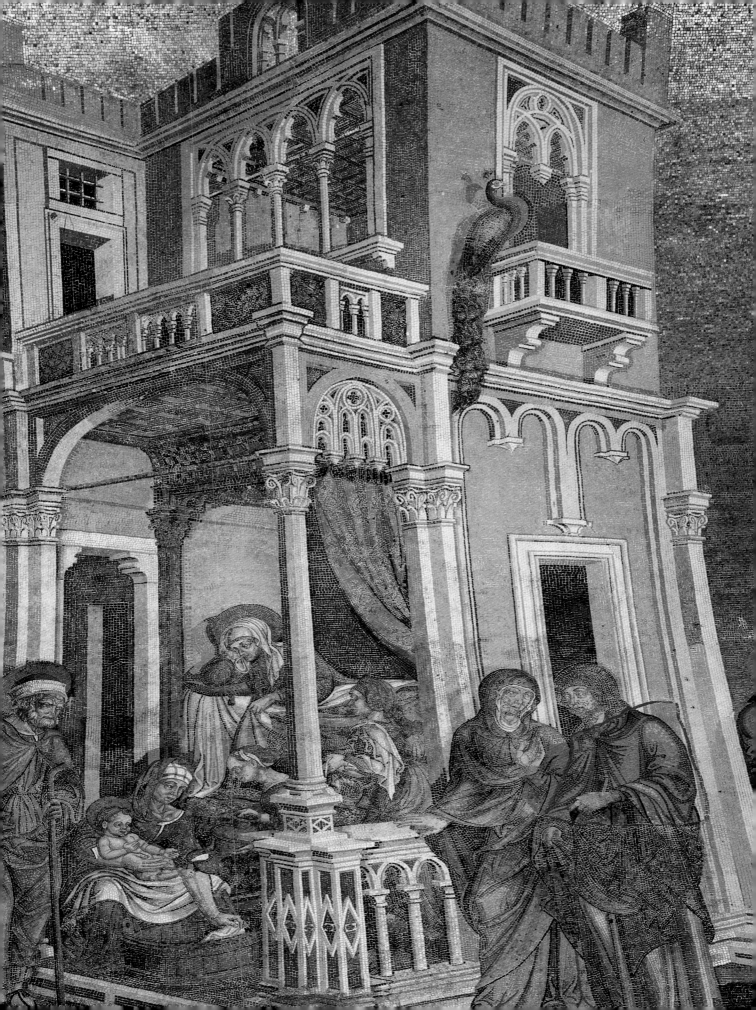

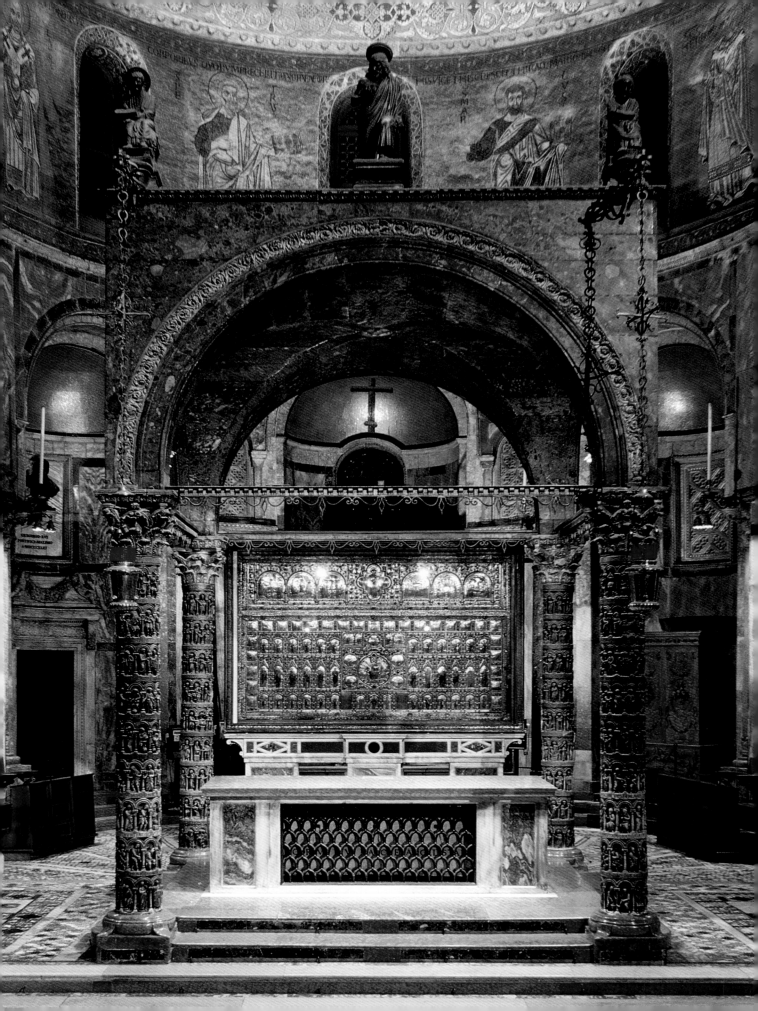

THE PALA D'ORO AND THE TREASURY OF ST. MARK'S

Ettore Vio

The Treasury of St. Mark's houses a rich collection of objects made from gold, silver, precious and semiprecious stones, rock crystal and worked and painted glass, along with finely made objects for the churches and palaces of Constantinople. The collection includes the most elegant and precious creations that Venetian craftsmen were able to produce in their desire to add to the glory of St. Mark's, seen as a metaphor for the Venetian duchy. It also contains examples of some of the most prestigious medieval and Renaissance art to have been created in Western Europe.

The oldest part of the collection was formed after 1204, following the conquest of Byzantium and the creation of the Eastern Latin Empire (1204-61) by the Crusaders, when many objects of sumptuary art were brought to Venice from Constantinople. It was further enriched with the conquest of Tyre and then with the abandonment of Candia (now Heraklion) by the Venetians, who sought to save as many of their valuable possessions as possible by taking them to Venice. Numerous precious gifts were also received from pontiffs and from the sovereigns of Western Europe.

Catastrophic fires like the one that broke out in 1231 and robberies – such as that plotted in 1449 by the Greek Stamati Crassioti, which was foiled by a tip-off from a friend, earning Crassioti the death penalty – have put the Treasury to a severe test. With the fall of the Republic, in 1797, it suffered a true *coup de grâce* and was reduced to its current 283 pieces.

Of all the objects, the most venerated and loved by the Venetian people is the *Nicopeia,* an image of the Madonna that was believed to bring victory to embattled armies, where it was set up in the front lines to protect them against the enemy. Set in a frame of gilded silver, enamel and precious stones, the icon was painted by a Byzantine artist in the tenth century and inspired by a mosaic Madonna located between the figures of Constantine and Justinian in the southern vestibule of Hagia Sophia in Constantinople. Its beauty was considered so divine that it was said to have been made not by ordinary human hand, but by St. Luke who, through divine inspiration, painted the first ever picture of the Mother of God (believed by some to be this very icon). Over the centuries it has accumulated a substantial amount of jewelry, now kept in a safe, testifying to the deep faith that the image has inspired.

The Pala d'Oro (Golden Altarpiece) is unanimously considered to be the most precious and refined object in the

124
Pala d'Oro

The Pala d'Oro, or Golden Altarpiece, was ordered by Doge Ordelaffo Falier in 1102 and finished in Byzantium in 1105. Later, enamels looted from Constantinople during the Fourth Crusade were added at the top. Originally set between two columns supporting statues of the Annunciation (now in the Treasury of St. Mark's), it folded back at the top and was covered by a so-called weekday altarpiece all year round except for on feast days. The present structure, made by the goldsmith Giovanni Paolo Bonesegna (1345), has been sealed inside a protective case with a wheel mechanism that allows the front of the altarpiece to be turned to face the nave on special occasions. The rest of the time the altarpiece faces toward the back of the presbytery, where it can be admired by tourists, while the weekday altarpiece, a panel painting of the 15th-century Venetian school, is visible from the altar. Two more weekday altarpieces were painted, the first by Paolo Veneziano in 1345 and the second by Maffeo da Verona in the 17th century. Both are now in the museum.

125 *following pages*
Pala d'Oro, detail

The altarpiece, about three meters long and two meters high, is exceptionally ornate, covered with precious stones, gold and enamels. It is composed of three different parts. In the lower central part, made in Byzantium (1102-05), the prophets foretelling the coming of Emmanuel are represented in three successive

rows starting from the lower edge. At the center, the Virgin, future Mother of God, is flanked by Princess Irene and Doge Ordelaffo Falier, who replaces the earlier figure of a Comnenus, probably the basileus of Constantinople at the time the altarpiece was ordered. In the central row we see the apostles, with Christ enthroned in the middle and surrounded by the evangelists. In the upper row the archangels sing the glory of God, with the throne of the *Hetoimasia* in the middle. The upper part was made with *cloisonné* enamels looted during the Fourth Crusade. It represents six of the church's festivals from the *Life of Christ,* with the archangel Michael, defender of the city and the church, at the center. It can be dated to the 10th century and is composed of the most splendid Byzantine enamels. A series of small panels with *Scenes from the History of the Church* and the *Life of St. Mark* are set along the sides of the altarpiece, in the lower part and along the line dividing the two parts. The *cloisonné* enamels are made using gold leaf as a ground. Different colours of powdered glass were placed inside cells formed by thin strips of gold and, after melting in the furnace, they took on their definitive color, forming a continuous sheet about five millimeters thick through which the gold ground gleams. The enamels are set in gilded frames of various shapes, embellished with semiprecious stones.

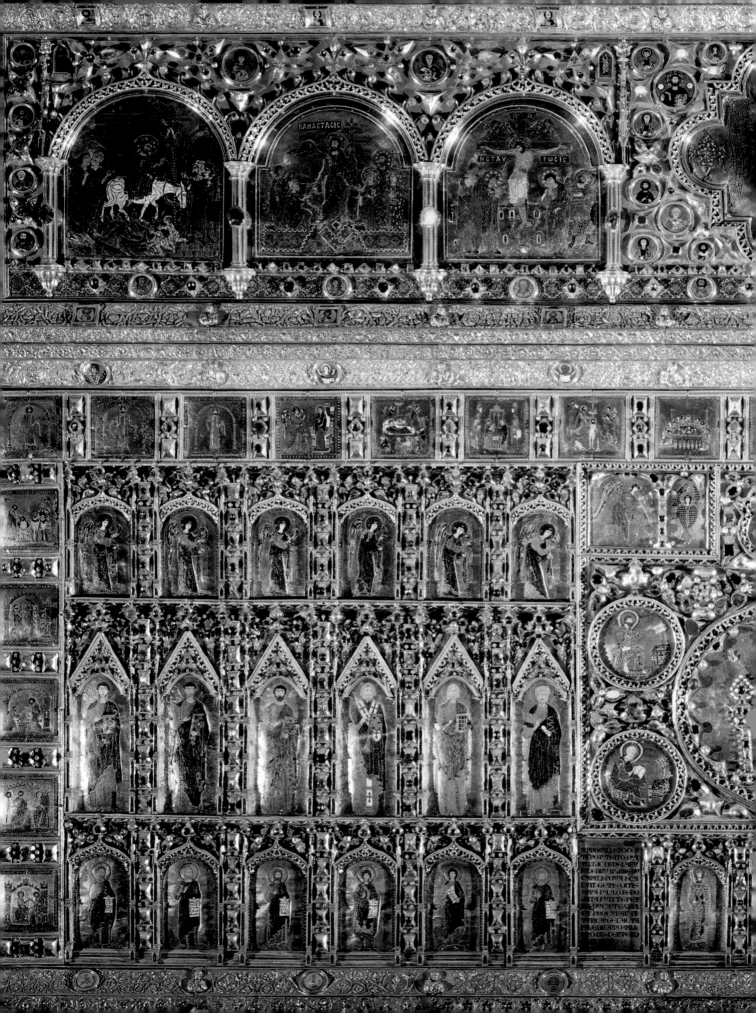

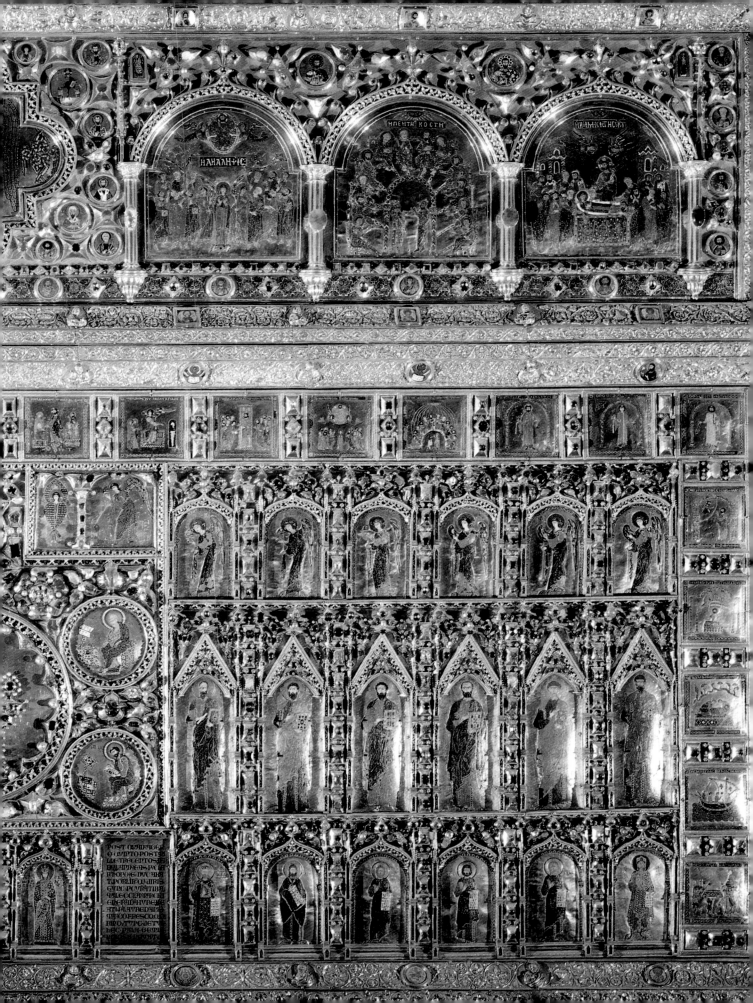

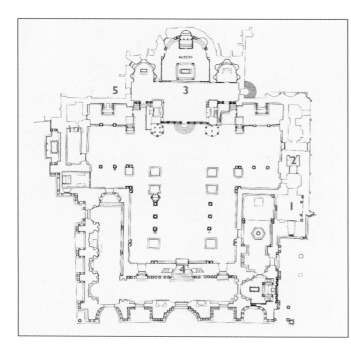

126

Plan of the basilica showing the route that has to be followed to reach the three areas used to house and display the basilica's various treasures

At the end of the south (right-hand) transept is set the entrance to the Treasury of St. Mark's (1), with objects brought back from the Fourth Crusade. These include works in rock crystal, glass vases, sardonyx amphorae, Persian ampullae and bowls (Fatimid period, 9th-11th centuries), Byzantine icons of the archangel Michael of extremely high value and quality, with *cloisonné* enamels, Byzantine chalices made by goldsmiths' workshops in the 9th-11th centuries and sardonyx goblets dating from the 1st-2nd century AD. The collection also houses candlesticks, crosiers, chalices from the Venetian Gothic period, articles made from rock crystal and filigree, the embossed and gilded silver casket or *artoforion* in the form of a basilica, and a whole series of other objects from different eras, including the golden rose given to Venice by a pope and the broadsword of Doge Francesco Morosini.

Next to the Treasury lies the Sanctuary used for the conservation of relics (2). These include Emperor Henry II's cross (1206-16), a relic of the True Cross, and a case of gilded bronze containing a golden reliquary with the wood of Christ's cross, made by the French goldsmith Gerardo. From the Chapel of St. Clement we move on to the Pala d'Oro (3), placed on the high altar.

In the atrium, at the sides of the central portal (4), along the staircase and in the museum above, where the chief exhibit is the four horses of St. Mark's, we find cases containing mosaics that have been removed from the walls of the basilica and other objects in stone.

Emerging from the Chapel of St. Peter and into the canon's courtyard, it is possible to take a lift up to the museum in the Banquet Hall (5). Here we can admire the tapestries of the *Passion* (15th century), the tapestries with *Scenes from the Life of St. Mark*, two ducal altar frontals (16th century), tapestries representing chivalric scenes from Flanders (15th century), Byzantine veils (13th century, restored in the 19th century), shirts and blouses with Burano lace (second half of 17th century), weekday altarpieces by Paolo Veneziano (14th century) and Maffeo da Verona (17th century), internal and external organ doors decorated by Gentile Bellini (15th century), Giovan Battista Tiepolo's *Nativity of Christ* (18th century), the golden lion of the left-hand organ, the doge's throne and other objects.

entire collection. An expression of the metaphysical genius of Byzantium and of the cult of light, seen as a means of elevating human beings toward God and a fundamental element in Western Gothic culture, it is set on the high altar of St. Mark's, glorifying the evangelist whose relics lie beneath. The enamels, executed in Constantinople in 1105 to a commission by Doge Ordelaffo Falier, were framed at the time in such a way that the square panels, now arranged vertically at the sides of the altarpiece, were lined along the base to tell the *Life of St. Mark*. The other square panels, with *Scenes from the Life of Christ*, now set horizontally in the fourth row from the bottom, were originally positioned above the scenes from the life of the evangelist so as to represent the Gospel according to St. Mark, an indispensable means of gaining access to the heavenly city depicted above. This predella made up of two rows of panels of *cloisonné* enamel constituted a sort of prologue to the vision of Paradise above. The center of the altarpiece is dominated by the figure of Christ enthroned, while his word is revealed by the four evangelists, depicted in round shields around him, and by the twelve apostles (six of them lined up to Christ's left and six to the right). The coming of the Son of God is now predicted in the lower level, underneath the apostles, by twelve prophets. Six stand to the left and six to the right of the central figure of the praying Virgin, who is flanked by the rulers of Venice and Byzantium

and by plaques with inscriptions recounting the history of the altarpiece itself. Above the central figure of Christ, we see the throne ready for the second coming of God on earth and reserved for the Last Judgment, adored by a line of cherubim, angels and archangels in the third row from the bottom.

The large frieze at the top, which comes from one of the three churches of the Monastery of the Pantocrator in Constantinople, showing the archangel Michael in the middle, and six panels depicting the *Entry of Christ into Jerusalem, Descent into Limbo, Crucifixion, Ascension, Pentecost* and *Death of the Virgin* were added to the altarpiece in 1209. In 1345 it was completed by the goldsmith Giovanni Paolo Bonesegna, with the addition of many precious stones and the new Gothic frame commissioned from him by the procurator Andrea Dandolo, who later became doge. A total of 1927 gems are mounted on it: 526 pearls, 330 garnets, 320 emeralds, 255 sapphires, 183 amethysts, 75 rubies, 175 agates, 34 topazes, 16 cornelians and 13 jaspers. The *cloisonné* enamels of the Gothic frame, with their precious colors set inside the gold wire around the cells, into which they were poured in a liquid state, perform the same function – that of emphasizing the abstract qualities of light – as the stained glass placed in cathedral windows. A material of uniquely Byzantine origin (enamel) mixed with the more exclusive creation of the Western sensibility (Gothic architecture), based on the manipulation of light, forms a perfect combination. The metaphysical qualities of the light in the enamel panels fuse with the anagogic ones (of mystical elevation to God) of the new Gothic framing. The altarpiece's image of Heavenly Jerusalem translates into a metaphor of Venice at a moment when the city seemed predestined to inherit the mantle of capital of the Eastern Roman Empire, which God had chosen as the seat for his Church and which Constantine had transferred from Rome to Byzantium.

In addition to such precious and venerated reliquaries as those of Christ's Blood, the Wood of the Cross, the Pillar of the Flagellation and the Sacred Purple, one of the most extraordinary objects in the Treasury, for its refinement, light and color, is the icon with a bust of the archangel Michael (tenth-eleventh century). The face, forearms and hands are all in gilded silver, the wings, halo and sleeves are made from *cloisonné* enamel, and the *loros* (a band around the bust) is studded with gems. The other icon representing the archangel Michael dressed as a warrior against a background decorated entirely with enamel, as is his cuirass, dates from the following century. Here the decorative and chromatic fantasy of the goldsmith seems inexhaustible and aims at the greatest possible abstraction of the image.

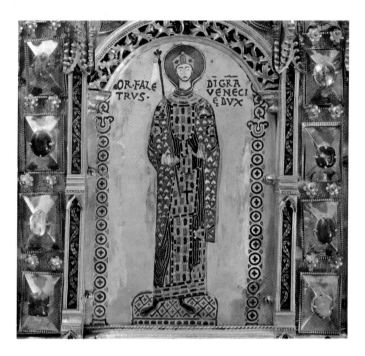

127

Doge Ordelaffo Falier, Pala d'Oro, detail

In the present organization of the altarpiece, the work of the goldsmith Giovanni Paolo Bonesegna (1345), Princess Irene and the doge are set in the bottom row, flanking the Blessed Virgin in an attitude of prayer. Since an examination of the material has shown that the doge's head is a replacement, it has been suggested that, prior to the Fourth Crusade, the figure represented a basileus of Constantinople, probably the princess's husband. After the breakdown of relations with the Byzantines, it seems that the Venetians substituted the head of the doge who had ordered the altarpiece from Constantinople in 1102.

Outstanding among the chalices is that of the Roman emperor, with a sardonyx bowl carved into stylized petals (first century AD) and a support of Byzantine silver gilt (tenth century). *Cloisonné* enamel panels, bordered by rows of pearls, depict Christ, the Virgin, John the Baptist, Peter, Paul, the evangelists, the Doctors and the archangels. They serve to sanctify the chalice and guarantee the invocation: "May the Lord aid the Roman Orthodox Emperor," which is written in Greek on the upper edge of the precious support. If it was ever used in Communion, the reddish-brown color of the sardonyx must have given the impression that the chalice, when lifted and viewed against the light, contained the precious blood that was shed for the salvation of humanity.

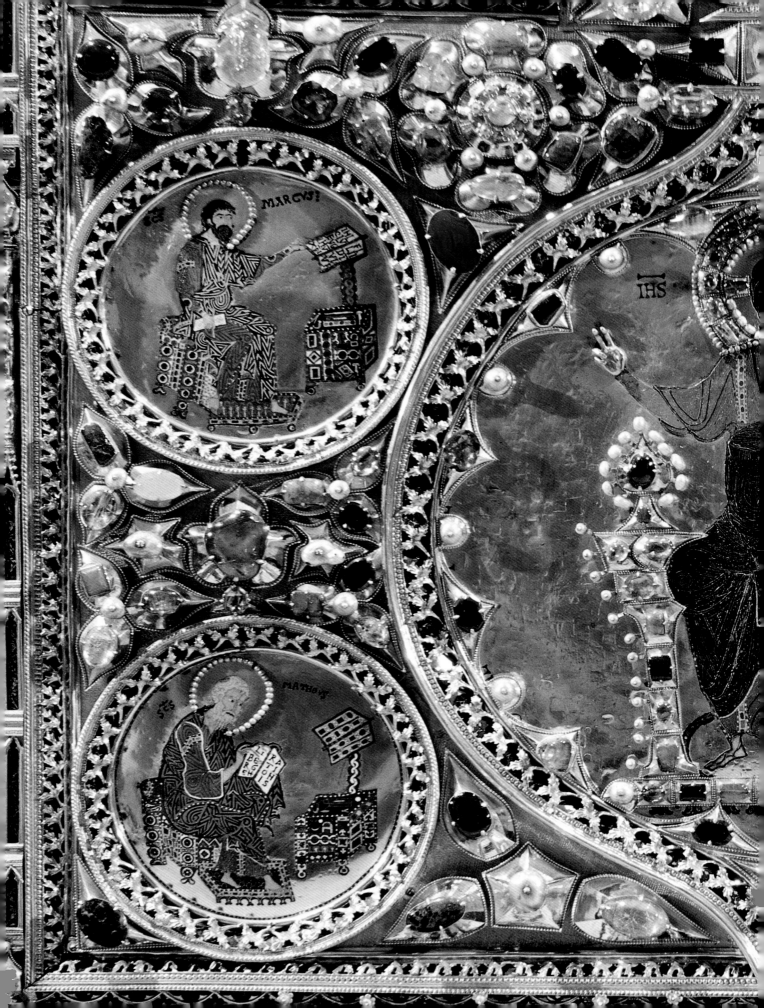

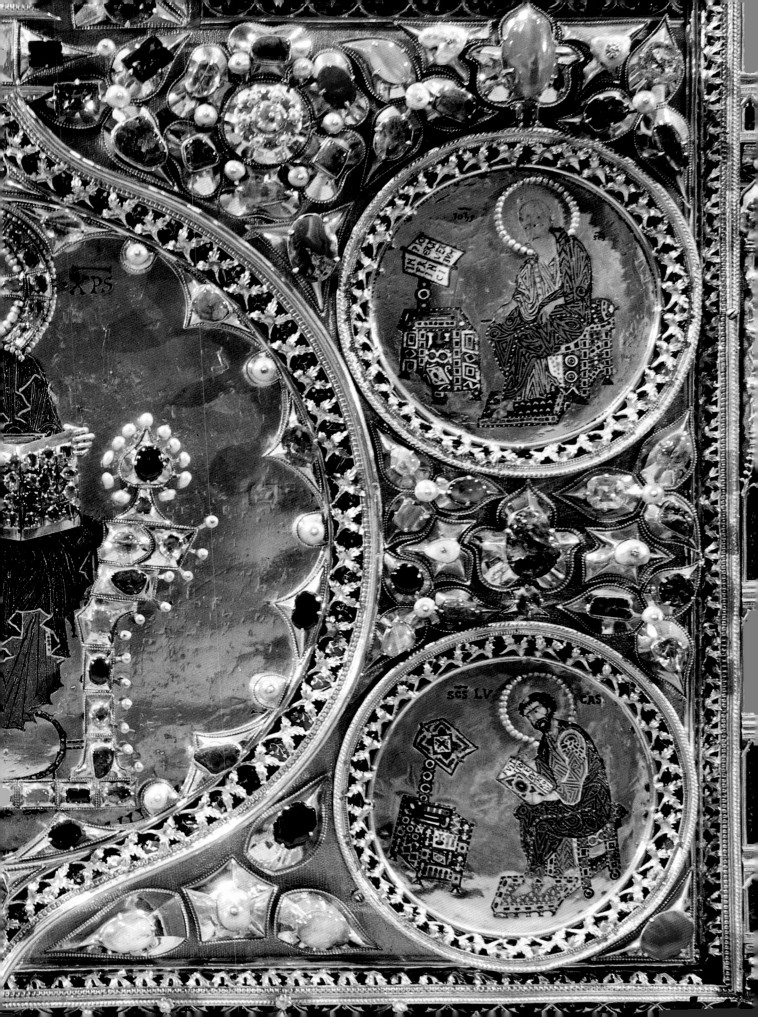

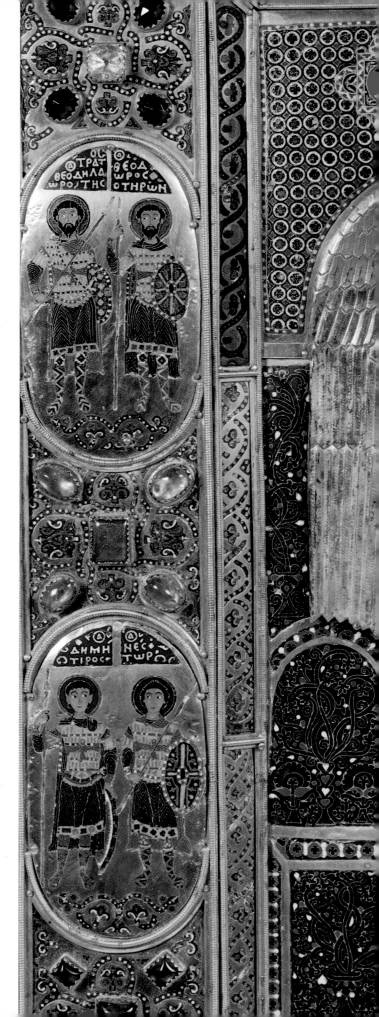

Symbolism and abstraction were the ultimate goals of Byzantine aesthetics and of the craftsmen who drew their inspiration from them. A similar effect is produced by another sardonyx chalice with handles (first century AD). It is supported by a stem and surrounded by a border, both of which are made of silver gilt and Byzantine *cloisonné* enamels representing Christ, the Virgin, John the Baptist, archangels, apostles, Doctors, bishops, deacons and martyrs. Under the base of the cup is set the Greek inscription: "May the Lord aid the Roman Orthodox Emperor" (tenth century).

These two chalices may have been the ones of deepest symbolic significance for the celebration of the Eucharist (although they were probably never used at St. Mark's), but the small temple of openwork silver gilt with a square and quatrefoil plan, five cupolas and four pinnacles topped by crosses was originally used to hold the Eucharistic bread. Its function is illustrated by the iconographic theme represented on the curved surfaces of the casket (formerly thought to be a perfume burner). The *Garden of Eden* and the *Tree of Life* are depicted at the top, while the fantastic animals on the base allude to the Vices, overcome by Courage and Prudence, embodied by the figures on the doors of a warrior and a woman with Greek inscriptions. It is these two virtues that permit entry into the temple and access to the Eucharist.

In any case, the refinement of the engraving and embossing, the gilding – that runs along the edges and corners and covers the allegorical figures – and the architectural elements (exedras, spires, domes and domed lantern) result in an object of totally abstract form, whose meaning is only comprehensible on a metaphysical level.

128 *preceding pages*
Christ the Pantocrator, Pala d'Oro, detail
The detail showing Christ the Pantocrator, surrounded by the evangelists, presents enamels of the highest quality. It is set in the central row of the original panel of the altarpiece ordered by Doge Falier.

129
The archangel Michael, standing and embossed, Treasury of St. Mark's
The Byzantine gold work of this icon in *cloisonné* enamels with gold and precious stones dates from the end of the 11th century. At the sides we can see pairs of warrior saints in enameled medallions, identified by inscriptions.

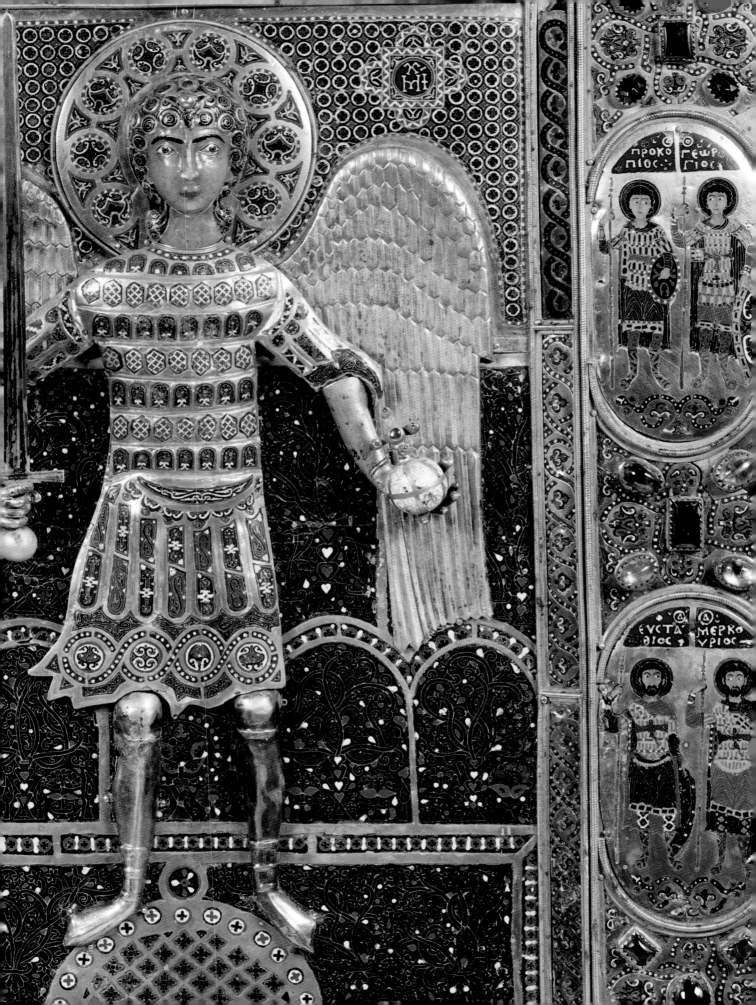

ΠΡΟΚΟΠΙΟC ΓΕΩΡΓΙΟC

ΕΥCΤΑΘΙΟC ΜΕΡΚΟΥΡΙΟC

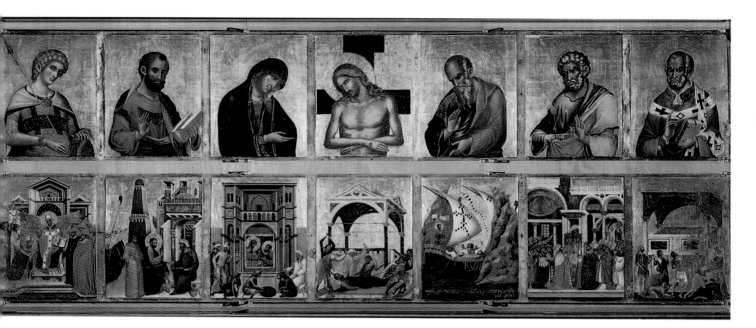

130 *above*

Paolo Veneziano and sons,
***Pala Feriale,* 1345**

The first and most important
weekday covering of the Pala
d'Oro. It is a wooden panel with
two registers of paintings: the
upper one represents *Christ and
the Virgin between Saints Theodore,
Mark, John the Evangelist, Peter and
Nicholas*; the lower one, *Scenes from
the Life of St. Mark*.

131 *right*

**Chalice of the Patriarchs,
Byzantine gold work,
Treasury of St. Mark's,
10th century**

Decorated with silver gilt, *cloisonné*
enamels and pearls, the chalice is
made out of a block of variegated
sardonyx. The mounting is typical
of the Byzantine era, when goblets
dating from the early centuries of
Christianity were reused.

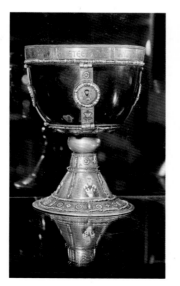

132 *right*

**Greek *artoforion*,
silver work, Treasury of
St. Mark's, 12th century**

A reliquary in the form of a small
domed church, made out of silver
and partially gilded, it dates from
the end of the 12th century. It
was originally used to hold the
Eucharistic bread.

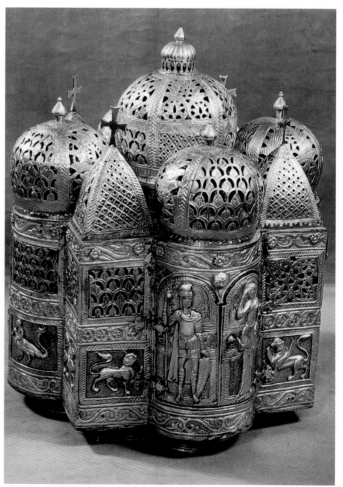

THE TAPESTRIES

Maria Da Villa Urbani

One of the chief delights of the Museum of St. Mark is its collection of fifteenth- and sixteenth-century tapestries. Having recently been completely restored, they have regained their original beauty, allowing us to appreciate once again the perfection of the workmanship and the preciosity of the materials, rescued from the damage wrought by the passage of time and by the effects of bad restorations over the centuries.

In addition to the fragments that come from the bequest of Cardinal Giovanni Battista Zen, four pieces of woolen cloth figuring *Scenes from the Passion*, originally used for religious services in Holy Week, also date from the fifteenth century. The thirteen scenes, from the *Last Supper* to the *Incredulity of Thomas*, are set in ten panels framed by plant borders. The symbol of the lion with folded wings — a form known to the Venetians as *in moleca*, referring to the shell-less phase of a crab — recurs frequently, underlining the fact that the images were woven for Venetian clients. The cartoons for these tapestries, executed in the flourishing manufactories of Arras in France in the early part of the fifteenth century, have recently been firmly attributed by art historians to the Venetian Niccolò di Pietro.

The four tapestries with *Scenes from the Life of St. Mark* and the two votive altar frontals of Doge Alvise Mocenigo (1571, to a cartoon by Jacopo Tintoretto) and Marino Grimani (1595, to a cartoon by Domenico Tintoretto) were made during the sixteenth century. All the sixteenth-century tapestries were woven in Florence and are characterized by their use of extremely precious and delicate yarn, such as silk and gold and silver thread.

The series of *Scenes from the Life of St. Mark*, depicting the miracles he worked, including the famous healing of the cobbler Anianus, and the saint's martyrdom, was commissioned by the procurators of St. Mark's from the Florentine tapestry manufactory, directed by the Fleming Giovanni Rost, on October 20, 1550, to decorate the sides of the presbytery. The statement in the contract that the tapestries were to be woven to a design that "will be sent by Master Jacopo Sansovino," *proto* of St. Mark's at the time, led people to believe that the cartoons were produced by Sansovino. However, critics have recently tended to see their style as having greater affinities with the works of Andrea Schiavone and Giuseppe Porta, known as Salviati.

Two other textiles in the basilica's museum are among the finest antique examples of the use of gold and silk embroidery for altar paraments to have come out of the workshops of Byzantium and can be dated to the twelfth or thirteenth century. The first is decorated with the figures of archangels Michael and Gabriel, while the other represents the dead Christ, watched over by two angels and surrounded by symbols of the evangelists.

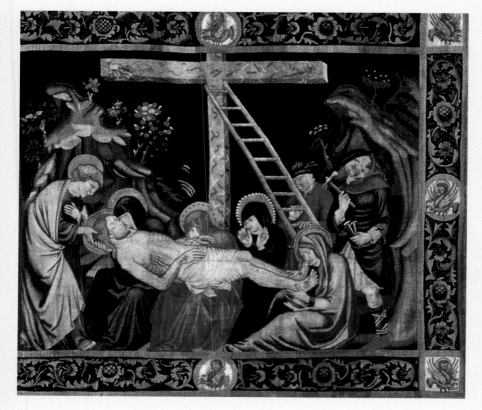

133

Deposition from the Cross, Scenes from the Passion, tapestry, Museum of St. Mark's, detail, first quarter of 15th century

The tapestries of the *Passion*, made abroad to cartoons by a Venetian painter in the first quarter of the 15th century, are the most important woolen hangings in Italy. There are four separate pieces of tapestry, two with three scenes and two with just two.

ESSENTIAL BIBLIOGRAPHY

1604
Venetia città nobilissima et singolare descritta già in XIIII. libri da M. Francesco Sansovino et hora con molta diligenza corretta, emendata, e più d'un terzo di cose nuove ampliata dal M.R.D. Giovanni Stringa. Venice.

1888-1892
La basilica di San Marco in Venezia, illustrata nella storia e nell'arte da scrittori veneziani, edited by Camillo Boito, Ferdinando Ongania Editore. Venice.

1946
SERGIO BETTINI, *L'architettura di San Marco: origini e significato*. Padua.

1960
OTTO DEMUS, *The Church of San Marco in Venice: History, Architecture, Sculpture.* Washington.

1965-1971
Il tesoro di San Marco: I. La Pala d'oro - II. Il tesoro e il museo, edited by Hans R. Hahnloser. Florence and Venice.

1975
FERDINANDO FORLATI, *La basilica di San Marco attraverso i suoi restauri.* Trieste.

1984
OTTO DEMUS, *The Mosaics of San Marco in Venice.* Chicago and London.

1984
The Treasury of San Marco, Venice, edited by David Buckton. Milan.

1986
I mosaici di San Marco: iconografia dell'Antico e del Nuovo Testamento, edited by Bruno Bertoli. Milan.

1990
Basilica patriarcale in Venezia. San Marco: i mosaici, la storia, l'illuminazione, edited by Ettore Vio. Milan.

1991
Basilica patriarcale in Venezia, San Marco: i mosaici, le iscrizioni, la pala d'oro, edited by Ettore Vio. Milan.

1991
RENATO POLACCO, *San Marco: la basilica d'oro.* Milan.

1992-1993
Basilica patriarcale in Venezia: San Marco: I. La cripta, la storia, la conservazione − II. La cripta, il restauro, edited by Ettore Vio. Milan.

1993
La basilica di San Marco: arte e simbologia, edited by Bruno Bertoli. Milan.

1993
MICHAEL JACOFF, *The Horses of San Marco and the Quadriga of the Lord.* Princeton.

1994
ANTONIO NIERO, *San Marco: la vita e i mosaici.* Venice.

1995
Le sculture esterne di San Marco, edited by Wolfgang Wolters. Milan.

1996
San Marco: aspetti storici e agiografici. Atti del convegno internazionale di studi, Venezia 26-29 aprile 1994, edited by Antonio Niero. Venice.

1997
Storia dell'arte marciana: I. L'architettura − II. I mosaici − III. Sculture, tesoro, arazzi. Atti del convegno internazionale di studi, Venezia 11-14 ottobre 1994, edited by Renato Polacco. Venice.

1999
Scienza e tecnica del restauro della basilica. Atti del convegno internazionale di studi, Venezia 16-19 maggio 1995, edited by Ettore Vio and Antonio Lepschy. Venice.